The
Essential
Guide to
SECOND EDITION
RF and Wireless

ISBN 0-13-035465-1

90000

9 780130 354655

Prentice Hall PTR
Essential Guide Series

THE ESSENTIAL GUIDE TO DATA WAREHOUSING

Agosta

**THE ESSENTIAL GUIDE TO WEB STRATEGY
FOR ENTREPRENEURS**

Bergman

**THE ESSENTIAL GUIDE TO THE BUSINESS
OF U.S. MOBILE WIRELESS COMMUNICATIONS**

Burnham

**THE ESSENTIAL GUIDE TO TELECOMMUNICATIONS,
THIRD EDITION**

Dodd

**THE ESSENTIAL GUIDE TO WIRELESS COMMUNICATIONS
APPLICATIONS: FROM CELLULAR SYSTEMS TO WAP
AND M-COMMERCE**

Dornan

THE ESSENTIAL GUIDE TO OPTICAL NETWORKS

Greenfield

**THE ESSENTIAL GUIDE TO INTERNET BUSINESS
TECHNOLOGY**

Honda & Martin

THE ESSENTIAL GUIDE TO COMPUTER HARDWARE

Keogh

THE ESSENTIAL GUIDE TO NETWORKING

Keogh

**THE ESSENTIAL GUIDE TO COMPUTER DATA STORAGE:
FROM FLOPPY TO DVD**

Khurshudov

**THE ESSENTIAL GUIDE TO DIGITAL SET-TOP BOXES
AND INTERACTIVE TV**

O'Driscoll

**THE ESSENTIAL GUIDE TO HOME NETWORKING
TECHNOLOGIES**

O'Driscoll

THE ESSENTIAL GUIDE TO KNOWLEDGE MANAGEMENT: E-BUSINESS AND CRM APPLICATIONS

Tiwana

THE ESSENTIAL GUIDE TO APPLICATION SERVICE PROVIDERS

Toigo

THE ESSENTIAL GUIDE TO STORAGE AREA NETWORKS

Vacca

THE ESSENTIAL GUIDE TO MOBILE BUSINESS

Vos & deKlein

THE ESSENTIAL GUIDE TO COMPUTING: THE STORY OF INFORMATION TECHNOLOGY

Walters

THE ESSENTIAL GUIDE TO RF AND WIRELESS, SECOND EDITION

Weisman

The
Essential
Guide to

SECOND EDITION

RF and Wireless

CARL J. WEISMAN

Prentice Hall PTR, Upper Saddle River, NJ 07458
www.phptr.com

Library in Congress Cataloging-in-Publication Data

Weisman, Carl.
  The essential guide to RF and wireless / Carl J. Weisman.—2nd ed.
    p. cm. — (Essential guide series)
  ISBN 0-13-035465-1
    1. Radio—Equipment and supplies. 2. Radio circuits. 3. Wireless communication
systems. I. Title. II. Essentil guide series (Prentice-Hall, Inc.)
TK6560.W39 2002
621.384 —2002020525

Editorial/Production Supervision: *Jane Bonnell*
Composition: *MetroVoice Publishing Services*
Publisher: *Bernard M. Goodwin*
Marketing Manager: *Dan DePasquale*
Editorial Assistant: *Michelle Vincenti*
Cover Design: *Bruce Kenselaar*
Cover Design Direction: *Jerry Votta*
Art Director: *Gail Cocker-Bogusz*
Manufacturing Manager: *Alexis Heydt-Long*

Prentice Hall books are widely used by corporations and government agencies for training,
marketing, and resale.

The publisher offers discounts on this book when ordered in bulk quantities.
For more information, contact Corporate Sales Department, Phone: 800-382-3419;
FAX: 201-236-7141; E-mail: corpsales@prenhall.com
Or write: Prentice Hall PTR, Corp. Sales Dept., One Lake Street, Upper Saddle River, NJ 07458.

Printed in the United States of America
10 9 8 7 6 5

ISBN 0-13-035465-1

Pearson Education LTD.
Pearson Education Australia PTY, Limited
Pearson Education Singapore, Pte. Ltd.
Pearson Education North Asia Ltd.
Pearson Education Canada, Ltd.
Pearson Educación de Mexico, S.A. de C.V.
Pearson Education—Japan
Pearson Education Malaysia, Pte. Ltd.

This book is dedicated to my parents,
Sylvan Weisman and Claire Weisman,
who taught me the joy of education
and the value of perseverance.

Contents

Preface   xvii

Part 1
Fundamentals

1   Basic Concepts   3

Introduction   4

Vocabulary   5

Prefixes   6

Basic Electronics Terminology   6

RF Basics   7

Transmitters and Receivers   7

Signals   8

2   RF Behavior   15

Loss and Gain   16

Devices   16

Attenuation   17

Insertion Loss   18

Decibels   19

Definition   19

Decibel Math   19

Bandwidth   22

Definition   22

Wideband and Narrowband   24

RF in the Environment   24

Signal Behavior   24

Match   28

What Is Match?   28

Consequences of an Imperfect Match   30

Part 2
RF Hardware

3 Basic System Components   35

Block Diagrams   36

Receiver   37

Transmitter   37

Antennas   38

Block Diagram   38

Antenna Characteristics   39

How Antennas Work   42

Antenna Performance   43

Polarization   45

Antenna Dimensions   46

Smart Antennas   48

Amplifiers   49

Block Diagram   49

Fundamental Properties of Amplifiers   49

How Amplifiers Work   54

Special Amplifiers   55

Filters   57

Block Diagram   57

The Filter's Function   58

Filter Types   59

Filter Performance   59

Special Filters   61

Mixers   63

Block Diagram   63

The Mixer's Function   64

How Mixers Work   65

Mixer Configurations   67

Sources   68

Block Diagram   68

How Oscillators Work   69

Different Kinds of Oscillators   70

A Special Oscillator—The VCO   71

Synthesizers   72

A Quick Review   73

Transmitter Block Diagram   74

Receiver Block Diagram   74

Review   75

4 Other Components   77

Switches   79

Block Diagram   79

Switch Function and Performance   79

Types of Switches   80

System Use   83

Attenuators   84

Block Diagram   84

The Attenuator's Function   84

Types of Attenuators   85

Dividers and Combiners   88

Block Diagram   88

The Dividers' and Combiners' Functions   88

System Use   89

Couplers   90

Block Diagram   90

How Couplers Work   90

Types of Couplers   91

Circulators and Isolators   93

Block Diagram   93

How Circulators Work   93

System Use   94

Isolators   95

Transformers   96

Block Diagram   96

The Transformer's Function   96

Detectors   98

Block Diagram   98

The Detector's Function   98

Phase Shifters   99

Block Diagram   99

The Phase Shifter's Function   99

Phase Detectors   100

The Phase Detector's Function   100

Review of Components   101

5 Circuits and Signals   103

Semiconductors   104

Materials and Devices   104

Diodes   107

Transistors   107

Integrated Circuits (MMIC)   110

Circuit Technologies   111

Lumped and Distributed Circuits   111

Discrete, Hybrid, and MMIC Circuit Choices   114

Subassemblies   117

Cavities   117

Modulation   119

What Is Modulation?   119

Types of Modulation   120

Modulators and Demodulators   127

Getting Around   128

Cables   128

Connectors   131

Waveguides   134

Circuit Traces   135

Part 3
RF Systems

6 Older Technology   141

Broadcasting   143

What Is Broadcasting?   143

The Role of Frequency   145

Tuning In   148

Television Delivery   149

Radar   153

What Is Radar?   153

How Radar Works   155

Different Radar Systems   159

Satellite Communications   162

Why Satellites?   162

How Satellites Work   164

Satellite Systems   171

A Special Satellite System—GPS   174

The Next Generation Satellites—LEO   179

The Internet from Above   181

Point-to-Point Microwave   187

What Is Point-to-Point Microwave?   187

Point-to-Point Operations   188

7 Mobile Telephony 191

A World of Choices 193

Differentiators 193

Worldwide Systems 194

The Cellular Concept 195

Topology 195

Infrastructure 197

Mobility 198

Adding Capacity 199

Underlying Technology 201

Frequency Reuse 201

Air Interface 203

Cellular Phone Block Diagram 206

CDMA Explained 209

Spread Spectrum 209

Channels 217

Cellular Evolution 218

Different Generations 218

Paths of Migration to 3G 221

8 The New World of Wireless 225

Broadband Fixed Wireless 227

Wireless Local Loop 227

Air Link Transmission Technologies 236

Wireless Networks 240

Local Area Networks 240

Personal Area Networks   247

Home Networks   249

The Mobile Internet   252

Technology   253

M-Commerce   255

The Bleeding Edge   256

Up-and-Coming Technologies   257

Security Issues   263

Health Concerns   266

Glossary   269

Appendix A—Acronyms   283

Appendix B—Specifications   293

Bibliography   297

About the Author   299

Index   301

Preface

A lot has transpired in the world of RF and wireless since I wrote the first edition of *The Essential Guide to RF and Wireless*. It seems as though this wonderful technology, which has actually been around quite a long time, has just begun to take off in the last two years. One thing is certain, there is no doubt that our lives will be forever changed by the wireless revolution we are now experiencing.

This book is written for all those who want to understand how this mysterious technology actually works, but did not have the good fortune (?) to get an engineering degree. Toward this end, the book's overriding goal is to simplify RF electronics and wireless technology with analogies, metaphors, and a minimum of mathematics. Many photographs and figures are included to help explain things further. Unlike other books of its kind, however, it takes a distinctly lighthearted approach to the subject by incorporating witticisms and sarcasm, occasionally directed at the book's hypothetical protagonist, the RF engineer. This book is intentionally made humorous because the subject matter is so dry. My feeling is, no matter how brilliantly written or factually correct an introductory book on RF is, if it is too long and boring, you will never get past the first chapter—which is really funny, by the way.

The Essential Guide to RF and Wireless takes an overly simplistic approach to the subject matter. In this vein, it accomplishes two main objectives: it provides a conceptual understanding of RF components and wireless systems, and it exposes you to the main vocabulary used in the industry. You can hardly expect to understand a topic as complex as wireless communications without first learning its *lingua franca*.

The Essential Guide to RF and Wireless is intended for non-technical people who know absolutely nothing about RF but need to or just want to. For every engineer working in the field of RF, there are many more non-technical people working in the field who can benefit from understanding and speaking RF. They include non-technical managers, sales administrators, distribution specialists, manufacturer's representatives, buyers, marketing and communications personnel, advertising agents, tradeshow booth staffers, executive recruiters, financial analysts, and technical writers. The first edition was especially popular among investment bankers and venture capitalists.

This book can be used three different ways. First, it can be read cover to cover as the book is organized in such a way where each successive chapter builds on the one before it, starting with basic concepts and terminology and ending with the various kinds of wireless systems. Second, each chapter can be read on a stand-alone basis, for those who need to quickly grasp a single subject or concept. Some of the subject matter is repeated in different chapters in an effort to make each chapter understandable by itself. Finally, this book can be used as a reference. The many tables, the Glossary, and Appendices A and B provide quick access to terminology, acronyms, and specifications used in the wireless industry.

Regardless of how you use this book, if you are new to the subject of RF, you should read all of Part 1 (Chapters 1 and 2), as the rest of the book builds on the fundamental concepts and vocabulary introduced there.

Part 2 (Chapters 3, 4, and 5) is primarily intended for those working in the RF and wireless industry, as it covers the underlying technology of an RF system in great detail. All of the important building blocks used to make RF hardware are explained, as are the different methods used to manufacture them. Also covered is the fascinating topic of modulation, which is how ground-based information gets prepared to enter the wireless world.

New items added to Part 2 in the second edition include smart antennas and superconducting filters. Other components new to the second edition are the phase shifter and phase detector (and the role they play in phase modulation). Consequently, a greatly expanded discussion and visual depiction of phase modulation has been added. Also new to the second edition is a discussion of some of the newer semiconductor materials used today.

Finally, Part 3 (Chapters 6, 7, and 8) is where the fun begins. This part of the book gives you an overview of several wireless systems. Chapter 6 discusses some wireless systems that have been around awhile. These are mostly systems with which you are already familiar but probably never knew how they worked. New additions to Chapter 6 include an expanded discussion of GPS as well as an introduction to satellite Internet delivery.

Chapter 7, which is completely rewritten in the second edition, is devoted entirely to mobile telephony. The chapter discusses the different mobile telephone choices worldwide and how they work. There is even a block diagram of a generic digital cellular phone. Because of its importance to the future of mobile telephony, an entire section in Chapter 7 is devoted to the workings of CDMA. The chapter concludes with a discussion about the future of mobile telephony.

Chapter 8, which is new to the second edition, is devoted to all those wireless technologies, systems, and applications that have exploded onto the scene since I published the first edition. These include developments in broadband fixed wireless, wireless networking, and mobile Internet access. The chapter concludes with discussions of leading-edge wireless technologies, wireless security, and health concerns.

I would like to thank everyone who took the time to provide me with feedback on the first edition. While I enjoyed receiving the complimentary feedback more, the critical feedback hopefully contributed to a better second edition.

If you would like to provide me with your feedback on this edition, feel free to contact me at cjweisman@yahoo.com

Enjoy.

Part 1

Fundamentals

1 Basic Concepts

In this chapter...

- Introduction   4
- Vocabulary   5
- RF Basics   7

This chapter introduces you to the minimum vocabulary and concepts you will need to learn the subject of RF. Before you learned to read and write, you needed to learn your ABCs. This chapter is the ABCs of RF. In it you will be reintroduced to terms you probably learned back in high school, like scientific prefixes. You will also be introduced to some terminology common to all fields of electronics, not just RF, like watts, circuit, and Hertz. And of course the term RF—with all its meanings—will be thoroughly explained.

An important concept introduced in this chapter is the block diagram, which is a graphical depiction used to illustrate RF hardware. In this chapter it is used to show the two basic building blocks of *all* wireless systems: transmitters and receivers. The two forms that electrical energy can take are discussed, along with the two types of electrical signals: analog and digital.

Frequency, the single most important concept to understanding RF, is explained in full detail. And finally, a surprising aspect of wireless communications is highlighted—the fact that wireless communication involves combining two different forms of electrical energy: one to store the information and one to carry the information.

INTRODUCTION..

WARNING! This book is an oversimplification of a very complex topic. (Your best bet is to keep it away from RF engineers.) When you are done with this book you will not be able to design RF circuits—nor should you want to. However, you should be able to converse intelligently about RF and wireless concepts, understand the lingo, and generally visualize what is going on.

The driving force behind this book is simplicity. It is meant to facilitate a qualitative understanding of an inherently quantitative topic. Many analogies and metaphors are used throughout the book to help you visualize concepts, and where there is a choice between simplicity and factual rigor, the book tends to err on the side of simplicity. My feeling is you don't need to know how to grow tomatoes to eat a pizza and you don't need to know Maxwell's equations[1] to understand RF.

---

1. Why are you looking down here? I just told you that you don't need to know it.

This book is intended for people working in and around the RF and wireless industry without a technical degree. The assumption I have made is that you know absolutely nothing about electronics, RF, or any other arcane science. And in an effort to keep things fun, I have included only one formula for you to memorize in the entire book. Here it is:

$$B = M$$

This equation means the more books which are bought, the more money I make. That's it—you can kick back and relax.

In this book the terms *RF* and *wireless* are used interchangeably just to break up the monotony. Wireless is primarily a marketing term used to describe a subset of newer, RF applications, which include things like cellular telephony and paging, to mention a few. In this book the cellular phone is frequently used as an example to help you visualize what is going on. In fact, it is beat to death. Oh well, it is simple, everyone knows what it is, and it gets the point across. Remember, the goal here is simplicity.

There are two things to note. First, this book uses block diagrams to describe RF systems. If there were another way, I would have chosen it. Unfortunately, it is the simplest way to explain what is going on. Block diagrams consist of strange symbols connected by lines in a systematic way. In some ways, block diagrams are like a foreign language that RF engineers use to communicate what is happening in their RF world. When you are done reading the book, you will be able to interpret rudimentary block diagrams. It will be like vacationing in France after listening to a Berlitz tape on French for half an hour. You will know just enough RF to get into trouble.

Second, every attempt is made in this book to keep the subject matter fun. Heaven knows the subject matter can use it.

VOCABULARY ....

Before you begin this journey, there are a few terms with which you need to become familiar. First and foremost is the term RF. The literal meaning of RF is *Radio Frequency*. However, it is more often used in its figurative sense as both a noun and an adjective. You can generate RF (a noun) or you can generate an RF signal (an adjective). (RF can also be used to describe a range of frequencies, but more about that later.) As will be explained shortly, when used in this book, it is best to think of RF as an electrical signal that is on the move.

Prefixes

Next, you will need to know the prefixes for the powers of ten (remember chemistry?). There are only four of any consequence and they are listed in Table 1–1.

Table 1–1   Some Useful Prefixes in RF

Prefix	Meaning	Example	Interpretation
milli (m)	1/1000th	5 mW	0.005 watts
kilo (k)	1000	3 kg	3000 grams
Mega (M)	1 million	2 MHz	2 million Hertz[a]
Giga (G)	1 billion	100 Gigabucks	Bill Gates' net worth

a. You don't know what this is yet.

Basic Electronics Terminology

Table 1–1 introduces you to another word you will need to know: watts. Watts are the unit of measure for power. If you don't know what watts are, just imagine touching a burning light bulb. A word related to power is energy, which is power times time. If a 100 watt light bulb burns for two hours, it equals 200 watt-hours of energy. If you want to envision what energy is, just imagine touching a burning light bulb for two hours. A word of caution, though—in the strange world that is RF, the words power and energy are often used interchangeably.

Two words closely related to power and energy are *voltage* and *current*. Voltage is just an electric potential, and there are two kinds: AC (alternating) voltage is the type found in a wall outlet; DC (direct) voltage is the type found in a battery. Current is simply electrons on the move. Like voltage, current can also be made either alternating or direct. The exact relationship between voltage, current, and power is simple: voltage times current equals power.

An important word related to current and voltage and one used quite often is *circuit*. A circuit is an interconnection of a bunch of electrical stuff. Electrical circuits are sometimes manufactured on something called *printed circuit boards*

(PCB). If you have ever seen the inside of a computer, VCR, or any other electrical appliance, you have seen a PCB. It is just a hard, thin, plastic board with electrical stuff mounted all over it.

A word you will see occasionally is *microwaves*. It is often used interchangeably with the term RF, but is mostly used to describe a range of frequencies. *Millimeter wave* is also used to describe a range of frequencies.

You have probably figured out by now that the word *frequency* is very important in the world of RF. This word will be explained in detail later, but its importance cannot be over-emphasized. If you are going to understand the concept of RF at any level, you will eventually need to grasp the concept of frequency. If you already understand what frequency is, you have it made. If you think it has to do with how often something occurs, you're right. Stay tuned.

Since I will be using the cellular phone to explain how RF things work, another word you will want to be familiar with is *basestation*. Cellular basestations consist of, among other things, those blue or gray steel towers by the side of the road, which are owned by the cellular providers and are used to communicate with cellular phones.

In the world of RF, all terminology eventually gets replaced by its acronym, and so it shall be in this book. After a concept is explained and the acronym noted in parentheses, the remainder of the book will use the concept and the acronym interchangeably. Cheer up. By choosing to use acronyms, several hundred pages are eliminated from your reading. Not to worry though, Appendix A contains nothing but acronyms to help you navigate the waters.

RF BASICS..

Transmitters and Receivers

Electrical energy moves from place to place in one of two ways. It either flows as current along a conductor (a bunch of electrons moving down a metal wire) or it travels in the air as invisible waves. In a typical wireless system, the electrical energy starts out as current flowing along a conductor, gets changed into waves traveling in the air, and then gets changed back into current flowing along a conductor again (see Figure 1–1).

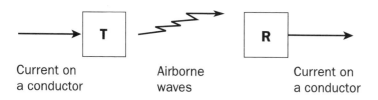

Figure 1–1
Block diagram of a generic wireless system.

In Figure 1–1, the electrical signal flows as current along a conductor (from the left) into the box marked "T." Inside box T, a bunch of stuff happens and out comes essentially the same electrical signal—only this time it is traveling through the air. Box T is known as the *transmitter*. It turns electrical current into airborne waves. Now traveling at the speed of light, the airborne signal reaches the box marked "R." Inside of the box marked R, some more stuff happens and out pops, you guessed it, the same electrical signal as current flowing along a conductor. Box R is known as the *receiver*. It turns airborne waves into electrical current.

Did You Know?

Sometimes RF engineers combine a transmitter and a receiver into a single functioning unit. Now what do you suppose they call this ingenious amalgam? A *transceiver*.

Signals

Analog Signals

Electrical energy (either current or waves) can store information if it is made to vary (in intensity) over time. When electrical energy varies over time in a controlled manner it is called a *signal*. Signals fall into one of two general categories: *analog* or *digital*. For those of you who were unfortunate enough to have suffered through high school trigonometry, you probably remember the sine wave. At the risk of stirring up horrible memories, there is a sine wave shown in Figure 1–2. As time goes by (moving from left to right in Figure 1–2), the intensity of a sine wave grows to some maximum at point B, then back to zero at point C, and on to some minimum value at point D, before finally returning to zero at point E and starting the whole process all over again and again and again.

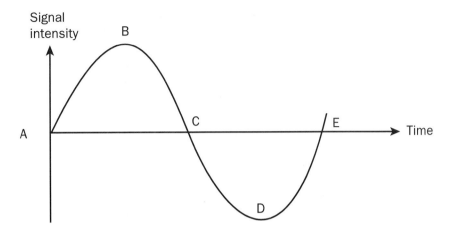

Figure 1–2
A sine wave.

  A sine wave is an example of an analog signal. Whether it is current flowing down a wire or a wave traveling in the air, a sine wave signal varies (in intensity) exactly as shown in Figure 1–2. In the RF world, the intensity of a signal is almost always a measure of power (in watts). The number of times a signal goes through a complete up and down cycle (from point A to point E) in one second is the signal's *frequency* (measured in Hertz[2] and abbreviated Hz). If you find it difficult to remember what Hertz means, every time you hear the word Hertz just replace it with the term "cycles per second." To get an appreciation for how fast these signals go up and down, a 900 MHz (megahertz) signal utilized in cellular telephony, not a particularly high frequency by today's standards, exhibits 900 *million* ups and downs in a single second. Wow!

Frequency

As mentioned in the introduction, the concept of frequency is key to understanding RF because all RF stuff is frequency-dependent. That is, it can distinguish between two different signals *solely* on the basis of their different frequencies. Frequency is what separates one RF signal from another and it is what distin-

---

2. Now you know what this is.

guishes one wireless application from another. Table 1–2 contains a sample of different electrical and wireless activities at different frequencies. You may not know what they all are yet, but you can still observe two things. First, notice how many different frequency-dependent applications there are—this is just a small sample—and second, the table is organized in such a way as to give you an appreciation for the difference in magnitude of all the frequencies.

Table 1–2   The Frequency of Various Activities

Frequency in Hertz	Application
60	Electrical wall outlet
2,000	The human voice
530,000	AM radio
54,000,000	TV channel 2 (VHF)
88,000,000	FM radio
746,000,000	TV channel 60 (UHF)
824,000,000	Cellular phones
1,850,000,000	PCS phones
2,400,000,000	Wireless LAN
2,500,000,000	MMDS
4,200,000,000	Satellite big dish
9,000,000,000	Airborne radar
11,700,000,000	Satellite small dish
28,000,000,000	LMDS
500,000,000,000,000	Visible light
1,000,000,000,000,000,000	X-Files

Table 1–3 uses frequency to quantify some terms introduced earlier. These are not strict definitions, but rather general guidelines.

Table 1–3 Some Frequency Range Definitions

Term	Frequency Range
RF frequency	Less than 1 GHz
Microwave frequency	Between 1 GHz and 40 GHz
Millimeter wave frequency	Greater than 40 GHz

Apparently back in the old days, describing a signal's frequency based solely on a number was too simple, so early RF engineers decided to use letters to reference certain frequency ranges called *bands*. To make matters worse, just when everyone memorized these bands, they went ahead and changed them all. Just by way of entertainment, I have included some of the more popular (old) band designations in Table 1–4. Now when somebody describes a satellite as working in "C-Band," you will at least have an idea what range the signal's frequency is in.

You now know that a signal at 3 GHz can be referred to as either a 3 GHz signal, a microwave signal, or an S-Band signal.

Table 1–4 Some Frequency Band Definitions

Band	Frequency Range
L-Band	1.0–2.0 GHz
S-Band	2.0–4.0 GHz
C-Band	4.0–8.0 GHz
X-Band	8.0–12.0 GHz
Ku-Band	12.0–18.0 GHz

Did You Know?

Somewhere around 1889 a German physicist named Heinrich Hertz succeeded in generating the first airborne RF waves in his laboratory. For all his daring and brilliance, the RF engineers of the world have honored him by using his name as the unit of measure for frequency. I guess we're lucky the first RF wave wasn't generated by Heinrich Schmellingstonberger.

Digital Signals

The other type of electrical signal is a digital signal, which is the same type used in a computer. Unlike the (analog) sine wave signal, which varies gradually between its high points and low points, a digital signal is one that varies instantaneously between two electrical values. For all practical purposes, there are no values between the high and low levels in a digital signal. A digital signal is shown in Figure 1–3. Notice there are only two signal levels: up and down (high and low). Digital signals can represent information in the pattern of highs and lows. For instance, a certain pattern of highs and lows can be used to represent your voice as you talk on a cellular phone.

While digital signals are used to "represent" information, they are not used to "carry" information over the air. Only analog signals (sine waves) are used to carry information "on their backs" as they travel through the air. These analog "carrier" signals can carry either analog or digital "information" signals. The process of combining information signals on top of carrier signals is called *modulation*, to be discussed later. When an information signal is combined with a carrier

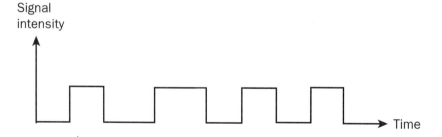

Figure 1–3
A digital signal.

signal the result is known as wireless communications, and the analog signal doing the carrying is called RF or the *carrier* (go figure). An example of analog wireless communications is cellular telephony, the first generation of cellular phones. An example of digital wireless communications is Personal Communication Services (PCS), the second generation of cellular telephony. Both generations use RF to carry different formats of information.

Did You Know?

When a transmitter is always on and the RF signal comes out uninterrupted or continuously, that RF signal is called a continuous wave (CW) RF signal. As you will learn later, there are wireless applications in which the transmitter is turned off and on rapidly, and the RF wave is not continuous. You might think that this type of RF signal would be called a "discontinuous" wave RF signal, but it is not. Just to keep things interesting, RF engineers refer to that type of RF signal as a pulsed RF signal.

You may be wondering which is better—analog or digital wireless communications? The simple answer is it depends, as both approaches have their pluses and minuses. Two things are certain, though. First, digital wireless communications is newer than analog so most older wireless systems are still analog, and second, digital wireless communication interacts seamlessly with all other digital appliances, like computers. For this reason alone, I think it is safe to say that most, if not all, new wireless communications systems coming on line in the future will be digital.

2 RF Behavior

In this chapter...

- Loss and Gain   16

- Decibels   19

- Bandwidth   22

- Wideband and Narrowband   24

- RF in the Environment   24

- Match   28

This chapter describes the behavior of RF energy, whether it is a signal in a circuit or a wave in the air. You are introduced to two fundamental concepts affecting all RF energy: loss and gain. RF energy is constantly changing as it moves around: it gets bigger, it gets smaller, and it gets distorted. Sometimes these changes are intentional and sometimes they are just an unwanted fact of life in the world of RF.

You will learn how the concept of frequency can be expanded to describe a very important parameter of all RF items called *bandwidth*. The performance of any RF item depends on its bandwidth. Bandwidth can also be used to define an RF application's "boundary." All wireless applications are restricted to their predetermined frequency boundaries. In the United States, these boundaries are determined by the Federal Communications Commission (FCC), which has the authority to not only select the exact frequencies and uses for each bandwidth, but also has the responsibility to enforce their declarations. It ensures that no party transmits an RF signal at an unauthorized power level or frequency, or for an unauthorized use.

In this chapter, the concepts of absorption and reflection are used to describe what happens to RF waves as they encounter solid objects, which they often do when traveling around as waves. Some applications are adversely affected by this behavior, while others depend on it.

Finally, this chapter introduces you to an interesting term called *match* and its two methods of measurement: VSWR and return loss.

LOSS AND GAIN ....

Devices

While an electrical signal is in the form of a current inside a transmitter or receiver, cruising around on some conductor, it encounters many different objects called *components* or *devices*. There are literally hundreds of different components that exist for some reason or another, but all components fall into one of two categories: active or passive. The difference is very simple. If it requires a power supply for it to work properly, it is an active component, otherwise, it is passive.

All components (active and passive) exhibit one of two properties: loss or gain. If the signal coming out is bigger than the signal going in, the device exhibits *gain*. If the device exhibits gain, it is called an *amplifier*. All amplifiers are active devices (i.e., they require a power supply). If you do not believe me, take the battery out of a cellular phone and try to make a call. In a cellular phone, the battery is connected to several amplifiers (among other things).

Attenuation

If the signal coming out is smaller than the signal going in, then the device exhibits *loss*. Any signal that passes through a device exhibiting loss is said to experience *attenuation* or is attenuated.

There are many different devices that exhibit loss; some are active and some are passive. You may be wondering (or maybe not), if a big RF signal goes in and a little RF signal comes out, what happens to the rest of the signal, the part that does not come out? It gets converted to heat. Components that exhibit loss warm up, components that exhibit a lot of loss get hot, and components that exhibit too much loss melt, which is why the power handling capability of passive devices is very important.

Figure 2–1 is a visual summary of gain and loss. The signal on the left experiences gain as it goes through the active device, as can be seen by the signal (represented by the sine wave) getting bigger. If the signal gets bigger, what must the device be? Here is a hint, it starts with "a" and ends with "mplifier." The signal on the right experiences loss, as the output signal is smaller than the input signal. If the signal gets smaller, what must the device be? This is a trick question, as it can be any one of a myriad of things, which will be discussed shortly.

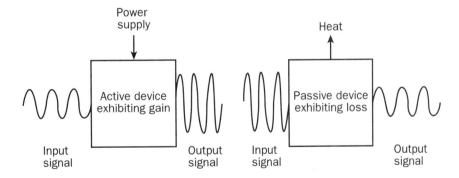

Figure 2–1
Devices exhibiting gain and loss.

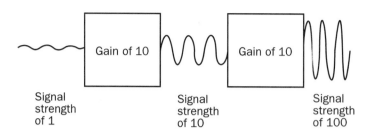

Figure 2–2
The result of multiple gain stages.

If a signal coming out of an amplifier is ten times bigger than the signal go-ing in, the amplifier has a gain of ten. If there are two of these amplifiers in a row, the resulting gain of both amplifiers is 100 (*not* 20!). If a signal is made ten times bigger and then that signal is made ten times bigger still, the final signal is 100 times bigger than the signal going into the first amplifier. It is simple multiplica-tion (see Figure 2–2).

Insertion Loss

Passive devices exhibit the exact opposite behavior of active devices. If the signal coming out of a passive device is 1/100th as big as the signal going in, then that device has a loss of 100 and the input signal is divided by 100 to find the magni-tude of the output signal. If a signal has a strength of 100 watts and experiences a loss of 100, the output signal will be one watt. The loss a signal experiences as it goes through a passive component is referred to by RF engineers as *insertion loss* (IL). (Apparently, the word loss by itself just isn't descriptive enough.)

Did You Know?

Because of their heat dissipating property, most passive RF components are now rated with something called thermal impedance. The thermal impedance of a device is simply a measure of how hot it gets, given a certain amount of input power. The unit of measure for thermal impedance is degrees Celsius per watt.

DECIBELS ....

Definition

If mathematicians had never come along, the story might stop right here and you would be an expert on loss and gain. Unfortunately, however, the signals leaving a transmitter can be literally a *billion* times larger than the signals arriving at the receiver, and the multiplication and division of such disparate numbers can be quite unruly. So mathematicians came up with a way of representing these big numbers with smaller numbers, which allows the use of addition and subtraction in place of multiplication and division. They call this little trick *logarithms*. (Or, as some people affectionately call them, those nasty little things that nobody understood in Algebra.) Before you panic and throw out the book, logarithms (or logs) are really very simple. Trust me.

There are only two things you need to know about logs when used in the context of RF. First, logs are *always* a ratio of two values, and second, this ratio has units of decibels (named after some guy with the last name Bel—really). Decibels are also referred to in the industry as dB (pronounced d´ b). For those of you who are gluttons for punishment, I have included the definition of dB here. Feel free to ignore it.

$$10 \times \log_{10}(\text{Power out}/\text{Power in})$$

Decibel Math

As mentioned above, if the signal coming out of an amplifier is 100 times bigger than the signal going in, then the amplifier has a gain of 100. Or using the definition above, the same amplifier has a gain of 20 dB. Before you start scurrying to find your high school calculator, let me make matters really simple. There are only two dB conversions you are ever going to need. Take my word for it.

+3 dB means 2 times bigger (multiply by 2)
+10 dB means 10 times bigger (multiply by 10)

There are also two corollaries (remember Geometry?) you will need to know. First, if the number gets smaller, the dBs are negative.

−3 dB means 2 times smaller (divide by two)
−10 dB means 10 times smaller (divide by ten)

Second, dBs are only added or subtracted, they are never multiplied or divided. There, you are done. That is everything you need to know about logarithms and decibels. Now for a single illustrative example, see Example 2–1.

Example 2–1   A simple decibel conversion.

If a signal experiences a gain of 4000 (gets 4000 times bigger), what is the gain in dB?

It is best to break up the gain of 4000 into its simplest factors as shown below.

$$4000 = 10 \times 10 \times 10 \times 2 \times 2$$

Now you simply replace the multiplication of factors by the addition of dB (from the only two that you know).

$$4000 = 10 \text{ dB} + 10 \text{ dB} + 10 \text{ dB} + 3 \text{ dB} + 3 \text{ dB} = 36 \text{ dB}$$

A gain of 4000 is equivalent to a gain of 36 dB. What if it were a loss of 4000 instead of a gain? Simple. A loss of 4000 is equivalent to –36 dB. What if it were a gain of 5000, how would you utilize the only two conversions you know? Be creative.

$$5000 = 10 \times 10 \times 10 \times 10 \div 2$$
$$5000 = 10 \text{ dB} + 10 \text{ dB} + 10 \text{ dB} + 10 \text{ dB} - 3 \text{ dB} = 37 \text{ dB}$$

What if it were a gain of 6000, which cannot be broken down into factors of 2 and 10? Approximate. From above, a gain of 4000 is 36 dB and it follows that a gain of 8000 is 39 dB. Since 6000 is half way between 4000 and 8000, pick the value half way between 36 dB and 39 dB (37.5 dB) as an approximation. The true value is 37.78 dB, which is pretty darn close. Now you are an expert.

Now that you know how to do this conversion, you can forget it, as you will never need it again. The world of RF only deals in dB, so all you will ever have to do is add or subtract dBs at any point in the system to figure out what is going on.

Note

When a device exhibits loss, it is said to have a "loss of 6 dB." You must understand that this is equivalent to a change of –6 dB. It will not be said to have a "loss of minus 6 dB."

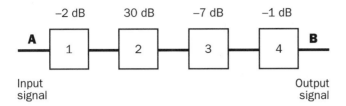

Figure 2–3
Totaling up the decibels.

Suppose there is a situation such as the one shown in Figure 2–3. An electrical signal at point A goes into component 1 with a loss of 2 dB, then goes to component 2 with a gain of 30 dB, then on to components 3 and 4 with losses of 7 dB and 1 dB, respectively. How big is the signal at point B with respect to the signal at point A? Has it experienced loss or gain? Since you are new at this, I will walk you through it, but in the future you are on your own.

The signal at point A minus 2 dB plus 30 dB minus 7 dB minus 1 dB equals the signal at point B. Therefore, the signal at point A plus 20 dB equals the signal at point B. Since 20 dB is being added to the signal at point A, the signal at point A gets bigger as it goes to point B, and therefore it experiences gain. In fact, it experiences exactly 20 dB of gain. Therefore, the signal at point B is 20 dB (or 100 times) bigger than at point A. If you understand this explanation, congratulate yourself, you have grasped a key element of RF.

But just to be sure, try one yourself. Referring to Figure 2–4, what is the size of the signal at point B with respect to the signal at point A?

The answer is –10 dB (1/10th the size). An interesting thing to note is that the lines connecting the devices in Figures 2–3 and 2–4 also exhibit insertion loss. Most of the time the loss in these "lines" is small and insignificant compared to the loss in the actual components, so it is ignored, but you should be aware of it. When a signal at one point in the system is 10 dB smaller than a signal at another point in the system, the smaller signal is said to be "10 dB down" from the larger signal.

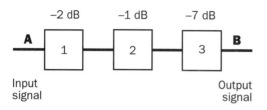

Figure 2–4
A decibel test.

Probably the most famous expression in all of RF is the term "3 dB down." When a signal is referred to as being "3 dB down" from some reference signal, it means it is half as big. Sometimes RF engineers use the expression jokingly like, "I need to get my weight 3 dB down." Funny, huh?

BANDWIDTH ....

Definition

Probably no word is used more often in the world of RF than the word *bandwidth*. Now that you know what frequency is, it is not too difficult to understand the term bandwidth. Bandwidth is a way of describing a range of frequencies. It equals the difference between the highest frequency and the lowest frequency of the device or application, and therefore two frequencies are required to define a bandwidth. For instance, if a particular device can accommodate all frequencies between 75 MHz and 125 MHz, it has a bandwidth of 50 MHz (125 MHz–75 MHz).

Sometimes bandwidth is expressed in terms of a percentage. In this case, the bandwidth is simply divided by the average of the upper and lower frequencies. A simple example will explain everything (see Example 2–2).

As you will learn in future chapters, there is a direct correlation between bandwidth and data carrying capacity (data rate). The wider the bandwidth (i.e., the greater the range of frequency) of a wireless application, the more data it can carry at a given time and therefore the higher the data rate.

Example 2–2   Calculating percentage bandwidth.

> If a device can accommodate all frequencies between 75 MHz and 125 MHz, what is its percentage bandwidth?
>
> First, you calculate the actual bandwidth. As noted above, the bandwidth for this example is 50 MHz (125 MHz – 75 MHz).
>
> Next, you calculate the average of the two frequencies. In this case it is 100 MHz (125 MHz + 75 MHz) ÷ 2.
>
> Finally, you divide the bandwidth by the average frequency and multiply by 100%.
>
> $$50 \text{ MHz} \div 100 \text{ MHz} \times 100\% = 50\%$$
>
> A device that operates from 75 MHz to 125 MHz has a 50% bandwidth.

Octaves and Decades

There are two other important descriptors of bandwidth: *octave* and *decade*. Octave and decade come from the world of logarithms in which octave means twice as big and decade means ten times as big. If the upper frequency of a device is twice as big as the lower frequency, then the device has an octave bandwidth. For instance, a device that operates from 100 MHz to 200 MHz has an octave bandwidth. The same is true for a device whose lower frequency is 1.2 GHz and upper frequency is 2.4 GHz. To really confuse you, if the lower frequency of a device is 100 MHz and the upper frequency is 400 MHz, the device has a *two* octave bandwidth. Any device that has a bandwidth greater than one octave is said to have a multi-octave bandwidth (as if it could be anything else).

If the upper frequency of a device is ten times the lower frequency, then the device has a decade bandwidth. An example of a decade bandwidth is a device that operates from 100 MHz to 1000 MHz (1 GHz).

WIDEBAND AND NARROWBAND ....

Why is all this important? It is important because all RF components are classified as either *narrowband* (meaning narrow bandwidth) or *wideband* (meaning wide bandwidth). There are no hard and fast rules for the separation between narrowband and wideband, so I will make one up. If the bandwidth of a component is less than 50%, it is narrowband. If it is greater than 50%, it is wideband.

Ok, so where is all this leading? Here is the key: The wider the bandwidth of a component, the more frequencies it can accommodate, but the more it costs and the worse it performs. For instance, a narrowband passive component might have 1 dB of insertion loss (good), where an identical wideband passive component might have 3 or 4 dB of insertion loss (bad). The trick in designing an RF circuit is to get away with the narrowest bandwidth device possible while still accommodating all the frequencies required. As an example, cellular phone conversations—from the phone to the basestation—cover the frequency range 824–849 MHz. The most intelligent designs cover just this frequency range and no more.

An interesting thing to note (if you are really bored) is that narrowband and wideband devices are manufactured entirely differently, which is why in the RF industry there are companies who specialize in either narrowband or wideband products.

Did You Know?

Today, when RF engineers want to impress people with the latest lingo, they refer to bandwidth as the "pipe." They will say something like, "If we want to transmit the data faster, we'll need a fatter pipe." What they are really saying is that if they want to transmit the data faster, they will need a wider bandwidth.

RF IN THE ENVIRONMENT ....

Signal Behavior

Skin Effect

As you have already learned, RF signals are either on a conductor or flying around as waves in the air. When an RF signal is on a conductor, which is just about any piece of metal, it only hangs out on the surface of the metal object itself. Picture a solid piece of metal the shape of a brick. If an RF signal were placed on the brick, the signal itself would only be present on the surface of the brick, none would venture inside. If a detector could somehow be placed inside the brick, it would not detect the presence of the RF signal. This behavior exhibited by RF signals is called the *skin effect*, which is self-explanatory.

The reason the skin effect occurs is simple to understand, if you have a degree in electrical engineering. But since the assumption is that you do not have an engineering degree—or you are an engineer with too much free time—I will explain the skin effect as follows. RF signals have a natural inclination to want to escape solid objects and fly around in the air, but for reasons that will be explained later, they cannot always do it. The next best thing these restless RF signals can do is to get as close to the outside of whatever it is they are on in the hope of ultimately escaping and fulfilling their true destiny: to be detected by aliens from another galaxy.

Free Space Loss

Once an RF signal does escape the bounds of a conductor and flies around in the air, it suffers from something called *free space loss*. To help you visualize it, think of a garden hose with a nozzle on the end. As the water comes out of the nozzle, it begins to spread out. If you make a circle by touching your thumb to your forefinger and hold it next to the nozzle, you can probably get all of the water to go through it. But as you move away from the nozzle, some of the water will undoubtedly miss the circle. In essence, all of the water is still there, it is just spread over a larger area. And if you think of the circle as a receiver, the further away it is, the less water (signal) there is to receive. So to the receiver, the signal appears to have lost its strength, relative to what is coming out of the nozzle (transmitter).

Ignoring everything else, the further away a receiver is from a transmitter, the smaller the received signal is due to free space loss. Now visualize the garden hose analogy, only this time instead of the thumb-forefinger circle, picture a square hoop, one meter on each side. Like before, as the hoop moves further away from a transmitter, the less RF energy will pass through it, only this time the amount of RF energy passing through it is meaningful. That value has the units of watts per square meter (or sometimes milliwatts per square meter) and is called *power density*. Power density is a measure of an airborne signal's strength and is used all the time in the RF world (take my word for it).

Absorption

If free space loss isn't bad enough, just about everything the RF signal encounters as it travels through the air changes it in some way. These changes tend to do one of two things to the RF signal: they either make it smaller or change the direction in which it is traveling.

Most of the "things" the RF signal encounters tend to make the signal smaller, including the air we breathe, rain, glass, wood, and even foliage. In a very real sense, all of these "things" can be viewed as types of passive devices with some amount of insertion loss (expressed in dB, of course). This insertion loss exhibited by things in nature is called *absorption*, because it absorbs the RF signal.

A perfect example to demonstrate absorption is the effect rain has on direct-to-home satellite TV, which is predominantly in the Ku-Band. It just so happens that the size of the RF signal carrying direct-to-home satellite television is just about the size of an average raindrop, which makes the conditions ideal for absorption. When the weather is clear, the signal makes it to the receiver with only free space loss and everything is fine. But when it starts to rain, some of the signal gets absorbed by the rain and, therefore, less of it finds its way to the little satellite dish on the roof. During instances of very heavy rain, it is entirely possible that absorption will be severe enough to wipe out the signal, leaving the direct-to-home satellite TV service out of order. This situation is not something the service providers advertise, but it is something you should be aware of if you live in, say, Seattle.

At the risk of insulting you, when an RF signal experiences loss as it travels through a rainstorm, where does the lost energy go? HEAT! Believe it or not, the rain actually warms up. Naturally the rise in temperature is so small it is difficult to measure, not to mention the darn raindrop would probably evaporate before you could get out the thermometer. Now for the $64,000 question. When does a cellular phone have the greater call range, on a sunny day or on a rainy day? I will leave the answer up to you.

Absorption explains exactly how your microwave oven works. An RF signal is radiated inside the microwave oven at a frequency that water really likes to absorb. As the RF signal encounters the water, the signal gets smaller and the water gets hotter. That is why objects with no water content will not get hot inside your microwave oven.

Reflection

Not everything an RF wave encounters absorbs RF energy. Some things that RF waves encounter send the RF signal in another direction. This change of direction is called *reflection*. As an approximation, RF signals tend to reflect off objects at the same angle at which they encounter them (see Figure 2–5).

Many objects reflect, at least partially, RF signals that hit them. The amount of reflection depends on two things: the frequency of the RF and the material of the object. Some materials reflect RF energy only moderately, like concrete, while others reflect it completely, like metal. For materials that only partially reflect the RF wave, what do you suppose happens to the rest of the signal? I will give you a hint. Go back a few paragraphs to the one that contains the word absorption. Now you have it. When an RF signal hits any material, the RF energy either gets completely absorbed (like water), partially absorbed and partially reflected (like concrete), or completely reflected (like metal). Congratulations, you now understand RF behavior.

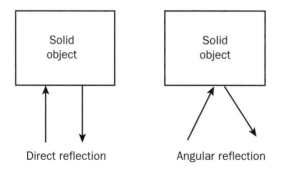

Figure 2–5
Direct and angular reflection.

MATCH ....

What Is Match?

The Meaning of 50 Ohms

Before an RF signal becomes airborne, it spends its existence cruising around on a conductor or inside some component. Every component has an entrance or exit, or both. It is easiest to think of the conductor and the components as parts of a garden hose system with the RF signal as the water inside. If an RF signal is to traverse a conductor and then enter a component, the conductor (garden hose) needs to be connected to the component (a sprinkler). That seems simple enough.

Because engineers run the RF world, no two garden hoses are exactly the same size. So no matter what conductor is connected to what component, some of the RF signal (water) leaks out. (No surprise there.) To make their lives easier, engineers in the RF world have standardized the size of the hose they all agree to use. In this way, a conductor (or component) made by one company will more or less work with a component made by another company—with only a little leaking. If I were actually talking about hoses, the standard size might be specified as "one half inch diameter." Since I am talking about RF, the standard (hose) size is specified as 50 ohms. Ohms (named after some famous engineer) are a measure of *impedance*, which describes the difficulty the RF signal (water) has in passing through the conductor (hose). The impedance of anything is dictated by its physical dimensions and the type of material from which it is made. Naturally a small-diameter hose would have a higher impedance than a large-diameter one.

Why 50 ohms you ask? The best I can tell, back around World War II the military needed to hook up some antennas (discussed in the next chapter) that just happened to have about 50 ohms of impedance. As a result, they developed some 50 ohm cable (discussed in Chapter 5), which was later given the name RG-58. Once they had all this cable, everything else they hooked up to it had to be 50 ohms. And because back then the world of RF was the military, the standard was set, and all because of a bunch of 1940's vintage antennas.

Is 50 ohms optimal? Not really. At least as far as cable is concerned, 75 ohms performs better (i.e., less attenuation) for a given amount of metal. Because it was developed more recently, 75 ohms is the impedance used in cable television (among other things). As a consequence, there are now two impedance standards:

50 ohms for the RF world and 75 ohms for the world of video. How is this resolved when the two worlds intersect? For low power and/or low frequency (<300 MHz), connecting a 50 ohm thing to a 75 ohm thing causes little problem. For higher frequencies or higher powers, however, an impedance matching circuit is needed, which you will learn about in exactly three pages.

The first thing RF engineers want to know, now that they have agreed to this standard size, is how much their hoses will leak when connected to someone else's. This is important to know because the goal is to get a certain amount of RF signal from one conductor or component to another, and if too much of it leaks out, the system will not work right.

VSWR

To measure the amount of leaking, RF engineers coined a term called *VSWR* (pronounced viz´ wär). Technically, VSWR stands for Voltage Standing Wave Ratio, but you will do yourself a favor if you pretend you never read that. VSWR is a numerical measurement of this thing called *match*. The better the match, the less the leaking.

The formula for VSWR is complicated, and to make matters worse, its unit of measure is nothing. It has no units. It does, however, have a format of X:1 (read "X to one"), where the bigger the X, the more it leaks (see Table 2–1).

Table 2–1   The Meaning of VSWR

VSWR	Meaning
1.0:1	Perfect match, a hose with no leaking, cannot be done.
1.4:1	Excellent match, very little leaking, often a design goal.
2.0:1	Good match, acceptable amount of leaking.
10:1	Horrible match, the result of designing a circuit after reading this book.
∞:1	The result of trying to hook up a garden hose to the Lincoln Tunnel.[a]

a. For those of you fortunate enough to have avoided calculus, ∞ means infinity.

Return Loss

Because RF engineers refuse to leave well enough alone, one measure of match is not enough. There is another measure of match called *return loss*, which is measured in, of all things, dB. There is a very straightforward formula for converting from VSWR to dB, but since no one can remember it (including most RF engineers), a conversion chart similar to the one shown in Table 2–2 is used. As you can see, the larger the VSWR, the smaller the return loss.

Table 2–2   *VSWR versus Return Loss*

VSWR	Return Loss (dB)
1.0:1	∞
1.4:1	15.6
2.0:1	9.5
10:1	1.7
∞:1	0

Consequences of an Imperfect Match

As much as I enjoy condemning RF engineers for unnecessarily complicating matters, there is a good reason for using the term return loss. When the match is not perfect and the hose leaks, the water (RF) does not actually leak out. In reality, the RF energy heads back down in the direction from which it came. When RF energy starts heading back down in the direction from which it came, it is called *reflection* (sound familiar?). Since no match is perfect, there is always some RF energy which is reflected. Frequently, the amount of RF energy reflected is small, in which case it goes unnoticed. In situations where the match is poor and a lot of RF energy gets reflected, the device it came from tends to blow up, which is generally how a bad match is discovered.

Did You Know?

There are two extreme cases for return loss: a perfect open and a perfect short. A perfect open occurs when someone forgets to connect the rest of the circuit to the output of a component and the RF signal encounters nothing but air. A perfect short occurs when someone lays a screwdriver across a perfect open. In both cases, almost all of the RF energy is reflected and the VSWR approaches ∞. Needless to say, this situation should generally be avoided, unless blowing up RF components seems like fun.

Impedance Matching

Quite often in the world of RF circuit design an engineer is forced to connect two things (a conductor to a component) with a bad match. For instance, the conductor may have the correct "size" (impedance) of 50 ohms, but the device it is attached to has a size (impedance) of 100 ohms. Connecting these two items as is would result in a bad match, and the circuit would not work very well, as there would be a great deal of power reflected. What do RF engineers do in this situation—after they get done crying? They insert, between the two disparate impedances, a neat little bit of technology called an *impedance matching* circuit. In the example above, the impedance matching circuit changes the 50 ohm impedance to 100 ohms, so the two items can be properly connected. Figure 2–6 is a graphical representation of an impedance matching circuit.

As will be discussed later, impedance matching circuits come in many different varieties, but they all serve the same purpose: to change some RF item's impedance to 50 ohms.

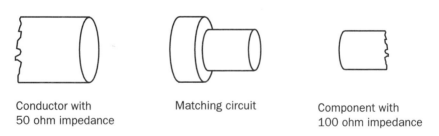

Conductor with   Matching circuit   Component with
50 ohm impedance   100 ohm impedance

Figure 2–6
A graphical representation of a matching circuit.

Part 2

RF Hardware

3 Basic System Components

In this chapter...

- Block Diagrams   36
- Antennas   38
- Amplifiers   49
- Filters   57
- Mixers   63
- Sources   68
- A Quick Review   73

This chapter begins by presenting block diagrams of the components that comprise the two basic building blocks in all wireless systems: transmitters and receivers. Once you understand how transmitters and receivers work, and the roles they play, you are well on your way to understanding wireless communications. And the good news is, both of these building blocks are fairly simple to look at and to understand because they consist of just *five* different RF components, which are covered in this chapter.

This chapter explains what roles antennas, amplifiers, filters, and mixers play in changing the nature, size, shape, and frequency of RF signals. It also points out where RF signals come from in the first place: sources. Each section within this chapter demonstrates that these five fundamental components all come in different variations, to accomplish very specific objectives. This usually involves manufacturing the device in such a way as to optimize one or two key performance parameters, which naturally increases its price. Appendix B is a comprehensive list of the many parameters used to quantify RF component performance.

Manufacturers in the RF industry are always trying to improve these five components by making them smaller, lighter, more energy efficient, and at lower cost. High-volume wireless products, like cellular phones, have increased the demand for these items, which has served to drive down their cost dramatically. State of the art is constantly changing for these items, as competition spurs innovation. For instance, there are at least 30 companies that manufacture high-power amplifiers for wireless infrastructure, which will ultimately translate to lower prices and more features for you, the consumer.

Finally, this chapter concludes with a review of the two basic building blocks just to make sure you were paying attention.

BLOCK DIAGRAMS ....

Transmitters and receivers are very complex systems with many internal components, but all transmitters and receivers perform the same basic functions and they can both be described by simple block diagrams (see Figures 3–1 and 3–2). In these figures, the signals flow from left to right. The weird shaped things are the components and the straight lines are the conductors that connect them. As can be seen in these block diagrams, a signal gets from one component to another by way of a conductor. Recall that a receiver turns an airborne wave into an electrical signal and a transmitter turns an electrical signal into an airborne wave.

Receiver

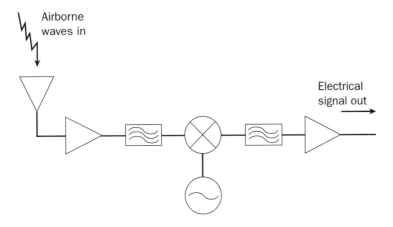

Figure 3–1
Receiver block diagram.

Transmitter

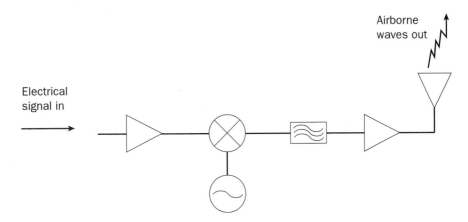

Figure 3–2
Transmitter block diagram.

At their simplest, all transmitters and receivers consist of just five basic building blocks. (Notice in Figures 3–1 and 3–2 there are only five distinct items in each block diagram, although some of them are repeated.) Once you understand these five building blocks and what functions they perform, you are halfway to understanding RF systems and wireless communications. (You will learn about the other half in the section on Modulation.) I will discuss each of these building blocks and what roles they perform in a wireless system.

ANTENNAS...

Block Diagram

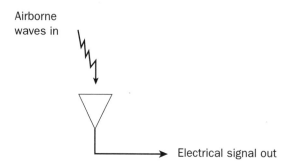

Airborne
waves in

Electrical signal out

Figure 3–3
Block diagram of an antenna.

This first device is called an *antenna* (see Figure 3–3). If you only learn one thing from this book, learn this: *Every wireless system has an antenna.* You may not see it, you may not recognize it, but it is there. The antenna's job is very simple—it converts electrical signals flowing down a conductor into airborne waves (in a transmitter) *or* it converts airborne waves into electrical signals flowing down a conductor (in a receiver) *or* both. It is the heart of the wireless system: no antenna, no wireless communications. Visually, it can be viewed as airborne waves entering (or leaving) the funnel-like structure at the top in the block diagram and leaving (or entering) as current along the conductor at the bottom of the block diagram. When airborne waves leave an antenna, they are said to *radiate* out from the antenna. Most antennas work equally well in both directions.

Antenna Characteristics

Active and Passive

Antennas can be active devices or passive devices. Passive antennas are just a hunk of metal, configured in a very specific way. If the antenna is active, it has a power supply attached somewhere. Active antennas are nothing more than passive antennas with amplifiers inside of them. You will learn more about amplifiers in the next chapter.

> **Did You Know?**
>
> Most active antennas have only one electrical connection. It carries both the RF signal *and* the power signal on the same conductor, which cuts down on material costs, not to mention the extra five seconds it would take to make another connection. Every little bit helps.

Sizes and Shapes

As you have probably already observed, antennas come in many shapes and sizes, from the super large towers transmitting AM radio signals, to the small and large dishes receiving satellite signals, to the little rubber ducky antennas on cellular phones. A variety of antennas is shown in Figure 3–4. Figure 3–5 shows a cellular basestation tower where the vertical structures at the top are the antennas.

The shape and size of any particular antenna depends on three things. The first thing an antenna's physical characteristics depend on is the frequency that the antenna is designed to handle. As a general rule, the lower the frequency the antenna must handle, the larger the antenna, which is one reason why AM radio stations, broadcasting at 530 kHz (530,000 Hertz), have antennas several hundred feet high while cellular phones, operating at 900 MHz (900,000,000 Hertz), have antennas only six inches long.

The second thing that determines the size and shape of an antenna is the direction of the airborne signal. If the objective is to transmit or receive the airborne signal in all directions equally, then the antenna will have a certain shape. Antennas of this type are called *omnidirectional* antennas, meaning "all directions." If, on the other hand, the objective is to transmit (or receive) the airborne signal in only one direction (north, for instance), then the antenna will have a completely different shape. Antennas of this type are simply called—don't laugh—directional antennas.

Figure 3–4
A sampling of antennas. *Courtesy of M/A-COM, Inc.*

Figure 3–5
Basestation antennas. *Courtesy of Alpha Industries.*

And finally the third thing that determines an antenna's size is the power it has to transmit or receive. As a rough approximation, the higher the power, the larger the antenna.

Signal Strength and Direction

Why do RF systems engineers choose one antenna type over another, besides the fact that they're bored? In the case of a transmitted signal, since there is only a finite amount of RF energy going into the antenna as current, unless you believe in the tooth fairy, there can only be a finite amount of energy coming out of the antenna as airborne waves. If an omnidirectional antenna is used, all of the RF energy must be evenly divided in all directions. If the antenna is in the middle of a big city or part of a cellular phone, then an omnidirectional antenna is fine. But what if the antenna is up against a mountain? Radiating some of the RF energy directly into the mountain is a waste—unless there are mole people living inside the mountain trying to pick up HBO.

A directional antenna, radiating RF energy strictly away from the mountain, will radiate more RF energy away from the mountain than an omnidirectional antenna. Both antennas will have the same amount of RF energy coming out, but since the directional antenna has to divide its energy over a smaller area, that area receives more RF energy. Here is an analogy to help you visualize this phenomenon. Suppose you were to bake two apple pies and the first pie is a normal one, with the ingredients covering the whole pie tin. This is analogous to the omnidirectional antenna as all the calories (RF energy) are spread evenly over the whole pie tin. The second pie has the same exact amount of ingredients as the first pie, but in this case the ingredients are somehow constrained to half the pie tin. This is analogous to the directional antenna. Each slice of the "half" pie will contain more calories (RF energy) than an equivalent size slice of the normal pie. This increased RF energy translates into increased range of the signal coming out of the antenna or increased data rate (or both).

As you probably know from personal experience, the signal strength radiating out of an antenna decreases in strength the farther away you get from the antenna. (You should recall from a previous chapter that this behavior is a result of free space loss, among other things.) That is why radio station reception fades as you get farther outside a city's limits. Therefore, a directional antenna with its higher power over a smaller area will have a greater signal range than an omnidirectional antenna with the same output power, which means you can listen to your favorite oldies station that much longer.

How Antennas Work

Wavelength

How the antenna does what it does requires a rigorous understanding of mathematics, physics, and electronics and is way beyond the scope of this book, but that will not keep me from trying to explain it. Assume for the sake of discussion that there is this thing called a *wavelength* that measures the length of an RF signal. Further assume that this wavelength is inversely proportional to the signal's frequency, which means the higher the frequency, the shorter the wavelength. To illustrate the point, a cellular phone's RF signal (900 MHz) is higher in frequency than an AM radio's signal (530 kHz), and therefore the cellular phone's signal has a shorter wavelength. Antennas begin to radiate RF energy (as waves) when the length of the wavelength of the RF signal it is carrying becomes similar in length to that of the antenna itself. The electrical current flowing into the antenna begins to radiate out of the antenna as invisible waves. Basically, it is magic. And the opposite is also true. Invisible waves, of appropriate wavelength, going into the antenna come out as current flowing down a conductor. All this explains why a cellular phone, which receives signals with a one foot wavelength, needs only a six-inch antenna. A six-foot antenna would not work very well and neither would a half-inch antenna.

Antennas explain how the RF energy "escapes" from solid objects as briefly mentioned during the discussion of skin effect. Naturally in this case the solid object is an antenna. In reality, any metallic object that is about as big as the wavelength of the RF signal on it will act as an antenna, and the RF energy will begin to radiate out from it. As hinted at before, if the object is much smaller than the wavelength it will not radiate RF energy at all, and if the object is much bigger than the wavelength, the object will radiate some RF energy, but not very efficiently.

Antenna Performance

Antenna Patterns

Because antenna design is still mostly an art requiring trial and error, RF engineers need a tool to know if the antenna they have designed really does what they want. The tool they utilize is called an *antenna pattern*. In its simplest form, an antenna pattern is nothing more than a birds-eye view of the RF energy radiating out from an antenna. In an antenna pattern, a solid dot in the middle represents the antenna and a line drawn around the antenna represents the power radiating out from the antenna. By convention, the line is drawn where the power radiating out from the antenna drops to one half that of the power at the antenna itself. Two representative antenna patterns are shown in Figure 3–6.

Did You Know?

What is true for antennas is also true for the RF world in general: the higher the frequency, the smaller things become. One of the reasons today's cellular phones are so small is that they operate at frequencies high enough to allow the components inside to be made small enough to fit inside the phone. Here are the wavelengths of three common wireless applications:

AM radio: 566 meters (3 city blocks)
Cellular telephony: 1 foot
Direct-to-home satellite TV: 1 inch

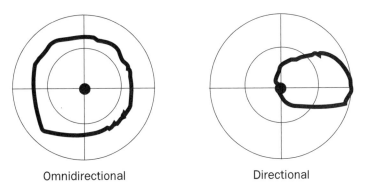

Omnidirectional   Directional

Figure 3–6
Antenna patterns.

As you can see on the left side of Figure 3–6, there is a (more or less) circular pattern drawn equidistant from the center, which is the antenna. This is a typical omnidirectional antenna pattern and shows RF energy radiated equally in all directions. On the right side of Figure 3–6 is one of many possible directional antenna patterns. Notice that all the RF energy is radiated to the right of the antenna, which is still in the center. This antenna pattern might be used for radiating RF energy down a narrow mountain pass between two tall mountains. Forget the mole people.

Antenna Gain

All antennas have gain, even passive ones. How is that possible, since gain always requires a power supply? What I forgot to mention is that gain always requires a power supply, EXCEPT when it comes to antennas. However, antenna gain is a little different in that the absolute value of the RF energy does not really get any larger.

As a way of explanation there is assumed to be a mythical antenna called an *isotropic* antenna. (It is mythical because you cannot actually build one, and neither can an RF engineer.) An isotropic antenna is a single point in space that radiates RF energy out in all directions. (Its three-dimensional antenna pattern is a sphere with the antenna as a point at the center.) Since the RF energy is radiating out in all three dimensions equally, it is spread about as thin as it can be (i.e., it has the lowest possible power density).

Now any antenna that radiates RF energy in just one direction would certainly send the signal further than an isotropic antenna would (in that same direction), using the same amount of RF energy (remember the pie). And since the directional antenna sends the same amount of RF energy further than the isotropic antenna, the directional antenna could be considered to have "gain" relative to the isotropic antenna. This is directional gain, rather than power gain. And not surprisingly, the more focused the (directional) antenna beam, the more (directional) gain it has.

One surprising result of comparing all antennas to an isotropic antenna is that even omnidirectional antennas have gain, albeit only a little. How is that possible? Do not forget, isotropic antennas radiate RF energy out in all three dimensions, omnidirectional antennas constrain the radiated RF energy to just two dimensions. An omnidirectional antenna's three-dimensional antenna pattern would look more like a cheesecake, with the antenna being a toothpick in the center.

So antenna gain is directional gain and is measured relative to an isotropic antenna. The gain is still measured in dB, but since it is relative to an isotropic antenna, the units of measure are dBi, where the "i" stands for isotropic. (Finally an i that has nothing to do with the Internet.)

This antenna gain raises an interesting question: what is the power coming out of the antenna? Is the antenna gain just added to all the other gains and losses (in dB) to determine the output power of a transmitter. Yes. But when the antenna gain is used to determine a transmitter's output power, the output power is given a very special name: *effective isotropic radiated power* or EIRP. You now know way too much about antenna gain.

Polarization

When RF waves travel in the air, the sine waves themselves have an orientation to them: either vertical or horizontal. This orientation is called *polarization*, which is very easy to visualize. If a cellular phone is held in such a way that the antenna is straight up and down, the RF (sine) wave coming out will be vertically polarized (the sine wave will vary up and down as it travels). However, if a cellular phone is held in such a way that the antenna is sideways, then the signal coming out will be horizontally polarized and the sine wave will vary from side to side as it travels.

Did You Know?

If you have ever watched a 3-D movie wearing those funny cardboard glasses, you have experienced the effects of polarization firsthand. All electromagnetic waves, not just RF, are comprised of traveling sine waves. Visible light is made up of horizontal and vertical sine waves. In 3-D movies, two slightly different images, with different polarization, are projected. Each side of the glasses lets only one type of polarization pass, which causes each eye to see a different image, tricking you into thinking you see an image with depth.

What is the purpose of all this? Polarization is a way to fit two different signals, of the identical frequency, in the same place at the same time. The goal of all RF systems is to fit as much information (phone conversations) as possible into the bandwidth it is allotted, and polarization does just that by allowing two otherwise identical signals to be differentiated solely by their different polarizations. In theory, by using horizontal and vertical polarization, twice as many conversations can take place in the same bandwidth.

You can witness this phenomenon first hand by observing the signal strength meter on your cellular phone. If the cellular signal you are trying to receive is vertically (up and down) polarized, as most cellular signals are, and you hold a cellular phone with the antenna horizontal, you will pick up a weak signal. As you turn the cellular phone's antenna upward, the signal strength will increase until it is fully upright.

Because RF engineers have too much free time on their hands, they figured out that if a vertically polarized signal is combined with a horizontally polarized signal, what results is a whole new type of polarization called *circular polarization*. In this form of polarization, the RF sine wave continuously varies from horizontal to vertical as it travels.

Did You Know?

There are two different kinds of circular polarization. (I told you they have too much free time.) One type is called Right Hand Circular or RHC and the other, naturally, is called Left Hand Circular or LHC.

Antenna Dimensions

One-Dimensional Antennas

As mentioned before, there are many different shapes of antennas, but they tend to fall into one of two categories: one-dimensional antennas and two-dimensional antennas. One-dimensional antennas are made from a hunk of wire in either a straight line, like those used on a cellular phone, or some clever shape, like the old rabbit ear antennas found on televisions before the advent of cable.

The two most basic one-dimensional antennas are the *monopole* and the *dipole*. A monopole is simply a straight wire antenna whose length is approximately one quarter of the wavelength of the RF signal it is intended to radiate. A dipole is just two monopoles connected together in a straight line. It follows that a dipole antenna is approximately one half wavelength (of the RF signal) long. Why a half wavelength? It turns out that antennas radiate RF energy really well when they are about a half wavelength long. (It's a physics thing.)

So if antennas work well when they are one half wavelength long, what is the purpose of a monopole, which is only a quarter wavelength long? Monopoles will radiate RF energy (although not as well as dipoles) but, when a monopole is used, it is generally sticking straight out of the ground. And because the ground is a conductor (if you do not believe it, try playing golf in a thunderstorm), it acts like an RF "mirror." In essence, a monopole that is buried in the ground acts just like a dipole, from an RF behavior standpoint. Using a monopole is important in lower frequency applications. Which would you rather erect, a 100-foot-high monopole or a 200-foot-high dipole?

Two-Dimensional Antennas

Two-dimensional antennas offer a lot more variety, from patches and arrays to horns and dishes. A patch antenna is essentially a square hunk of metal, while an array is a bunch of patches in an organized, two-dimensional pattern. Examples of both can be seen in Figures 3–7a and 3–7b. Horn antennas resemble the megaphones used by old-time high school cheerleaders.

Figure 3–7a
Patch antennas. *Courtesy of Alpha Industries.*

Figure 3–7b
An array antenna. *Courtesy of Epsilon Lambda Electronics.*

Dish antennas act as big funnels collecting the RF energy that comes their way, mostly from satellites. Dishes come in many sizes—from the ultra-huge ones employed by the local television stations to the little 18-inch ones used for direct-to-home satellite (DTH) TV. The size of the dish depends on two things, the first of which you should know by now: frequency. The higher the frequency, the smaller the dish required. The second thing that affects the size of the dish is the power transmitted or received. For instance, the greater the other party's transmitted power, the smaller your dish needs to be. As you can now appreciate, DTH satellite TV, with its small dish, was only made possible by the latest generation of satellites capable of transmitting at higher frequency and higher power. A large dish antenna is shown in Figure 6–9 (in the Section on Satellite Communications).

Smart Antennas

There is a whole new category of antennas called *smart antennas*, which are used primarily in mobile telephony. If you look closely in Figure 3–5, you can see that the basestation antennas are in reality three sets of antennas. In most cellular systems, the (circular) cell is divided into three 120° sectors. Each set of antennas is responsible for 120° of coverage, and therefore have a beamwidth of 120° when viewed on an antenna pattern.

There are two problems that occur when a single antenna (or set of antennas) is responsible for 120° of coverage. The first problem is wasted RF energy. There may be only one or two mobile phone users in the entire sector and yet there is RF energy being radiated everywhere.

The second problem is something called *interference*. At its simplest, interference is just any unwanted signal. Since the antennas do not know where in the sector a particular mobile user is, they must transmit the signal everywhere. And while this signal is quite useful to the person using it, it is interference to every other mobile user in the sector.

It seems like a simple solution is to break up the 120° sector into a bunch of smaller sectors, each with its own antenna. Not only would this reduce interference, but it would increase the range of the cell itself. That is more or less what smart antennas do. The smart part comes from the antennas' ability to "track" the users as they move within the sector. This breaking up of sectors into smaller sectors and tracking the mobile user is referred to as *spatial division multiple access or SDMA* (what else?).

There are two types of smart antennas: switched beam and adaptive array. Switched beam uses many narrow beam antennas, each pointed in a slightly different direction, to cover the entire 120° sector. The smarts within the system switches from one antenna to another as the mobile user moves within the sector. Adaptive array uses a single array antenna, like the one shown in Figure 3-7b, along with sophisticated digital signal processing (DSP) to electronically "swing" the antenna beam from one position to the next.

AMPLIFIERS ....

Block Diagram

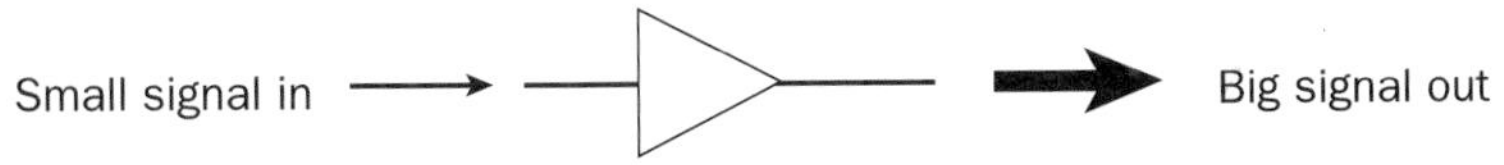

Small signal in $\longrightarrow$ $\longrightarrow$ $\blacktriangleright$ Big signal out

Figure 3–8
Block diagram of an amplifier.

This next device, shown in Figure 3–8, is called an amplifier, which makes signals bigger. RF signals constantly need to be made bigger as they move from place to place. It is just like driving a car. You drive around from place to place using up gas, and when you run low, you fill up. An amplifier is a filling station for RF signals. They move around from place to place (either in the air or along a conductor) and when they need a boost, hopefully there is an amplifier around. Visually, a small signal enters the large end of the block diagram (left side) and leaves as a large signal from the pointy end.

Fundamental Properties of Amplifiers

Gain

There are three fundamental properties of all amplifiers: gain, noise figure or output power, and linearity. Gain is a measure of how much bigger the output signal is than the input signal, and is measured in, as you may have guessed, dB. Some places in an RF system need a lot of gain (40 or 50 dB), and some places only need a little (5–10 dB).

Amplifiers fall into three main categories: low noise, high power, and "other." A low noise amplifier is the very first amplifier a signal encounters after it comes through the antenna in a receiver. A high power amplifier is the last amplifier a signal goes through before it flies out the antenna in a transmitter. Every other amplifier is an "other."

Noise Figure

Low noise amplifiers (LNA) listen for very small RF signals so they must be vewy, vewy, qwiet. A measure of an LNA's quietness is called *noise figure* (NF) and is measured in, of all things, dB. The fundamental property of an LNA is noise figure. The lower the NF of an LNA, the better. Some RF engineers pay big bucks for an LNA with super low NF. (The rest of us just invest in mutual funds.) What is a good NF? It depends. Think of it this way: the lower the noise figure, the smaller the signal that the LNA can hear, the further away the LNA can be, and thus the greater the range of, say, a cellular phone.

Output Power

High power amplifiers (HPA) boost the RF signal as big as possible (or allowable) just before it is shot out of the antenna. The bigger the signal, the farther it travels and the greater the range of, say, a cellular phone. The second fundamental property of an HPA is output power, measured in watts. Generally speaking, the higher the power, the better.

Unfortunately, RF engineers insist on making things difficult and tend to express output power in *dBm*. What the heck is dBm you ask? It literally means "dB above one milliwatt." For instance, 10 dBm is a signal 10 dB above (or bigger than) 1 mW, 30 dBm is 30 dB bigger than 1 mW, and so on. A 30 dBm signal, which is 30 dB (or 1000 times) bigger than 1 mW, translates to one watt (1000×1 mWatt). So 30 dBm is the same as 1 watt. Damn engineers. See Table 3–1 for some common conversions.

Table 3–1   Watts to dBm Conversion

Power in Watts	Power in dBm
0.1 mW	–10 dBm
1 mW	0 dBm
1 watt	30 dBm
1000 watts	60 dBm

Figure 3–9a shows an example of an LNA and Figure 3–9b shows an exaggerated example of an HPA. The two were chosen to demonstrate how much bigger HPAs can be compared to LNAs. This situation arises out of the need to remove heat from the HPA. Because amplifiers are not 100% efficient, some of the energy that goes into the amplifier comes out as an RF signal, but the remainder comes out as heat, which is why many HPAs contain fans to provide internal cooling, like the fan in a car's engine. If the HPA's fans stop working, you might as well get out the marshmallows.

When discussing the output power of an HPA you need to know that everything is relative. For instance, while the output amplifier in most cellular phones puts out less than 1 watt, the output amplifier at the basestation end puts out 50 watts and both amplifiers are HPAs. Just because it is an HPA does not mean it puts out a lot of power, but it does mean that it is the last amplifier in a transmitter.

Figure 3–9a
An LNA. *Courtesy of Mini-Circuits.*

Figure 3–9b
An HPA. *Courtesy of Amplifier Research.*

Linearity

In this age of digital communications, there is a third fundamental property of amplifiers called *linearity*. One of the implications of digital wireless communications is that when a digital signal rides on top of an RF carrier, any amplifier that the signal goes through must be really linear. Linearity is a measure of how much the amplifier distorts the shape of the signal. As you will learn in the future section on modulation, tiny changes to the shape of the RF carrier (sine wave) actually contain information; therefore, unwanted changes in the signal's shape serve only to distort the information. What RF engineers want at the output of their amplifiers is a signal that is bigger than, but identical in shape to, the input signal. As a way of visual introduction to the concept of linearity, I present you with the single most important piece of information about any amplifier, the *transfer curve* (see Figure 3–10). A transfer curve is a graph of the output power versus the input power of an amplifier. All amplifiers display this type of behavior.

Referring to Figure 3–10, as the input power to an amplifier increases (moving to the right on the horizontal axis), the output power from the amplifier increas-

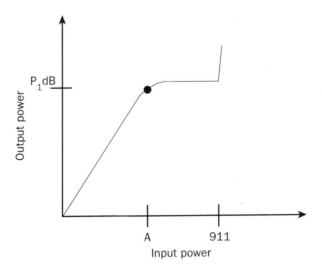

Figure 3–10
Output power versus input power of an amplifier.

es by a like amount, at least until the point marked "A." Everything up to point A is known as the linear region of an amplifier. It is in this region that the amplifier must operate if it is to avoid distorting the RF signal. The output power at point A is referred to as the P_1dB (pronounced p wun´ d b) point or the P_1dB power or the one dB compression point. P_1dB has an exact definition, but it will only cause confusion. It is much simpler to think of the P_1dB point of an amplifier as the highest power the amplifier can put out *and* still be in the linear region. Or another way of viewing it, P_1dB is the highest linear power an amplifier can put out.

Beyond point A on the horizontal axis (increasing the input power further), notice that the output power no longer rises, but stays flat. In other words, an increase in input power no longer results in an increase in output power. The amplifier stops amplifying. After point A, the amplifier is said to be in *saturation* and enters the non-linear region. It is in the non-linear region where all the signal distortion occurs and messes up a digital cellular phone call. Output power greater than P_1dB is called saturated output power. In some instances, saturated output power is useful, but not in digital wireless communications. Just as a note: if the input power is increased further, eventually a point is reached where the output power of the amplifier increases rapidly, as shown. Of course at this point the output power is in the form of flames shooting out of the amplifier, which is why it is referred to (jokingly) as the 911 point.

One method of measuring an amplifier's linearity is by its *intercept point* (also called the *third order intercept point*). The higher the intercept point, the more linear the amplifier. The intercept point is represented by the symbol Ip3 (pronounced i´ pee three). (Sometimes an amplifier's Ip3 is referred to as its *dynamic range*.) Like power, the intercept point is also measured in dBm. An amplifier with a 40 dBm intercept point is more linear than an amplifier with a 30 dBm intercept point. A rule of thumb used by all RF engineers is that an amplifier's Ip3 is 10 dB greater than its P_1dB point. There is no need to go any further.

Did You Know?

The third order intercept point is a mythical point that does not really exist and cannot be measured directly. Instead, a bunch of other measurements are made and then the Ip3 of an amplifier is calculated using these other measurements. Leave it to RF engineers to base the performance of this critical component on something that does not even exist.

How Amplifiers Work

How an amplifier supplies gain to an input signal is an interesting process. The input signal itself does not really get bigger per se as it moves through the amplifier. Instead, the input RF signal acts to control another type of power called DC power, where DC stands for direct current. (DC power or DC voltage, unlike a sine wave, does not vary with time, but is constant, just as the voltage from the battery in a flashlight.) Similar to turning the tires of an automobile, as you drive you are not really turning the tires themselves, you are controlling the tires' movement with a controller called the steering wheel. If the automobile were an amplifier, the driver would be the input RF signal, the tires would be the DC power, and the steering wheel would be the controller called a *transistor*, which you will learn about in a later chapter. In an amplifier, the RF input signal tells the transistor to "shape" the DC power to exactly reflect the shape of the input signal. In this way, the output signal has the same exact shape as the input signal, only bigger. How much bigger? It depends on how much DC input power there is. The main difference between HPAs and every other amplifier is that HPAs have greater DC input power.

Special Amplifiers

Limiting Amplifiers

There are two special cases of amplifiers that you should be aware of if you really want to impress an RF engineer. The first type is called a *limiting amplifier* and, as the name implies, it limits the output power. This type of amplifier is used in places where the component that follows it will be damaged if its input power is too high. The limiting amplifier provides a sort of protection for the next component. You may recall from Figure 3–10 that all amplifiers behave somewhat as limiting amplifiers. At a certain input power, the output power levels off. Basically, the only difference between a limiting amplifier and any other amplifier is that limiting amplifiers do not blow up at the 911 point—in theory.

Balanced Amplifiers

The other type of amplifier is called a *balanced amplifier*. It is not so much a different amplifier as it is a different amplifier design. In a balanced amplifier, there are two amplifiers in parallel (see Figure 3–11).

Referring to Figure 3–11, in a balanced amplifier design the RF signal enters at the left side as usual. Once inside, the signal gets split in two, with half going to one amplifier and half going to the other amplifier. Once inside the amplifiers, both "half" signals get amplified and are then added back together before leaving at the output on the right side. From the outside, a balanced amplifier looks and behaves just like a regular amplifier.

At this point you must be wondering why go through all that if one amplifier will do. Well, there are two advantages to the balanced amplifier design that just

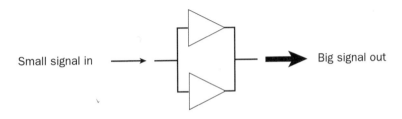

Small signal in   ⟶   Big signal out

Figure 3–11
Block diagram of a balanced amplifier.

cannot be realized from a single amplifier. The first advantage is that there are two amplifiers. If one fails, there is still one working, albeit with reduced performance. Balanced amplifiers are often used in circumstances requiring a high degree of reliability or fault tolerance.

The second advantage—and you are going to have to take my word for it because it is too complicated to explain—is that balanced amplifiers provide a better match (lower VSWR) than regular amplifiers. They leak less, and less leaking is premium performance, which some RF systems simply must have to function properly.

Did You Know?

Amplifier prices vary dramatically. In general, the higher the frequency or the wider the bandwidth or the greater the output power, the more the amplifier costs. Also, super low-noise figure amplifiers are expensive. Just as an example, some low-cost surface-mount amplifiers sell for as little as 50¢, while some high-power, wideband amplifiers sell for as much as $50,000. Just be glad you don't have an RF engineer on your Christmas shopping list.

Variable Gain Amplifiers

There is one last amplifier type you should know about, the *variable gain amplifier* or VGA. Most amplifiers have fixed gain (i.e., the gain has one single value). A fixed gain amplifier with 10 dB of gain will make all input signals ten times bigger. Variable gain amplifiers have an external control that allows the user to vary the gain over some predefined range. All VGAs come specified with a "gain range" like 10–20 dB, for example. A VGA is like a gas range, where the heat (gain) varies from simmer to boil and the external control is the knob on the stove. The block diagram of a VGA is shown in Figure 3–12 and, as you can see, it is nothing more than a regular amplifier with an arrow through it.

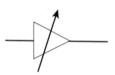

Figure 3–12
Block diagram of a variable gain amplifier.

In practice, rarely is a VGA's external control connected to the outside world, like the knob on a stove. More often than not, the VGA's control is connected to some other point in the RF system that senses what is going on and changes the VGA's gain accordingly. Whenever a component changes its own performance based on something happening somewhere else in the system, it is known as *feedback*. VGAs frequently sense an RF signal "farther down the line." If the signal it is sensing is too big, it lowers its own gain, and if the signal is not big enough, it cranks it up. It continues changing its own gain until the signal it is sensing is just right, and then it keeps its gain right at that point.

Did You Know?

There is an entire branch of electronics called feedback theory, which predicts the behavior of feedback circuits. The thermostat controlling a home's temperature is a classic example of feedback theory. All feedback circuits work the same way, by sensing an output (room temperature) and varying an input (furnace flames) to achieve a specific outcome (desired temperature). RF systems, like all electrical systems, make extensive use of feedback circuits. I guess the components don't like it when it gets too cold.

FILTERS ....

Block Diagram

Figure 3–13
Block diagram of a filter.

This next device in the lineup is called a *filter* (see Figure 3–13). The filter does just what you think it does—it filters out all the signals that are not wanted. Visually it can be viewed as a bunch of signals at different frequencies entering the filter on the left (f_1, f_2, and f_3) and only the desired signal (at the desired frequency) coming out the right side (f_2). Where do all these unwanted signals come from? Everywhere.

The Filter's Function

There are tons (in reality they don't weigh anything) of these invisible RF waves cruising around in the air at any moment in time at all different frequencies. These waves come from all of the RF transmissions taking place, like cellular phones, satellite communications, radar, even sunspots. All of these waves cruising around try to get into the receiver by way of the receiver antenna, and many do. Some of the signals even get past the LNA, but that is where the filter comes in. It acts like a bouncer at a nightclub letting all of the "acceptable" signals in and turning away all of those other "loser" signals. Instead of selecting people by attractiveness or wealth, the filter selects signals by their frequency.

In an ideal (and simplified) world, when the filter gets done doing its thing, the only signal still standing is the exact signal desired. But alas, the world is not ideal, which is why you will often see several filters in both the transmitter and receiver.

It is simple enough to understand what the filter's purpose is in a receiver, but why is one needed in a transmitter? As you will soon learn, there is an evil component in all RF systems known as a mixer. And what this evil mixer does, (among other things), is inject unwanted signals (at unwanted frequencies) into the signal to be transmitted. But alas, the transmitter gets the last laugh, because just before the signal gets amplified by the HPA on its way out the antenna, a filter is used to eliminate all of those unwanted signals the evil mixer injected into the original signal in the first place. Ha ha ha ha ha.

The Role of the FCC

In most cases, the filter on the transmit side is required by the Federal Communications Commission (FCC). When someone is given permission to transmit a signal at a particular frequency, they are prohibited from transmitting at any other frequency, for fear it will mess up someone else's signal. The transmit filter makes sure none of these "illegal" signals ever leave the transmitter.

Did You Know?

The FCC, which has the power to allocate all airborne transmission in the U.S., gave away—for free—the right to the cellular frequency bands by way of lottery many years ago. After discovering that this little ploy netted the U.S. Government exactly zero dollars, they wised up. All rights to wireless transmission since then have been auctioned off to the highest bidder. Cha ching.

Filter Types

There are so many different filters that someone could write an entire book on the subject, which probably explains why there are entire books on the subject. But all filters, no matter how they are constructed, fall into one of four categories, as detailed in Table 3–2.

Table 3–2   Different Filter Types

Filter Type	Explanation
Low pass	Allows all frequencies below a certain frequency to pass while rejecting all others. It is like letting only short people into the bar.
High pass	The opposite of a low pass.
Bandpass	Allows all frequencies between two specific frequencies to pass while rejecting all others. It is like letting only people between 5'10" and 6'2" into the bar.
Band reject	The opposite of bandpass. It is also called a *notch filter*.

Several filters are shown in Figure 3–14. Notice all the different shapes and sizes (how pretty!). Filters share the same common frequency property as all other RF stuff: the higher the frequency, the smaller the filter.

Filter Performance

Frequency Response

Generally speaking, filters are passive devices and therefore do not require a power supply. In fact, filters operate by varying their insertion loss as a function of frequency (see Figure 3–15). Figure 3–15 is known as the *frequency response* of the filter. (Could it be called anything else?) Every filter has a frequency response, which is all that is required to describe the filter's performance. Figure 3–15

Figure 3–14
Filters. *Courtesy of K&L Microwave, Inc.*

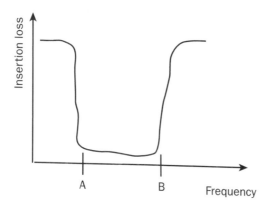

Figure 3–15
A band pass filter's frequency response.

shows the frequency response of a bandpass filter. With frequencies less than point A and greater than point B, the insertion loss is high. High insertion loss for a filter might be 30 dB, which means at those frequencies, the filter wipes out 99.9% of the RF signal. Conversely, frequencies between points A and B experience a low insertion loss. Low insertion loss might be one dB, which only wipes out about 20% of the signal.

Referring once again to Figure 3–15, the frequencies between points A and B are known collectively as the *passband*, because the filter allows frequencies in this band to pass on through. Likewise, the frequencies outside of the points A and B are collectively known as the *stopband*. What happens to the RF energy in the stopband if it is not allowed to pass? Shame on you. It gets converted to heat, which explains why RF engineers prefer to do all of their signal filtering when the signal is still at very lower power (i.e., before the HPA). Many times this is possible, but you will soon learn that there is at least one popular wireless system where this is not the case. Hint: think cellular.

Special Filters

Duplexers

You may hear the word *duplexer* (or *diplexer*), which is a fancy device that combines two filters into a single component. These are mostly used in conjunction with basestation antennas. By combining both the transmitter and receiver filters into the same device, the same antenna can be used for transmitting and receiving, thereby reducing the number of antennas required at the basestation. If a duplexer combines two filters in a single device, how many filters do you suppose get combined in a *triplexer*?

SAW Filters

There is another type of filter you should be aware of, the *SAW filter*, and no, it is not made out of the wood cutting tool. "SAW" stands for surface acoustic wave, which is a fancy way of saying sound wave. Remember that RF devices get bigger as the frequency gets smaller, and below a certain frequency, standard RF filters become prohibitively large. One day some bright RF engineer discovered that if the RF signal is first converted into a sound signal, the components required to filter this "acoustic" wave are much smaller, which is how SAW filters work. First, they convert the RF signal into a sound signal, then they filter the sound signal, and finally, they convert the sound signal back to an RF signal.

Because SAW filters are manufactured very much like semiconductors, they can be made (in volume) very inexpensively. So SAW filters are an excellent choice when small size and low cost are a premium (when aren't they?), which is why they are used extensively in mobile phones. Unfortunately, due to manufacturing limitations, SAW filters are only really practical between 10 MHz and about 3 GHz.

One other thing needs to be mentioned about filters in particular, and passive devices in general. Amplifiers are not the only components that have a 1 dB compression point (P$_1$dB) and a third order intercept point (Ip3). Passive components like filters, as well as others, also have these parameters. In the case of passive components, these two parameters do not measure how much power the components put out (they don't—they're passive), they measure how much power the components can handle without distorting the signal. You can imagine that if a very large signal is put into a small filter, something bad will happen. In fact the "bad" thing that happens is signal distortion, which is any unintended change in a signal's size or shape. Of course, if the signal becomes much too big for the filter, the filter might catch on fire, which is also a form of signal distortion.

Superconducting Filters

If you recall from Figure 3–2, the last thing an RF signal passes through on its way out the transmitter (before the antenna) is an HPA. In some instances, the power is great enough and the FCC's requirements are strict enough to require a filter AFTER the HPA, so the output does not interfere with any other wireless systems. The most common occurrence of this is in the output of the transmitter in a cellular basestation. This is one instance where all of the filtering cannot be done at low power.

Recall that in the passband, even the best filters have some (insertion) loss. And when the filter comes after the HPA, this filter loss is a bad thing. It unnecessarily attenuates the signal, which translates to decreased range of the wireless system. But what if there were a way to eliminate the filter's insertion loss?

Enter the *superconducting filter*. If you have done any reading at all, you probably know that superconductors are special materials that exhibit no electrical resistance (among other properties). What if someone made a filter out of a superconductor? It would have no (or very little) insertion loss.

As a way of example, let us assume a typical filter used at the output of a cellular basestation has about 0.5 dB passband insertion loss (which is not bad), and that the basestation puts out 40 watts of RF power (before the filter). The power lost due to the filter's insertion loss is over 4.5 watts. This means that the true output power of the transmitter is less than 35.5 watts.

Now what if we replaced this filter with a superconducting filter that, say, had only 0.1 dB of insertion loss. You are probably thinking, what is the big deal, we are only going to save 0.4 dB. Well the true output power in this case is almost 39 watts, or an increase of over 3.5 watts. Now 3.5 watts may not sound like a lot, but take my word for it, it is. It can dramatically increase the range of the cellular basestation, or better yet, it can dramatically increase the life of your mobile phone's battery. Now I've got your attention.

More and more superconducting filters are finding their way into cellular basestations—their only real application at present. The reason they are only being used in cellular basestations (right now) and not in, say, mobile phones, is that they are very large. What I neglected to mention is that for superconducting filters to work, they need to be kept really cold—like several hundred degrees below zero (Celsius or Fahrenheit) cold. And for them to be kept really cold, they must have their own cooling system. So not only are they large, but they tend to be relatively expensive too. Nevertheless, there are situations where they make financial sense and so they are used there.

MIXERS..

Block Diagram

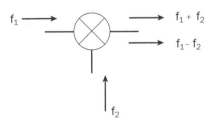

Figure 3–16
Block diagram of a mixer.

Ah, the evil *mixer*. The mathematics and physics underlying the functioning of a mixer (see Figure 3–16) are so complex, a spreadsheet is required to describe it. Fortunately, it is easy to explain conceptually.

The Mixer's Function

The Mathematics

The purpose of a mixer is to change the frequency of a signal while hopefully keeping everything else about the signal the same. Visually, one signal enters the mixer at the left side at one particular frequency (f_1), while another signal enters the bottom of the mixer at a second frequency (f_2), and what comes out of the right side are two different signals. One signal has a frequency equal to the sum of the first two frequencies ($f_1 + f_2$) and the second signal has a frequency equal to the difference between the first two frequencies ($f_1 - f_2$). A simple example will clear everything up (see Example 3–1).

Example 3–1   Mixer mathematics.

> Two signals are going into a mixer. One signal has a frequency of 500 MHz and the other signal has a frequency of 400 MHz. What are the frequencies of the two signals coming out of the mixer?
>
> The first frequency can be calculated by adding the two numbers.
>
> $$500 \text{ MHz} + 400 \text{ MHz} = 900 \text{ MHz}$$
>
> The second frequency can be calculated by subtracting the two numbers.
>
> $$500 \text{ MHz} - 400 \text{ MHz} = 100 \text{ MHz}$$
>
> The two signals coming out of the mixer have frequencies of 900 MHz and 100 MHz.

This raises three questions. 1) Why does a signal's frequency need to be changed? 2) How does the fact that there are now two signals get resolved? 3) What makes mixers evil?

Changing Frequencies

First, a signal's frequency must be changed because the signals that you and I encounter in everyday life are at different frequencies from the signals used to carry information over the air. For instance, when you speak you create sound waves in the neighborhood of 2 kHz (2000 Hertz). However, if you hope to talk on a cellular phone, the frequency of your voice (2 kHz) needs to be changed to the frequency used in cellular communications (900 MHz). In order to change the frequency of a human voice to that of the cellular carrier, one or more mixers is required.

Second, the two signals coming out of the mixer are dealt with by getting rid of the unwanted one. In the example above, if the desired signal is the 900 MHz signal, then the 100 MHz signal is eliminated. Now for the Final Jeopardy question of the day, how is the 100 MHz signal eliminated? Do do do do do do do, do do do do doo-da do do do do. With a filter, which is why there is always a filter right after a mixer, because the mixer puts out two signals and the filter gets rid of the one that is not needed. This stuff all makes sense, if you give it a chance.

And finally, why are mixers evil? If mixers worked exactly as described above they would not be evil. As you have already learned, in the world of RF, things are not that simple. In reality, when two signals are fed into a mixer what comes out is not just two nice clean signals. Dozens of signals come out, at all different frequencies, which drive RF engineers crazy. (Come to think of it, that is one of the mixer's greatest benefits.) These unwanted signals are loosely defined in engineering parlance as *noise*. Noise in an RF system is either a signal at a frequency which is unwanted, or an imperfection in the RF signal which is wanted. Mixers are notorious for injecting noise into RF systems, which is another reason why they are followed by a filter.

Other Names for Mixers

It needs to be pointed out that mixers are sometimes called *upconverters* or *downconverters*. If the mixer is part of a receiver, then it is a downconverter. If it is part of the transmitter—well, you can figure out the rest.

How Mixers Work

Three Ports

In an effort to expand your already vast RF vocabulary, the two inputs and one output (called *ports*) in a mixer are referred to as the RF, LO, and IF. The RF is the

Figure 3–17
A mixer. *Courtesy of Mini-Circuits.*

port with the higher frequency signal (900 MHz in the previous example). The IF, or *intermediate frequency*, is the port with the lower frequency signal. The LO will be explained later in this chapter. As you might suspect, the RF, IF, and LO ports have very limited frequency ranges over which they work. Trying to operate a mixer outside one of its ports' frequency range will result in poor electrical performance. And, just like every other RF component, the wider the frequency range of the three ports, the more the mixer costs and the worse its performance is. Every attempt is made by RF engineers designing with mixers to choose the ones with the narrowest possible frequency ranges that will accomplish the task. A typical mixer is shown in Figure 3–17 (not much to look at). Make a note that the mixer does, in fact, have three ports.

There are both active mixers and passive mixers, but if the truth be told, 95% of all mixers used are passive. While active mixers do have gain, which is generally a good thing, the rest of the active mixer's performance parameters stink, so hardly anyone uses them.

Conversion Loss

Like all passive components, passive mixers exhibit insertion loss. Now RF engineers do not call it insertion loss, which would be too easy. Insertion loss in a mixer is called *conversion loss* (CL), just to be different. Conversion loss is one of the two most important parameters of a passive mixer. The lower the CL, the better. The other key parameter of a passive mixer is noise figure (NF). (Remember noise figure?) You thought only amplifiers have an NF. Not true. And just like LNAs, the lower the NF in a mixer, the better. Also, as indicated above, the wider the frequency ranges of the RF, IF, and LO ports, the worse will be the CL and the NF, and if you can understand this sentence with all its acronyms, you have truly grasped mixer terminology.

Mixer Configurations

Two-Stage Mixers

Here is one last attempt to complicate things. If there are two mixers in a transmitter or receiver, which is usually the case, the signal between them is the IF and the lowest frequency signal is called the *baseband* signal (see Figure 3–18).

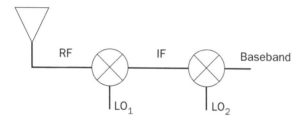

Figure 3–18
Block diagram of a two-stage mixer in a receiver.

Note that the baseband is just a lower frequency version of the RF signal. It still has the "information" signal riding on top of it. A complete receiver can be thought of as performing two functions. The first function is to lower the frequency of the carrier, and the second function is to strip off the "information" signal from the baseband signal. The second function is discussed in more detail in the section on modulation. Both of these steps also happen in the transmitter, only in the opposite order.

Did You Know?

When a receiver uses two mixers in a row, as shown in Figure 3–18, it is called a *superhetrodyne* receiver. Knowing that, plus two nickels, will get you a dime.

Mixer Types

Just to mention in passing, you should know that mixers come in three flavors: single-ended, double-balanced, and triple-balanced. These distinctions have to do with how the mixers are built internally and, for the sake of this book, have no effect on a mixer's function. All this is a long-winded way of saying when you hear any of the mixer descriptions mentioned above, ignore them and just think to yourself, mixer.

Frequency Doublers

There is another component that is closely related to the mixer: the *frequency doubler*. At the risk of insulting you, the output frequency of a frequency doubler is twice that of its input. Remember how mixers produce all sorts of unwanted signals at different frequencies? Frequency doublers use this behavior to double a signal's frequency. Enough said.

SOURCES ....

Block Diagram

Output
signal

Figure 3–19
Block diagram of an oscillator.

The last of the major building blocks is called a source or an *oscillator* (see Figure 3–19). An oscillator that provides one of the inputs to a mixer is called a *local oscillator* or LO. (I guess this is to distinguish it from a remote oscillator, which is located on Venus.) Now you know what the LO port in a mixer does: it gets connected to an oscillator.

How Oscillators Work

While the actual workings of an oscillator are somewhat involved, they are very simple to understand conceptually. A power supply is connected and, in an ideal world, out comes a perfect sine wave signal at a predetermined frequency. (That is why there is a little sine wave inside the circle.) Needless to say, all oscillators are active devices.

Oscillators are where the RF comes from in the first place. They are the "source" of the RF. Visually, it is simply a sine wave signal coming out the top of the oscillator, as shown in Figure 3–19. Several surface mount oscillators used in today's wireless systems are shown in Figure 3–20. Notice how small they are.

Did You Know?

Almost every solid object that exists has what is known as a *self-resonant frequency*. What that means is if you can excite the material with electrical energy (or by tickling it), the material will produce a sine wave! No kidding.

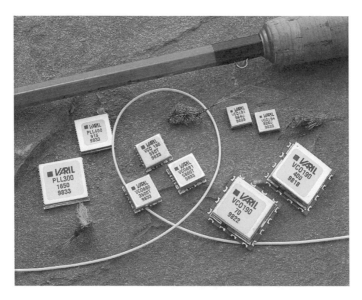

Figure 3–20
Surface-mount oscillators. *Courtesy of VARI-L Company, Inc.*

Different Kinds of Oscillators

There are many different oscillator types, which make up an alphabet soup of acronyms, a selection of which is detailed in Table 3–3. Every one of these oscillators has the same objective: to provide the most perfect sine wave under the given conditions (temperature, frequency, etc.). It is imperfections in the sine wave that cause problems and require the use of additional filters.

Table 3–3   Types of Oscillators

Acronym	Oscillator	Use
DRO	Dielectric Resonator Oscillator	Accurate, high frequency
DTO	Dielectrically Tuned Oscillator	Variable DRO
OCXO	Oven-Controlled XO	Accurate, with a built-in oven
SAW	Surface Acoustic Wave	Low cost, small size
TCXO	Temperature-Compensated XO	Accurate over temperature
VCO	Voltage-Controlled Oscillator	Variable frequency
VCXO	Voltage-Controlled XO	Very accurate and variable
XO	Crystal Oscillator	Very accurate
YIG	Yttrium-Iron-Garnet	Accurate, very high frequency

The Reason for the Different Oscillators

The reason for all the different oscillators comes down to how "perfect" the sine wave must be. Naturally the more perfect the sine wave, the more the oscillator is going to cost. The actual sine wave requirement is dictated by the system's requirements. For instance, digital wireless communication systems, like the newer cellular phones, require a more perfect sine wave from their LO than the communication systems of FM radio stations. Imperfections in the LO's sine wave show up as noise in the system and degrade the system's performance.

What Distinguishes Them

Inside the oscillator, the thing that determines the actual frequency and "perfect-ness" of the sine wave is just some small piece of material like ceramic or crystal. The exact frequency is determined by the composition and size of the material, and you should know by now that the higher the required frequency, the smaller the given piece of material will be.

Did You Know?

There is a type of oscillator called a YIG (rhymes with pig) oscillator. YIG stands for Yttrium-Iron-Garnet, which is a metallurgical compound that just happens to produce an incredibly perfect sine wave. How some RF engineer stumbled onto this little tidbit of information is beyond me.

How the Frequency Is Determined

What frequency should the oscillator be? To answer this question, you have to go back to the operation of a mixer. A mixer adds and subtracts frequencies, which in the case of a transmitter is used to raise the frequency of the RF signal before shooting it out the antenna. In this case, the mixer is used to add two frequencies together (rather than subtract them). If the signal going into the mixer (IF) is 400 MHz and the signal we want out (RF) is 900 MHz, what must we make the frequency of the LO? I will wait for you to get your calculator. The answer is 500 MHz. But the mixer gives two frequencies and the unwanted one (100 MHz) is eliminated with a filter, but you already knew that.

A Special Oscillator—The VCO

A special subset of oscillators is known collectively as *voltage-controlled oscillators* or VCOs. A VCO is an oscillator that can vary the frequency of its output sine wave in response to a change in input voltage. A block diagram of a VCO is shown in Figure 3–21.

Frequency
out

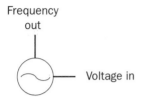
Voltage in

Figure 3–21
Block diagram of a VCO.

How They Work

As the voltage applied to the VCO changes, the output frequency of the VCO
changes. Unlike oscillators with a single fixed frequency, VCOs have a range of
frequencies over which they operate. All the same rules apply to VCOs: the wider
the frequency range, the more they cost and the poorer their performance. In this
case, poor performance means imperfections in the sine wave. When RF engineers design a system that requires a VCO, they choose one with a wide enough
frequency range to accommodate their requirements, but no wider.

Where are VCOs used in RF systems? As you will learn later in the section
on modulation, there is a type of modulation called *frequency modulation*, or FM,
which is the modulation used in FM radio signals (duh). Frequency modulation
works by taking the information to be transmitted wirelessly and "imprinting" it
onto the RF carrier by varying the RF carrier's frequency. What device do you
suppose the RF system uses to vary the RF carrier's frequency? Hint: look at
Figure 3–21.

Synthesizers

The Use of Feedback

There is another type of device related to the oscillator known as a *synthesizer*. In
some circumstances the sine wave coming out of a normal oscillator is just not perfect enough. Eventually, RF engineers discovered that if an oscillator is combined
with a bunch of other electronic circuitry and it utilizes feedback, it can make the
sine wave even more perfect, which is what a synthesizer is: an oscillator plus
some other circuitry that employs feedback to make a more perfect sine wave.

Phase-Locked Loops

As mentioned previously, feedback in any electrical system is nothing more than sensing the output of some component and, if it is not exactly the way it should be, changing the input to make it so. That is basically how synthesizers work—by sensing the output of an oscillator and, if the sine wave is not perfect enough, making a slight modification to something inside the oscillator to improve it. When synthesizers perform this feedback activity they are sometimes referred to as *phase-locked loops* or PLLs. (Apparently the word synthesizer is just too simple.)

Real life synthesizers can become pretty sophisticated and quite costly. They also perform many more functions than just simple feedback. One of the functions a synthesizer can perform is frequency programmability. The output frequency of a synthesizer can be made to vary gradually or it can made to jump from one discrete frequency to another very quickly. With discrete frequencies, a synthesizer acts like a box with several oscillators inside, all at different frequencies. The system can then select which frequency the synthesizer puts out, and in this way, the synthesizer can instantaneously switch between different (oscillators) frequencies. The ability to instantaneously switch between different frequencies is useful in secure military communications, as well as the newest digital wireless communication technologies.

A QUICK REVIEW ....

To quickly review all that has been covered to this point, I will follow an RF signal through the general transmitter and receiver block diagrams introduced in Figures 3–2 and 3–1, repeated here for convenience.

Transmitter Block Diagram

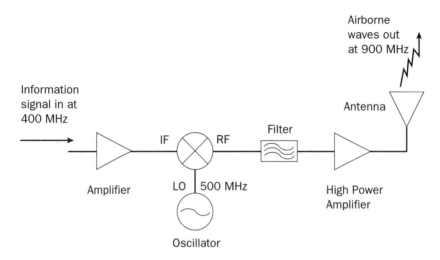

Figure 3–22
Transmitter block diagram.

Receiver Block Diagram

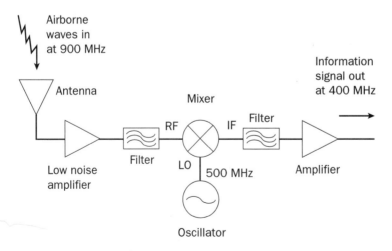

Figure 3–23
Receiver block diagram.

Review

Transmitter

Starting with the transmitter in Figure 3–22, a power supply is connected to the oscillator and out comes a perfect sine wave (hopefully) at 500 MHz. Next, another signal is injected, which is already carrying the information to be transmitted (at 400 MHz). The injected 400 MHz signal first gets amplified, because it probably is not big enough for the mixer to use as is. In this case, the mixer is an upconverter. Out of the mixer comes two signals (sum and difference) at 900 MHz and 100 MHz and, since this is the transmitter, the lower frequency signal is eliminated with the ensuing filter. Finally, the signal gets amplified by the HPA before it gets shoved into the antenna (as current on a conductor) and comes out as an invisible wave traveling through the air. Voilá!

Antenna

If the antenna is an omnidirectional antenna, then the transmitted signal is traveling all over the place and, if the signal is strong enough and there are no obstructions, the signal will find its way into the intended receiver's antenna. Just as a note: the signal also finds its way into a bunch of unintended antennas, like a neighbor's cellular phone. In fact, the signal makes it all the way through the unintended receiver, but that is where it stops, as the digital signal processor (DSP) inside the cellular phone knows to ignore the unintended signals. A brief overview of one way that the DSP does its thing is covered in the section on Spread Spectrum in Chapter 7.

Receiver

At this point, the intended receiver antenna turns the invisible wave into a current on a conductor. The signal is very weak from path loss and absorption. Before it can be of any use, it needs to be made bigger (amplified). So it gets sent through the LNA, after which it is big enough to "see," then the filter eliminates all of the unwanted signals (noise) that made it through the antenna.

It is now time to recover the original information signal at 400 MHz by subtracting out 500 MHz from the 900 MHz signal. This is done by sending the signal through another mixer (downconverter), which is fed by an oscillator at the same exact frequency as the one in the transmitter (500 MHz). Out of this mixer also comes two signals (sum and difference), one at 1400 MHz and the other 400 MHz. This time the higher-frequency signal is eliminated with a filter. And, finally, because the signal has just been through hell, it gets a little boost with a final amplifier. The original 400 MHz information signal just moved from one point to another *wirelessly.* Ain't life wonderful?

Did You Know?

For a wireless signal to be properly received, it does not need to be very powerful. Because of path loss and absorption in a wireless communications system, the received signal is usually on the order of a millionth of a watt (called a microwatt). It's invisible, it's infinitesimal, and yet it's still useful. I love RF.

4 Other Components

In this chapter…

- Switches   79
- Attenuators   84
- Dividers and Combiners   88
- Couplers   90
- Circulators and Isolators   93
- Transformers   96
- Detectors   98
- Phase Shifters   99
- Phase Detectors   100
- Review of Components   101

There are many other components used in RF systems beyond the five basic ones covered in the previous chapter. Some of these components are very simple to understand while others are more complex. Most of these other components exist to accomplish one of two objectives. They either send the RF signal in a different direction—or in multiple directions—or they change the size or shape of the signal. All of these "other" components are used in RF systems to effectively implement wireless communications, keeping in mind that the objective at any moment is to have a perfect sine wave, of the exact size required, at only one frequency.

This chapter covers eleven more components, and their derivatives, used in RF systems. Switches, dividers, combiners, couplers, circulators, and isolators all reroute the RF signal in one or more directions within the system. A major design objective for these components is to minimize insertion loss while rerouting the signal. On the other hand, attenuators, transformers, detectors, phase shifters, and phase detectors change the size and/or nature of the RF signal while keeping its shape unchanged. And, like the components covered in the previous chapter, each of these other components can be manufactured to optimize one or two key parameters. At least one example is given where each of these is used in a wireless system.

Unlike the five components covered in Chapter 3, these listed here tend to be manufactured by fewer companies, since they are used less frequently. This offers smaller manufacturers an opportunity to carve out small, but profitable, niches producing these devices.

There are other, more esoteric, components used in RF that are outside the scope of this book. (If you really want to learn about them, get an engineering degree.) The goal of this chapter is to give you an appreciation for how the complexity of an RF circuit can grow beyond that of the five basic components used in a transmitter and receiver.

SWITCHES ···

Block Diagram

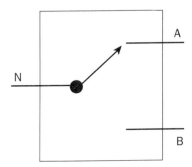

Figure 4–1
Block diagram of a single-pole, double-throw switch.

Switch Function and Performance

Function

Switches do what you think they do: they change the path that the RF signal is on, just like a switch on a train track. Referring to Figure 4–1, an RF signal cruising down "track" N is headed to track A, unless the path is switched to track B at the last minute. One interesting thing to note is that some switches work in both directions. Any component that works equally well in both directions is conveniently referred to as *bidirectional*. If the switch in Figure 4–1 is bidirectional, then two trains (RF signals) could be coming down tracks A and B at the same time, but only the one whose path is connected to N will get through. All switches are active devices (i.e., they require some sort of power supply to function properly).

Performance

There are two key performance parameters that RF engineers look for when designing with RF switches. The first performance parameter of importance is loss. Because they are so fickle, RF switches just happen to have two different kinds of loss. In the case of Figure 4–1, an RF signal going from N to A will only experience a little bit of loss. The path from N to A is the low-loss path and the loss the RF signal experiences is called insertion loss (remember insertion loss?). Insertion loss in the (closed) low-loss path of an RF switch is 1 dB or less. On the other hand, if the signal at N tries to make its way to B, it will not make it because the path from N to B is open and is therefore a high-loss path. You may think that the open path also has insertion loss (only much higher than the closed path) and you are right. RF engineers being who they are, however, felt the need to call this "higher" insertion loss in the open path *isolation*. Isolation in a switch can be thought of as the insertion loss of the open path. Isolation in an RF switch depends on a lot of things, but the minimum useful isolation is about 20 dB.

In almost every case, RF engineers try to design switches with the lowest possible insertion loss and the highest possible isolation. And just like everything else in RF, RF switches can be made with super low insertion loss and/or super high isolation (for a price).

The other important performance parameter is switching speed, which is a measure of how long it takes for the switch to go from one position to another. In general, RF engineers want the fastest possible switching speed, for the price, given the type of switch they are using.

Types of Switches

Electromechanical Switches

There are two basic types of switches in RF systems: electromechanical and solid state. Electromechanical switches are similar to the wall switch that controls a dining room light. In electromechanical switches, a control signal causes the contact to physically change positions during the switching process. The advantage to electromechanical switches is that they can handle high-power RF signals because their insertion loss is very low and their isolation is very high. For this reason, they are quite often used in RF test equipment. In contrast, everything else about electromechanical switches is bad. They are big and heavy, they are slow in switching, and they cost a lot. (Other than that, they're terrific.) Switching speed for an electromechanical switch is in the order of milliseconds (thousandths of a second), which is an eternity in the RF world. Three electromechanical switches are shown in Figure 4–2.

Figure 4–2
Electromechanical switches. *Courtesy of Dow-Key Microwave Corp.*

Solid State Switches

The other type of switch is solid state, which means that at the heart of the switch is some kind of semiconductor device. Unlike electromechanical switches, nothing inside solid state switches actually moves when they switch. This makes them very fast, although they cannot handle the large signals electromechanical switches can. Switching time for solid state switches is in the order of nanoseconds (billionths of a second), which is fast by anybody's measure. A solid state switch is shown in Figure 4–3. Solid state switches are either made from diodes or transistors, which you will learn about in the section on Semiconductors in Chapter 5. Why two choices? Diode switches have lower insertion loss, while switches made from transistors are faster.

Figure 4–3
A solid state switch. *Courtesy of JFW Industries, Inc.*

Poles and Throws

All RF switches come in different flavors categorized by their number of *poles* and *throws*. (It sounds like an Olympic event.) Referring to Figure 4–1, the big dot in the middle of the switch is known as a pole. The pole is the thing to which the "moving" part of the switch is hinged. A switch can have one or more poles. In essence, each pole represents a separate switch within the switch, but different poles within a single switch are not independent. They all switch at the same time.

Throws are all the different positions that the switch can switch to. In Figure 4–1, the switch can be "thrown" to two different positions, A and B, and this switch is therefore a two-throw switch. In fact, the switch in Figure 4–1 is called a single-pole, double-throw switch. A switch can have any (practical) number of throws. A ten-throw switch will have ten different positions it can switch to, labeled A through J. A block diagram of a double-pole, double-throw (DPDT) switch is shown in Figure 4–4. Notice it has two poles (big dots) and each pole has two throws (positions). Ergo double pole, double throw.

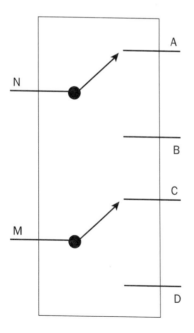

Figure 4–4
Block diagram of a double-pole, double-throw switch.

Here is an interesting question. If a double-pole, double-throw switch is abbreviated DPDT, how is a single-pole, double-throw switch, like the one shown in Figure 4–1, abbreviated? SPDT. Here is a tricky one. How is a single-pole, four-throw switch abbreviated? SP4T. I think I have beaten this to death, and will therefore assume you can figure out any switch abbreviation you are likely to encounter for the rest of your life, for whatever that's worth.

Did You Know?

There is a type of RF switch called a single-pole, *single*-throw (SPST), which means the switch has one input (the pole) and only *one* output (the throw). This invites the question, when the SPST switch is not connected to its one output and an RF signal is applied to the input, where does the signal go? The signal gets reflected, which is why SPST switches are only used in very low power applications.

System Use

Where is a switch used in a RF system? Suppose a cellular phone wants to use its antenna for both transmitting and receiving. The phone could utilize a T/R switch, where the antenna is connected to the N path, the receiver to the A path, and the transmitter to the B path, as shown in Figure 4–5. Furthermore, the antenna could be made to switch to the receiver path every time a signal is coming in (the other person is talking), and it could be made to switch to the transmitter every time a signal is going out (you are talking).

Not only would that work very well and eliminate the need for a second antenna, but that is precisely how many cellular phones work.

Any switch that is connected to both a transmitter and receiver, like the one shown in Figure 4–5, is conveniently referred to as a transmit-receive switch, or T/R switch for short.

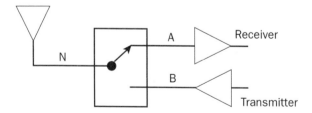

Figure 4–5
A T/R switch between an antenna, a transmitter, and a receiver.

ATTENUATORS ....

Block Diagram

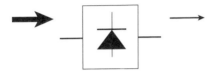

Figure 4–6
Block diagram of a generic attenuator.

The Attenuator's Function

Think of *attenuators* as anti-amplifiers. A block diagram of a generic attenuator is shown in Figure 4–6. As hard as it is to believe, sometimes in a wireless system the darn signal is just too big, which is where attenuators come in. They make a signal smaller by attenuating it. You may recall from an earlier chapter that attenuation is the result of insertion loss. Attenuation and insertion loss mean the exact same thing. Attenuators allow RF engineers to install a known amount of insertion loss into a circuit.

Visually, a big signal enters the attenuator on the left side and leaves as a smaller signal on the right. Where does the rest of the signal go? You should know that by now: heat, which is why attenuators always come with a maximum power rating. It states the greatest amount of RF input power the attenuator can handle without melting. Attenuators can also be represented by the block diagram shown in Figure 4–7.

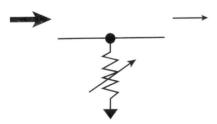

Figure 4–7
Alternative block diagram of a generic attenuator.

To demonstrate the complex nature of the average RF engineer, there are some RF systems in which an amplifier is immediately followed by an attenuator. Talk about indecision. They cannot decide whether they want the signal bigger or smaller. There really are good electrical reasons for doing this, but the explanation is way beyond what you need, and besides, it's just easier to think of RF engineers as complex.

Types of Attenuators

Fixed Attenuators

Attenuators fall into two categories: *fixed* and *variable*. Fixed attenuators, as the name implies, cause the signal to experience a fixed amount of loss, measured in dB. Sometimes fixed attenuators are called *pads*. A typical fixed attenuator might exhibit 3 dB of insertion loss and is therefore a 3 dB pad. In this case, the signal coming out is half as big as the one going in. (–3 dB is the same as dividing by 2.) A couple of fixed *coaxial* attenuators are shown in Figure 4–8. Notice that they look just like cylindrical hunks of metal, which is essentially what they are. Fixed attenuators are passive devices.

Figure 4–8
Fixed coaxial attenuators. *Courtesy of JFW Industries, Inc.*

Voltage Variable Attenuators

The other kind of attenuator is called a variable attenuator. Variable attenuators allow the RF engineer to control the exact amount of attenuation (or insertion loss), at any moment through the use of an external control. There are two different kinds of variable attenuators: voltage variable attenuators (VVA) and digital attenuators, both of which are active devices.

Voltage variable attenuators vary the attenuation over a specified attenuation range and are controlled by a single external control voltage. (I guess that's why they call them voltage variable attenuators.) For instance, a VVA may be specified with an attenuation range from 2 to 30 dB, which means that by varying the control voltage, any value of insertion loss from 2 dB all the way to 30 dB can be obtained. It could even be adjusted to π (Pi) attenuation (3.14 dB) if the need arose. VVAs are used where exact amounts of insertion loss are needed in the system, usually in conjunction with feedback.

Digital Attenuators

The other type of variable attenuator is a digital attenuator. Unlike the VVA, which has a single input control, digital attenuators have multiple input controls, each controlling a different value of attenuation. It is easiest to think of a digital attenuator as a bunch of fixed attenuators, all in a row, which can either be switched into or out of the circuit at any time. The trick is that each subsequent "fixed" attenuator has twice the attenuation of the previous attenuator. A quick look at Figure 4–9 will clear everything up.

An RF signal enters the digital attenuator at the left and goes through four fixed attenuators before it emerges on the right. Each attenuator that the signal goes through either has the attenuation value shown if it is on, or a value of zero if it is off. Each attenuator is turned on and off with their respective control lines A, B, C, and D. In this way, the total attenuation a signal experiences can range from 0 dB, if all the attenuators are off, to 30 dB, if all the attenuators are on. Note, however, that the attenuation value does not vary continuously from 0 to 30 dB. It cannot take any value between the two extremes, but only those that can be made by adding up various combinations of the four attenuators. For instance, 20 dB of attenuation is possible (by turning off the 2 dB and the 8 dB attenuators and turning on the 4 dB and 16 dB attenuators), but, alas, π dB of attenuation is not. For that you will need a VVA.

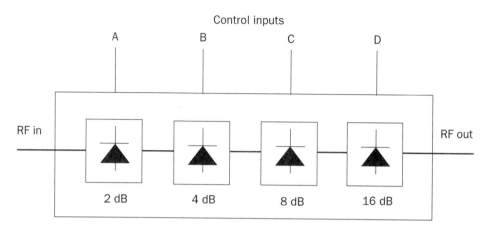

Figure 4–9
Block diagram of a digital attenuator.

Digital attenuators can be controlled by the same types of (digital) signals that run around inside a computer, which is why digital attenuators are used when RF engineers want to "program" the amount of attenuation in a circuit. A digital attenuator is shown in Figure 4–10. It cannot be seen from the outside, but inside is a very sophisticated electrical circuit. Also, compare the digital attenuator in Figure 4–10 with the fixed attenuator in Figure 4–8. They look so different, it is hard to believe they are both attenuators.

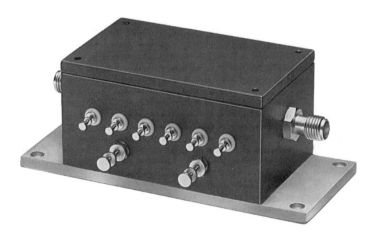

Figure 4–10
A digital attenuator. *Courtesy of Mini-Circuits.*

The key performance parameter for all types of attenuators is accuracy. Not only must the attenuation be the exact amount required—whether fixed or variable—but the attenuation must not vary over time, temperature, or anything else.

DIVIDERS AND COMBINERS ....

Block Diagram

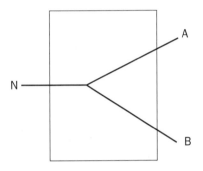

Figure 4–11
Block diagram of a two-way power divider.

The Dividers' and Combiners' Functions

Dividers divide. Visually, a signal goes cruising down path N (see Figure 4–11) and half the signal's power goes down path A, while the other half goes down path B. The signal gets divided in half. Its shape stays the same, but the power is reduced. Dividers are also called *power dividers*.

Dividers can divide by numbers other than two. A four-way power divider has paths C and D and one quarter of the original signal's power goes down each path. Dividers always divide the input signal equally among all of the outputs.

If it were flipped over and two different signals were sent down paths A and B, then the signal on path N would become a combination of the two signals. What do you suppose RF engineers call this flipped-over divider? A *combiner*. A two-way power divider (or combiner) is shown in Figure 4–12. All power dividers and combiners are passive devices.

Figure 4–12
A two-way power divider. *Courtesy of TRM, Inc.*

System Use

Why are dividers needed? Perhaps there is a wireless system that requires the use of two identical transmitters in the same place (don't ask why). Two transmitters require two of everything, including two power amplifiers, two mixers, two sources, etc. Or do they? What if a single oscillator is used and its output is divided in half (by the divider). Then one of the signals is sent to one mixer and the other signal is sent to the other mixer. Assuming dividers are cheaper than oscillators (which they are), this reduces the cost of the hardware. Dividers are used when RF engineers want to send the same signal to more than one place in an RF system.

The key performance parameter for combiners and dividers, as well as most other passive devices, is insertion loss. The lower the insertion loss, the more of the signal that makes it through the device, which is a good thing.

COUPLERS..

Block Diagram

Figure 4–13
Block diagram of a directional coupler.

How Couplers Work

To understand how *couplers* function, I will use the analogy of wine tasting. Before you buy an expensive bottle of wine, you want to taste a sample. The sample does not have to be very big for you to know whether you are going to enjoy the whole bottle. This is how couplers work; only instead of sampling wine, they sample the RF signal.

Visually, a signal enters the coupler at point A (see Figure 4–13) and generally makes its way to point C and along its merry way somewhere else in the system. Except, as it goes from A to C, a tiny fraction of the signal is siphoned off and brought out at point B, called the sample port. The signal at point B is the sample. What can be done with the sample? Lots.

Imagine RF signals having color. Suppose the goal is to transmit an orange signal out of the antenna. A coupler could be placed just before the antenna to sample the signal before it gets radiated out. As long as the sample is orange, everything would be fine. But what if the signal that the coupler samples turns red? At that point, the sample could be used to tell some other part of the circuit to crank up the yellow, which is exactly the purpose of a coupler. A coupler samples an RF signal and yells back to some other component to change something if everything is not just right. And if you have been paying attention, you will recognize this as an explanation of feedback. Couplers are often used as part of feedback circuits in RF systems. A directional coupler is shown in Figure 4–14. Couplers are passive devices.

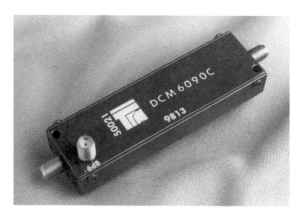

Figure 4–14
A directional coupler. *Courtesy of TRM, Inc.*

Types of Couplers

Directional and Bidirectional Couplers

The coupler discussed above is a *directional coupler*, which means that it has one sample port and only works in one direction. A cousin to the directional coupler is the *bidirectional coupler*. The bidirectional coupler works in both directions and has two sample ports. (Because of the quirky nature of RF, separate sample ports are needed for waves traveling in opposite directions.)

Another way to think of directional couplers is as two-way dividers in which the power is divided unevenly: 99% of the power goes to the output and 1% goes to the sample port.

The key performance parameter for a directional coupler, in addition to insertion loss, is coupling accuracy. For the coupler to function properly, the amount of signal that comes out of the sample port must be known exactly and must not vary (too much) over frequency, time, temperature, or anything else.

Quadrature Couplers

Just when you thought you had mastered the subject of couplers, RF engineers came along and invented a whole new breed of coupler called a *quadrature* or *Lange coupler*, also called a *quadrature hybrid* or *quad hybrid*. Unlike directional

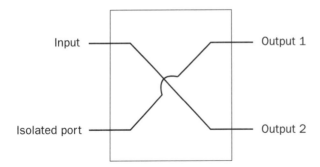

Figure 4–15
Block diagram of a Lange coupler.

couplers with their sample port, quadrature couplers are almost identical to two-way power dividers. Their output power is divided evenly between the two outputs. The block diagram for a Lange coupler is shown in Figure 4–15.

There must be some difference between a quadrature coupler and a two-way power divider, right? There is, and the difference between the two concerns subtleties of RF that are way beyond the scope of this book; but as you know, that will not keep me from trying to explain it. The difference between a two-way power divider and a quadrature coupler is that in a quadrature coupler the two outputs are "out of phase." (Do not fret if you don't know what that means because you soon will.)

Do you recall the balanced amplifier from the previous chapter? In a balanced amplifier, the input signal is divided in two, sent through two parallel amplifiers, and then combined again at the output. Well, that divider and combiner are, in reality, quadrature couplers. To simplify matters, quadrature couplers are used in balanced amplifiers because they improve the amplifier's match (remember match?). They are also used in digital modulation, which you will learn about in the next chapter. And just as a point of information, with reference to Figure 4–15, the isolated port does not necessarily do anything. It's just there for confusion.

CIRCULATORS AND ISOLATORS ....

Block Diagram

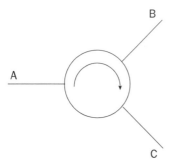

Figure 4–16
Block diagram of a circulator.

How Circulators Work

These devices are real special. You will understand *circulators* perfectly if you can picture a traffic circle, which automobiles sometimes find themselves trapped on in cities on the east coast of the U.S. and in Europe. A traffic circle or rotary is a circular roadway, in the middle of a highway, with several exits on the outer periphery. All the cars travel around the circle in the same direction, and if they are lucky, they are on the outside of the circle when it is time for them to exit. A block diagram of a circulator is shown in Figure 4–16.

Circulators work the same way. All the RF signals travel in the same circular direction (see the arrow), but there is only one catch. All the RF signals have to get off at the very first exit they encounter. For instance, an RF signal getting on the circulator at point A and going clockwise around the circle must get off at point B. Those are the rules. A circulator is shown on the right side of Figure 4–17. See the three connections (called ports)?

How do circulators do what they do? By building on the laws of electricity and magnetism, circulators combine magnets and a special type of material called *ferrite* to perform their magic. (Ferrite is just a material that magnetic fields really like to hang out in.) You can now impress your friends by casually dropping the word ferrite into a social conversation.

Figure 4–17
An isolator and a circulator. *Courtesy of Nova Microwave.*

System Use

Where is a circulator used in an RF system? Think back to the example in which the switch is used to connect the antenna to the transmitter and receiver. What if the switch were replaced with a circulator as shown in Figure 4–18?

As shown in Figure 4–18, following the rules of a circulator, any signal coming from the antenna gets routed by the circulator to the receiver, which is desired. Any signal coming out of the transmitter gets routed by the circulator to the antenna, which is also desired. And finally, any signal coming out of the receiver—wait a minute, there should not be any signals coming *out* of the receiver. The circulator acts as kind of an intelligent switch, without actually having to switch anything. And, oh, by the way, circulators are passive devices.

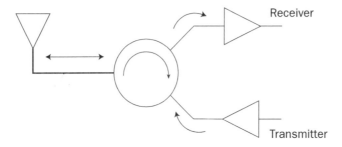

Figure 4–18
A circulator between an antenna, a receiver, and a transmitter.

Isolators

There is a particular type of circulator in which only two of the three ports are utilized, called an *isolator*. In reality, the third (unused) port is fed into a hunk of some material (called a *resistor* or load) for the sole purpose of dissipating heat. The reason it is called a load is because it "loads" the circuit down. Recall from the discussion on match that if a circuit is left open, all the RF energy gets reflected back. Rather than getting reflected back, the load accepts the RF energy and converts it entirely to heat. Okay, I explained my way out of the circulator, but what possible use might there be for an isolator?

Back during the discussion on match, it was pointed out that when two RF components are connected, some of the RF energy leaks. In fact it does not leak out, but gets reflected back from where it came. Picture the point in a transmitter where the power amplifier (PA) is connected to the antenna. The power amplifier puts out a lot of power and some of it gets reflected right back to the amplifier. PAs are just like schoolyard bullies, they can dish it out but they can't take it. So while a PA may put out 50 watts, if only 2 or 3 watts get reflected back, they go off crying to their mother amplifier. What really happens is they blow up.

Figure 4–19 shows an isolator placed between an antenna and a PA (in a transmitter). In this situation, most of the high-power RF signal from the PA makes its way to the antenna and out as invisible waves. A small portion, however, gets reflected back from the antenna toward the PA. But before the reflected signal can get to the PA and cause damage, it gets rerouted by the isolator into the load where it gets dissipated harmlessly as heat. Tah dah. Isolators act to protect some RF devices from reflected RF power by "isolating" them from the reflected power. An isolator is shown on the left side of Figure 4–17.

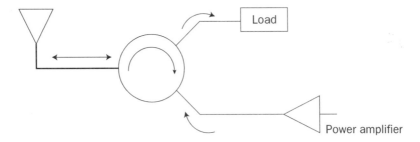

Figure 4–19
An isolator between a power amplifier and an antenna.

The primary performance parameter for isolators and circulators is insertion loss. RF engineers want the insertion loss to be as small as possible so that only a small amount of the signal is lost (as heat) and the majority of the signal makes it through to its intended destination.

TRANSFORMERS ....

Block Diagram

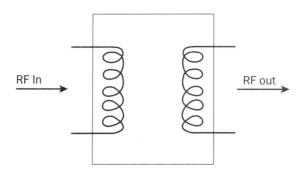

Figure 4–20
Block diagram of a transformer.

The Transformer's Function

During the discussion about match, it was mentioned that there is a standard "size" of inputs and outputs for all RF components, which is 50 Ω (ohm) impedance. When the output of one device and the input of the next device are both 50 Ω (or nearly so), then the two devices are connected directly and the slight mismatch (leaking) is tolerated. However, sometimes one of the devices has an input or output that is so far from 50 Ω that trying to connect it to another device with the proper input (50 Ω) causes a horrible mismatch (leaking). What is needed in this situation is a matching circuit, and so in steps the *transformer*. It "transforms" the wrong impedance (maybe 100 Ω) into the right impedance (50 Ω). That way the device with the wrong impedance can be utilized. A transformer is the actual device represented by the impedance matching circuit graphically depicted in Figure 2–6. A block diagram of a transformer is shown in Figure 4–20.

Recall the garden hose analogy and imagine trying to connect two garden hoses with different size openings. A transformer is needed between the two hoses to adapt the hose with the bigger opening to that of the hose with the smaller opening, which is exactly the function of an RF transformer. Two small surface-mount transformers are shown in Figure 4–21. If you look closely, you can see the wires wrapped around like a coil, which is what the squiggly lines represent in Figure 4–20.

Did You Know?

In the world of RF, the prefix "trans" is used so frequently that RF engineers abbreviate it with the letter "X." Therefore, the word transformer is abbreviated as xformer, transmitter is abbreviated as xmitter, and so on. Now you can xlate from RF to English.

Impedance Ratio

As you might imagine, there are a lot of "wrong" impedances out there and so there are many different transformers. The key performance parameter of a transformer is its *impedance ratio*. The impedance ratio dictates what "wrong" impedance the transformer will make "right." If the impedance ratio is specified as 2:1, then the transformer will "transform" 100 Ω into 50 Ω. Therefore, a 2:1 transformer is used when the "wrong" impedance is 100 Ω.

Figure 4–21
Surface-mount transformers. *Courtesy of Coilcraft, Inc.*

There are some other uses for transformers, but they depend more on the subtleties of electronics. For the sake of this book it is easiest to ignore them. In the world of RF, transformers are most often used to "transform" impedances, which is the best way to think of them.

DETECTORS ....

Block Diagram

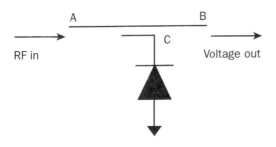

Figure 4–22
Block diagram of a detector.

The Detector's Function

A block diagram of a detector is shown in Figure 4–22. If you think a detector looks like a cross between a coupler and attenuator, you are right, but that will not help you much. A *detector* is essentially a power-to-voltage converter. RF power enters at point A and what comes out at point B is a voltage that is proportional to the RF power.

The reason a detector is used in place of a coupler is that there are certain pieces of test equipment and non-RF components (like microprocessors) that cannot handle RF power directly, but can handle an electrical voltage. In these instances, the detector is used to convert the RF power to voltage, which is then sent somewhere else (either within the RF system or to a piece of test equipment) so that a decision can be made based upon it.

If you want to know what a detector looks like, look at the picture of the fixed attenuator in Figure 4–8. They look almost exactly alike. In fact, even RF engineers sometimes confuse the two, which makes for interesting circuit behavior.

PHASE SHIFTERS......................................

Block Diagram

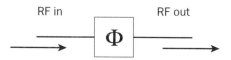

Figure 4–23
Block diagram of a phase shifter.

The Phase Shifter's Function

Your patience will now be rewarded. Here is where you learn what "out of phase" means. The first thing you will need to know is that sine waves (and therefore RF signals) have a phase associated with them. The phase of a sine wave is measured in degrees and one complete cycle covers 360°. Referring back to Figure 1–2, from point A to point E is 360°.

In a phase shifter (a block diagram of which is shown in Figure 4–23), the input signal acts as a reference signal and the output signal is phase shifted with respect to the input signal. Imagine viewing both signals on a piece of test equipment, with the input signal above the output signal, like that shown in Figure 4–24. If the phase shifter were to shift the output 0° (no phase shift), both sine waves would exactly line up with one another (left side of the figure). In this case, the two signals are "in phase." As the phase shift is increased to 90°, the output signal viewed on the test equipment will move to the left (right side of the figure) by one quarter of a sine wave. These two signals are 90° out of phase.

For many reasons that will soon become apparent, it is often useful to be able to accurately control the phase of one signal with respect to another and that is where the phase shifter comes in. Phase shifters can be variable or fixed. In a variable phase shifter, the phase can be made to vary continuously by the use of some external control. This is often required when testing an RF circuit, to help optimize its performance, or when using feedback (and you know what that is). A fixed phase shifter has a set value, with the more common ones being 90° and 180°. Phase shifters can be active or passive and like many other RF components, phase shifters are often made from diodes.

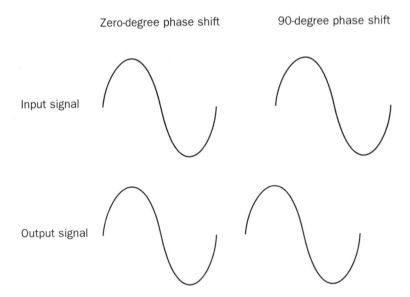

Figure 4–24
An example of phase shift.

The symbol in the center of the phase shifter block diagram is the Greek letter (Φ) phi. Phi is used by RF engineers the world over to represent this thing called phase. Many other Greek letters are also used in the world of RF such as lambda (λ) for wavelength and omega (ω) for frequency. And you thought they were only used by fraternities.

PHASE DETECTORS......................................

The Phase Detector's Function

It would do no good to impart a phase shift onto an RF signal if that phase shift could not somehow be detected. That is where the phase detector comes in. A phase detector has two inputs and one output. (The reason there is no block diagram of a phase detector is that it is usually just a box with the words "phase detector" on it.) Two different sine waves act as the two inputs and what comes out is a voltage that is proportional to the difference in their phases.

Phase detectors are different from the detectors discussed earlier in the chapter. The detectors mentioned previously convert a single RF signal into an equivalent voltage, whereas a phase detector converts the difference in phase between two sine waves into an equivalent voltage.

Phase detectors can be used in the demodulation process (be patient) to separate out a digital information signal from an RF carrier. What are phase detectors made of? In their simplest form, phase detectors are nothing more than doubled balanced mixers, where the RF and LO ports are the inputs and the IF port is the (voltage) output. Really.

REVIEW OF COMPONENTS.......................................

I thought it might be valuable at this point to review all of the components you've learned about in the last two chapters. Table 4–1 is a quick review by type and function.

Table 4–1   Review of Components

Component	Active/Passive	Primary Function
Antenna	Both	Convert to and from airborne waves
Amplifier	Active	Make signals bigger
Filter	Passive	Separate signals by frequency
Mixer	Both	Increase/decrease a signal's frequency
Oscillator	Active	Create a perfect sine wave
Switch	Active	Change the direction a signal travels
Attenuator	Both	Make signals smaller
Divider	Passive	Split up a signal
Combiner	Passive	Add signals together
Coupler	Passive	Split up or add 2 signals in unequal proportion
Circulator	Passive	Control signal flow among 3 components

Table 4–1   Review of Components (Continued)

Component	Active/Passive	Primary Function
Isolator	Passive	Protect adjacent components from signal reflection
Transformer	Passive	Change impedance
Detector	Passive	Convert an RF power signal to its equivalent voltage
Phase shifter	Both	Change the phase of 1 sine wave with respect to another
Phase detector	Passive	Produce a voltage proportional to the difference in 2 phases

5 Circuits and Signals

In this chapter…

- Semiconductors 104

- Circuit Technologies   111

- Modulation   119

- Getting Around   128

This chapter ties together, literally, all the components discussed up to this point. Three different circuit technologies used to manufacture RF components are introduced: discrete, hybrid, and MMIC. Their differences are noted, as well as the reasons why one is chosen over another in a particular situation. The three are also viewed from the standpoint of both performance and cost impact. Additionally, this chapter covers three different component interconnection schemes: cable, waveguide, and traces. Once again, the reasons why one is chosen over another are pointed out.

This chapter also introduces you to two different circuit philosophies: lumped element and distributed. With these you will see how some RF components can be realized two different ways, the choice of which depends heavily on their frequency of intended use.

RF semiconductor devices are covered in detail, including the primary materials used in RF electronics and the two main devices used in all RF hardware: diodes and transistors. Also included is a discussion on integrated circuits and their advantages and disadvantages when compared to other options.

This chapter also deals with the very complicated subject of modulation, which is the term used for combining the information signal with the carrier signal in wireless communications. The major modulation techniques are discussed, along with some of their variations. You also will learn of the role that digital technology has played in the evolution of the modulation schemes prevalent in today's most sophisticated wireless systems.

SEMICONDUCTORS...

Materials and Devices

Solid State Technology

The world of wireless communications really began to take off with the development of semiconductor technology. Another name for semiconductor technology is solid state technology. The reason it is called solid state is that semiconductors are a solid material. (It also helps distinguish it from liquid state technology, in which the electrical components are made out of chocolate milk.) The other type of technology, soon to be extinct, is tube technology. In tube technology, all the electrical stuff happens in a vacuum. An example of a tube technology is the old vacuum tube found in the television sets of the sixties. Many of those old tubes were in fact RF amplifiers in disguise. In those tubes, the RF signal got bigger (amplified) while it floated around in a vacuum in the tube.

Vacuum-based electrical products (tubes) are, with only a few exceptions (like very high power requirements), no longer used in RF communications. It is not that the old tubes cannot do what semiconductors can—they can, it is that semiconductors have two really attractive properties that tubes do not: they can be made very small and very cheap (not to mention they don't break when you drop them).

Silicon and Gallium Arsenide

There are two primary semiconductor materials used to manufacture RF components: *silicon* (Si) and *gallium arsenide* (GaAs), also known as "gas." In general, GaAs is used for higher frequency applications. If some RF component utilizes GaAs, chances are that silicon did not work at the (high) frequency of intended use. When given a choice, an RF engineer will choose a silicon device over a GaAs device because it is less expensive.

Newer, More Exotic Materials

There are two new materials making their presence felt in the world of RF and they are *silicon germanium* (SiGe) and *indium phosphide* (InP). The driving force behind SiGe is the handheld mobile phone. Until recently, the output power amplifier in a handset was almost always made of GaAs. But SiGe not only has better linear performance than GaAs (which is important in digital wireless communications), but it is more efficient. And better efficiency translates into longer battery life. Expect to see more and more SiGe components in the next generation of mobile wireless devices as they can be made about as inexpensively as plain silicon devices.

The driving force behind InP is high frequency—specifically performance at millimeter wave frequencies (> 40 GHz). InP has amongst the best low noise performance of any material today at very high frequencies. InP can also be used to make power amplifiers, of course at millimeter wave frequencies, high power isn't all that high. Unlike SiGe however, for the time being, InP is still relatively expensive to manufacture.

Diodes and Transistors

There are only two basic semiconductor building blocks used in the RF world: *diodes* and *transistors*. Before you start thinking that things are pretty simple with only two basic building blocks, know that there are a lot of different kinds of diodes and transistors and they are all used for different reasons. Table 5–1 highlights the most popular diodes and transistors used in RF systems.

Table 5–1   RF Diode and Transistor Types

Diode Types	Transistor Types
PIN	MOSFET & MESFET
Schottky	Bipolar
Gunn	HBT
Impatt	HEMT & PHEMT
Tunnel	JFET
Varactor	LDMOS

Before you start feeling overwhelmed with all the different types of diodes and transistors, understand that the primary difference between them is in how they are fabricated and from what material they are made. All the diodes pretty much do the same thing, but because they are fabricated differently, they have superior electrical performance in different areas. For instance, Schottky diodes are fabricated to be fast, while PIN diodes are fabricated to handle a lot of power. The same goes for transistors. Most diode types indicated in Table 5–1 can be made of either silicon or GaAs, while the transistors are made of one material or the other, but not both.

For instance, you can buy a PIN diode made from silicon or one made from GaAs (although why you'd want to is beyond me). Each has their advantages but you know the rule of thumb: silicon is for lower frequencies, GaAs is for higher frequencies. And now with the newer, more exotic materials, you can get diodes made from them also.

Transistors are a little trickier. Like diodes, they too can be manufactured from different materials, but unlike diodes, when the material type changes, so does the type of transistor. This is discussed in greater detail below.

Diodes

Diodes are used in many different components in the RF world, but they are primarily used in three components: switches, mixers, and voltage variable attenuators (VVA). (If you want to know what a diode looks like in block diagram form, it is the weird shape on the attenuator shown in Figure 4–6.) If Schottky diodes are fast and PIN diodes can handle substantial amounts of power, what diode is used if the switch needs to be fast? How about if it has to handle a lot of power?

As mentioned in Chapter 3 in the section on sources, most oscillators utilize some sort of material to determine the actual frequency of oscillation. This technique works well for "lower" RF frequencies. For "higher" RF frequencies (greater than 10 GHz), material choice is limited and so oscillators frequently use a diode to determine the frequency of oscillation. Gunn, Tunnel, and Impatt diodes are all used to generate these "higher" RF frequencies in oscillators, especially Impatts, which are used for super high RF frequencies (greater than 100 GHz).

Varactor diodes can be thought of as "variable diodes" and are used in voltage controlled oscillators (VCO). Recall from Chapter 3 that VCOs are oscillators whose output frequency can vary over some range. Well, the reason it can vary is because it utilizes a "variable diode" (varactor) to determine its frequency. (All of this stuff really does make sense.)

Transistors

Transistors are used extensively in RF for everything from low noise amplifiers to high power amplifiers to switches, attenuators, mixers, oscillators, you name it. Transistors are the work horse of RF. Transistors are fabricated one of two different ways. They are either made as bipolar junction transistors (BJT) also called bipolars—or they are made as field effect transistors (FETs). The only difference you need to know about the two structures is that bipolars have junctions (duh) in them where the material changes abruptly and FETs do not. Block diagrams of these two common transistor types are shown in Figure 5–1, strictly for entertainment purposes.

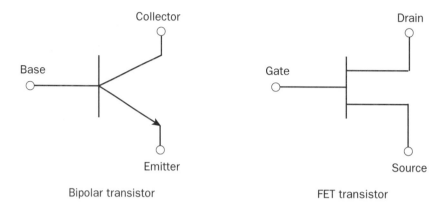

Figure 5–1
Circuit representation of a bipolar and FET transistor.

HBT Transistors

There is a new type of bipolar transistor available today called the *heterojunction bipolar transistor* or HBT. Originally, BJT transistors were only made from a single material, usually silicon. However, some physics PhD somewhere discovered that if you make a BJT from more than one material, you can often times improve its performance in some meaningful way. Enter the HBT. In simplified terms, an HBT is just a BJT made from more than one material. So a BJT made from Silicon is called a BJT, but a BJT made from GaAs is called an HBT. As mentioned above, when the material changes, the transistor type changes.

Transistor Usage

Here is a great rule to know: if there is gain, there is at least one transistor. All solid state amplifiers use transistors of one kind or another. To produce a lot of gain, amplifiers require two or more transistors.

The lowest frequency (less than 1 GHz) transistor used in RF is the MOSFET, which stands for Metal Oxide Semiconductor Field Effect Transistor. (Can you guess whether this is a BJT or an FET?) Your intuition should tell you that MOSFETs are made from silicon (hint: low frequency). Also, they are primarily used in high power amplifiers (HPA).

Above 1 GHz, RF engineers choose between bipolar transistors and MES-FETs, which stands for Metal Semiconductor Field Effect Transistor. As you already know, BJTs are always made from a single material, usually silicon. Likewise, MESFETs are always made from GaAs. Which transistor type is better? Well if cost is an issue then (Silicon) BJTs are the better choice because they are cheaper. If on the other hand, the transistor needs to operate at a particularly high frequency, then the (GaAs) MESFET is the better choice. As another consideration, at frequencies where either transistor type can be used, bipolar transistors are manufactured to produce more RF power than MESFETs while MESFETs provide a lower noise figure (NF) than bipolars. In summary, bipolars are less expensive and produce high power while GaAs MESFETs cost more, but work better at higher frequencies while delivering lower noise figures.

There is a new type of FET transistor on the block which is known as LD-MOS (pronounced l dee´ mäs), which stands for Laterally Diffused Metal Oxide Semiconductor. (I couldn't make this stuff up.) Some bright young RF engineer discovered that if a MOSFET is fabricated a little differently, it can be made to work at frequencies above 1 GHz. Where do you suppose these LDMOS transistors get used? If you said high power amplifiers above 1 GHz, give yourself a prize.

HEMT Transistors

There is yet another new family of transistors, specifically designed for super high frequency applications, known as HEMT and PHEMT, which stands for High Electron Mobility Transistor and Pseudomorphic HEMT, respectively. (How many people do you suppose you would have to ask before you could find one who knows what Pseudomorphic means?) HEMT transistors are just MESFETs that have an added layer of some super-fast semiconductor material, like InP. (This is another example of a transistor type changing when the material changes.)

Picture the electrons in an ordinary MESFET as cars traveling on a regular highway (speed limit: 55 MPH). HEMT transistors are nothing more than MES-FETs in which the electrons have been given their own InP autobahn. If the electrons can travel faster, then the transistor can work at higher frequencies. HEMT transistors are particularly suited to high-frequency, low-noise applications.

Something to note: When I say certain transistors "work" at higher frequencies and others do not, what I really mean is that certain transistors work well at higher frequencies and others perform poorly, even though technically they "work" at higher frequencies. Poor performance manifests itself as degraded electrical parameters like power, gain, and noise figure.

Integrated Circuits (MMIC)

Some clever engineers figured out a while back that if an amplifier (or other device) needs, say, three transistors, two diodes, and a bunch of other electrical components, why not just put all of these goodies onto a single piece of semiconductor (silicon or GaAs). There are many advantages to doing this, including lower cost and smaller size. When more than one electrical device (transistor, diode, etc.) is combined onto a single piece of semiconductor, it is called an *integrated circuit* (IC).

Now RF engineers could not let their devices be called just integrated circuits for fear that people might confuse them with other integrated circuits, like the Pentium microprocessor in a PC. RF engineers complicate matters by calling their ICs *Monolithic Microwave Integrated Circuits* or *MMIC*s (pronounced mim´ iks). (Whatever.)

Most of the components covered to this point can be made as MMICs. A MMIC is not a particular device, it is a manufacturing technology used to realize particular components. For instance, a MMIC that uses a bunch of transistors to make an amplifier is called a MMIC amplifier, while a MMIC that uses a bunch of transistors to make a switch is called a MMIC switch. (You get the idea.)

MMIC Performance

If a component can be made as a MMIC, which is smaller and cheaper (per unit) than other approaches, why are not all components made as MMICs? There are two drawbacks to MMICs. First, since they involve the semiconductor manufacturing process, they are very expensive if only a few will be needed. Therefore, MMIC technology is only used when the volume requirement is sufficient enough to justify the initial investment to develop the MMIC. Second, quite often MMICs have worse performance (on key parameters) than the same device made out of individual components. Where performance is at a premium, like low noise in a low noise amplifier or high power in a high power amplifier, the devices are made out of individual transistors (or diodes). When performance is not as critical and cost is, the devices used are MMICs.

To quickly review, there are two main semiconductor materials used in the RF world: silicon and gallium arsenide. Silicon and gallium arsenide are used to make two basic building blocks: diodes and transistors. RF devices can be manufactured two ways: by combining individual diodes and transistors or as integrated circuits (MMICs).

Did You Know?

There is a special class of RF MMICs called ASICs, which stands for *application specific integrated circuit*. ASICs are nothing more than custom MMICs, designed to accomplish one specific task and usually intended for only a single customer. Because they are custom-made, ASICs must be used in high volume to justify the design expense. Cellular phones are the ideal candidate for ASICs. In fact, some people believe that to get the cost of cellular phones down even lower, in the not-too-distant future, cellular phones will have just a single component inside of them: an ASIC. I say, what's the holdup?

CIRCUIT TECHNOLOGIES ....

Lumped and Distributed Circuits

RF components are frequently made up of several different electrical components called *discrete* components. For instance, while an RF amplifier is an RF component, it is made up of several discrete electrical components like diodes, transistors, and the big three: *resistors*, *capacitors*, and *inductors*. Resistors, capacitors, and inductors are small, inexpensive passive electrical components used to shape electrical signals and are utilized in some combination in every electrical circuit.

When electrical components are combined together in a defined area to perform some prescribed function, the components are said to form a *circuit*. In the world of RF, there are two philosophies behind circuit design: *lumped element* circuits and *distributed* circuits.

Lumped element and distributed circuits both use the same semiconductor devices (transistors, diodes, and MMICs) in their designs. Where they differ is in the nature of the passive components they use, specifically the big three, as well as others like transformers and couplers.

Lumped Element Circuits

In lumped element circuit designs, the capacitors and inductors are real things that can be seen and touched. A sampling of "real" capacitors and inductors is shown in Figure 5–2. In lumped element designs, couplers are really just transformers. (I told you they were used for other things.)

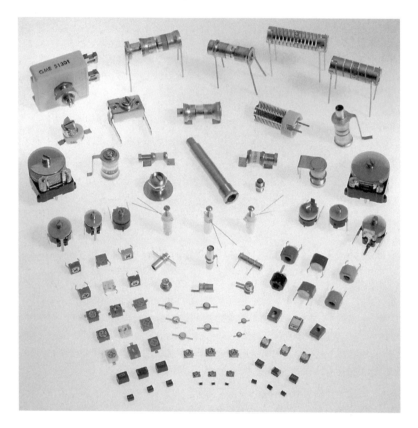

Figure 5–2
Lumped element ("real") capacitors and inductors. *Courtesy of Sprague-Goodman Electronics, Inc.*

Distributed Circuits

Distributed circuits are where things get interesting. As you recall from the introduction, signals in the RF world get around in a circuit by cruising around on a conductor, which is often just a small, thin piece of metal (called a *trace*) on a printed circuit board (PCB) or other substrate. An interesting thing happens to these metal traces at RF frequencies: they begin to act as discrete components. In distributed circuits, RF engineers can shape the metal traces in very specific ways to make them behave like capacitors, inductors, transformers, and even couplers, which is why in pure distributed circuits the only "real" devices are semiconductors, the rest are just a bunch of odd-shaped metal traces. Figure 5–3 shows an example of a distributed circuit. The circuit traces in the small square area on the left side of the figure actually form a coupler, which looks quite a bit different from a lumped element (transformer) coupler. (Compare this to Figure 4–21 in the previous chapter.)

How is the choice made between circuit philosophies when designing a circuit? While both have their advantages and disadvantages, the decision is usually very simple. In the RF world, the higher the frequency, the smaller things get, and vice versa. If a circuit is to operate at a "low" RF frequency, then the components will be relatively bigger. And if the components need to be bigger, then the size and shape of the circuit traces needed to realize the components in a distributed design become prohibitively large. All this is a long-winded way of saying below a certain frequency, the only circuit choice is a lumped element design. Conversely, above a certain frequency, the only reasonable choice is a distributed circuit design. In between, you flip a coin.

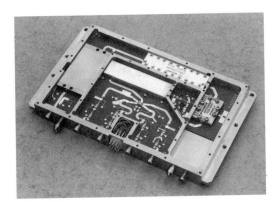

Figure 5–3
A distributed circuit. *Courtesy of JCA Technology.*

Discrete, Hybrid, and MMIC Circuit Choices

Once a circuit philosophy is selected (or dictated), the next choice is what circuit technology to use. Once again there is a choice to be made, this time from three different circuit technologies: discrete, hybrid (also called MIC, for microwave integrated circuit), or MMIC (microwave monolithic integrated circuit). Table 5–2 details the three choices and their respective advantages and disadvantages. An example of each type is shown in Figures 5–4a, 5–4b, and 5–4c. Figure 5–4b (the MIC) contains both packaged and bare "chip" semiconductors.

Table 5–2   Discrete, Hybrid, and MMIC Circuit Technology Comparison

Technology	Description	Advantages	Disadvantages
Discrete	Combines semiconductor devices (diodes, transistors and MMICs) and lumped passive devices as individually packaged discrete components onto a printed circuit board (PCB).	Utilizes existing discrete components; fast design time; superior performance at high power.	Takes up a lot of space; reduced performance at high frequency; expensive in large quantity.
Hybrid (MIC)	Combines both packaged and "chip" semiconductor devices (diodes, transistors, and MMICs), and passive devices (both lumped and distributed), along with metal traces onto a ceramic substrate.	Smaller and better high-frequency performance than discrete; cheaper than discrete in large quantity; superior high-frequency performance.	Expensive in small quantity; longer design time than discrete; more delicate handling and troubleshooting than discrete.
MMIC	Combines semiconductor devices (diodes and transistors) and distributed passive devices onto a single piece of semiconductor.	Smaller than any other approach; less expensive than any other approach in high volume.	Very expensive in small quantity; very long design time; some degradation in performance compared to hybrid approach.

Figure 5–4a
A discrete circuit. *Courtesy of Alpha Industries.*

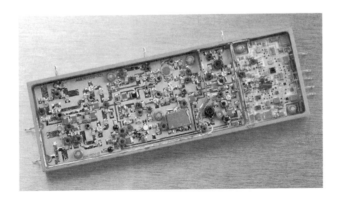

Figure 5–4b
A hybrid circuit. *Courtesy of Micro Networks.*

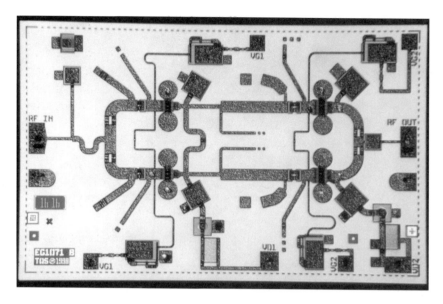

Figure 5–4c
A MMIC. *Courtesy of TriQuint Semiconductor, Inc.*

Did You Know?

The predominant way that discrete components get mounted onto RF printed circuit boards (PCB) today is by what is known as *surface mount technology* (SMT). In SMT, the individual components get soldered right to the surface of the PCB. Now this may seem obvious, but in the early days of electronic manufacturing, another technique called feed-through technology was used in which the individual components were fed through little holes drilled in the PCB. So if nothing else, SMT saves on drill bits.

Did You Know?

The newest MIC technology used today is called *low temperature co-fired ceramic*, or LTCC for short. LTCC is just like a PCB (with its multilayer traces), only it is made from ceramic instead of a plastic composite. LTCC allows the MIC to be made very small, which is ideal for use in very high frequency components.

Subassemblies

There are certain RF manufacturers who make a living by combining more than one RF component to perform more than one RF function into a single package. When a box of RF "stuff" performs more than one basic function, like a single mixer or a single amplifier, the box of stuff is referred to as a *subassembly*.

Did You Know?

> Sometimes a subassembly is called a *subsystem*. Now there is no technical difference between the two descriptions, but companies selling subsystems have been known to fetch a higher price than those selling subassemblies. That's marketing for you.

As an example of a subassembly, refer back to the block diagram of a receiver in Figure 3–1. A receiver has a mixer that is fed by an oscillator and followed by a filter. If some enterprising RF manufacturer thought it made good business sense, they might combine all three components (mixer, oscillator, and filter) into a single box and call it a mixer-oscillator-filter subassembly (or a mixoster?). The good news regarding subassemblies, at least as far as the manufacturer is concerned, is that because they are complicated to make, they fetch a high price. On the flip side, however, subassemblies take a long time to develop, require a lot of engineering and, because they are so specific, tend to have only a single customer. Because of this, manufacturing subassemblies is considered risky business. Of course, that doesn't keep a lot of manufacturers from trying.

Cavities

There is one final way an RF component can be manufactured. Unlike the other technologies (discrete, hybrid, and MMIC), *cavity* type components do not use conductors to carry the RF signal. Instead, RF signals move as waves inside cavity components.

A cavity circuit is some sort of hollow container made out of metal with the RF signal bouncing around on the inside. Cavity technology is a fairly old RF technology and many different RF components can be made as cavity components, like couplers, oscillators, and even amplifiers. When an amplifier is of the cavity type, it is called a *traveling wave tube amplifier* or TWTA (or TWT for short). (It makes sense: an amplifier with a wave traveling around inside a tube-shaped cavity *should* be called a traveling wave tube amplifier!) A TWT is shown in Figure 5–5.

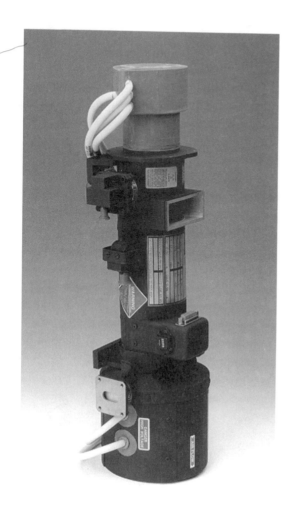

Figure 5–5
A traveling wave tube. *Courtesy of Litton Electron Devices.*

Cavity components are used for one reason and one reason only: high power. When RF engineers need to amplify a signal really big—bigger than any transistor can amplify it—they use a cavity amplifier (TWT). When they need to couple a high-power signal or filter a high-power signal, they use cavity components. Until very recently, all of the output filters of cellular basestations were (guess what?) cavity filters because the output power of basestations is relatively high. (Cavity filters also happen to have the superior filtering characteristics required by cellular transmitters, but that's another story.)

MODULATION ·······································

What Is Modulation?

Modulation is a mathematically complex subject that is difficult to explain quantitatively because it is easy to get lost in all of the formulas. Fortunately, it is simple to understand visually, which is how it is covered here.

Earlier, I described a digital signal as "riding on the back of the RF." Modulation is the way the information signal (analog or digital) is made to ride on the back of the carrier signal (the RF). This is done by taking the RF signal and superimposing the information signal onto it. The act of superimposing the information signal onto the RF (carrier) signal is called *modulation,* and the device that does the superimposing is called a *modulator.* In RF systems, the RF first gets modulated and then sent through the transmitter and out the antenna. After the signal arrives at the receiver, the process is done in reverse. The received signal gets *demodulated* (the RF carrier gets stripped away), leaving only the information signal.

As a way to visualize modulation, think of mailing a letter as wireless communication. The envelope is the RF (the carrier) and the letter inside is the information. To get a letter (the information) from point A to point B, a letter is placed in an envelope (the signal gets modulated) and dropped into the mailbox. Once the envelope arrives, the envelope is opened (the RF is stripped away) and voilá, the letter (the information) has moved from point A to point B. When something is transmitted wirelessly, two signals are sent: the RF carrier (the envelope) and the information signal (the letter). The act of combining these two is called modulation.

You will recall from Chapter 3 that the goal of every source (oscillator) is to produce a perfect sine wave, which is the RF. The reason why a perfect sine wave is needed is because modulators superimpose the information signal onto the (perfect) RF signal by making tiny modifications to it. If the RF signal is not perfect, the imperfections may be incorrectly interpreted as modifications (information), which is unwanted.

Modulators and demodulators do what they do by changing some aspect of the RF signal (a perfect sine wave) in some specific way. Technically, they are not really considered devices or components. They are better thought of as *subsystems*, which are combinations of two or more components.

Types of Modulation

In the world of wireless communications today there are literally dozens of different types of modulation used (and more being created every day). The good news is that all forms of modulation fall into one of three general categories: *amplitude modulation* (AM), *phase modulation* (PM), and *frequency modulation* (FM), which is used to broadcast FM radio. AM and FM are older forms of modulation that have been around since the early days of wireless communication. PM is the new kid on the block and the one which is used most frequently in today's (advanced) digital wireless communication systems.

The reason AM and FM came into being first is that the sophisticated digital chips needed to implement PM just were not around at the beginning of wireless communication. Digital wireless communication and PM evolved as a direct result of the advances in digital semiconductor integrated circuits.

AM, FM, and PM describe the three ways in which the perfect sine wave changes as it accepts the information signal. AM changes the height of the sine wave (as time goes by), FM changes the frequency of the sine wave (as time goes by), leaving the amplitude unchanged, and PM changes the phase of successive sine waves. These changes contain the information.

Amplitude Modulation

AM changes the amplitude of the perfect sine wave RF carrier as shown in Figure 5–6. The left side of Figure 5–6 shows how an unmodulated sine wave appears. Note that the sine wave is repeated many times. The right side of Figure 5–6 shows what happens to the sine wave after it has been amplitude modulated. Notice that the sine waves are still there and that the frequency is still the same (the space between successive sine waves is unchanged), but the amplitude (height) of each successive sine wave varies. The amplitude changes (or is modulated) from sine wave to sine wave, but the frequency is unchanged. If you trace your finger over the top of the signal on the right side you will notice that it follows the path of a sine wave, which is no coincidence.

AM has been around longer than any other modulation scheme, primarily because it is easy to implement. Unfortunately this ease of implementation comes with a price. All RF signals pick up noise as they move around. As mentioned in Chapter 3, noise is any imperfection in the (RF carrier) sine wave. More often than not, these imperfections manifest themselves as random changes in ampli-

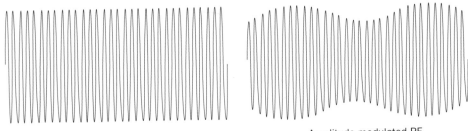

Unmodulated RF   Amplitude modulated RF

Figure 5–6
An unmodulated and an amplitude modulated RF carrier.

tude. So when noise changes the amplitude of the RF carrier, the RF system does not know whether the change is intended (as a result of amplitude modulation) or unintended (as a result of noise). What all this means is that AM signals are very susceptible to being distorted by noise.

The AM depicted in Figure 5–6 is a type of "analog" AM. In analog AM, the system modulates the RF carrier with an analog signal (e.g., a sine wave). In essence, it superimposes a sine wave onto a bunch of other sine waves, as can be seen in the figure. AM has been around for a long time and not much has changed—until very recently.

Binary Amplitude Shift Keying

There is a new generation of AM, which is digital in nature, known as Binary Amplitude Shift Keying (BASK). Unlike "analog" AM, which superimposes an analog (sine wave) signal onto the RF (sine wave) carrier, BASK superimposes a digital signal (like the one in Figure 1–3) onto the RF (sine wave) carrier (see Figure 5–7). Notice how the shape of the RF carrier mimics the shape of the digital signal.

BASK is less noise-sensitive than analog AM. BASK signals are still susceptible to random changes in amplitude from noise, but since the "smarts" of the RF system only have to differentiate between a "high" and a "low," slight changes in either amplitude (high or low) will not cause the system to misinterpret one as the other. BASK is used in today's digital wireless systems because it is less susceptible to noise.

By the way, whenever you hear the term "shift keying," you should think two things. First, it involves modulating a digital signal onto an RF carrier and second, the changes are discrete in nature, as opposed to continuous (as in analog AM).

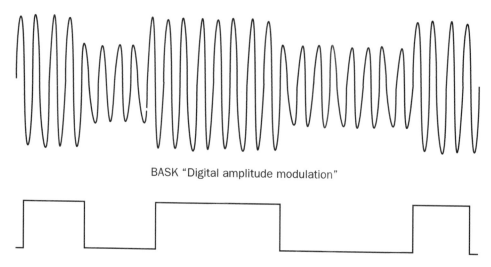

BASK "Digital amplitude modulation"

Figure 5–7
Binary Amplitude Shift Keying (BASK).

Frequency Modulation

FM is the second way a perfect sine wave can be made to vary (see Figure 5–8). Notice in this case that the amplitude remains the same (from unmodulated to modulated), but the frequency changes (the space between successive sine waves changes). This change in frequency (as time goes by) contains information, like a human voice on a cellular phone call. (As hard as it is to believe, it's true.)

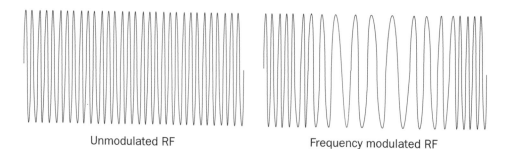

Unmodulated RF   Frequency modulated RF

Figure 5–8
An unmodulated and a frequency modulated RF carrier.

Since the world is going digital, you must have guessed that there is a type of frequency modulation especially for digital information signals. There is and it is called *frequency shift keying* (FSK). FSK uses two completely different frequencies to represent a one and a zero. It quickly switches between these two frequencies depending on the incoming digital bit stream. What sophisticated piece of hardware is used to quickly switch between two frequencies? Go back and read the section on synthesizers.

FM is not as sensitive to noise as AM, which is why it came about. Like AM signals, FM signals are still susceptible to random changes in amplitude from noise, but since the "smarts" of the system are only looking for changes in frequency, the system disregards changes in amplitude. Before you start thinking that FM sounds like a free lunch—you should know better, there is also a type of noise that affects a signal's frequency, but that's another story.

Phase Modulation

PM is the third way a perfect sine wave can be made to vary. Most of the digital information that gets sent wirelessly today is modulated onto the RF carrier by way of phase modulation (or some variation thereof).

As mentioned previously in the section on phase shifters, sine waves (and therefore RF signals) have a phase associated with them. The phase of a sine wave is measured in degrees, and one complete cycle covers 360° (see the top of Figure 5–9). Phase shift is always measured with reference to some other signal. Figure 5–9 shows the result of four different phase shifts with respect to a reference signal. Notice that the 0° phase shift is identical to the reference signal (as it should be) and that the 180° phase shift is a mirror image of the reference signal. The 90° and 270° phase shifts are also mirror images of each other. In fact, any two signals 180° out of phase are mirror images of each other. In essence, each 90° phase shift shifts the sine wave one quarter of a sine wave to the left.

Did You Know?

You can add or subtract 360° from any phase shift and get the same exact phase shift. That is, two sine waves phase shifted by 360° are in phase. For instance, a 270° phase shift is the same as a –90° phase shift. Likewise with 180° and –180°. This explains why you will never see a phase shift greater than 360° in an RF textbook. That and the fact that you'll probably never open one.

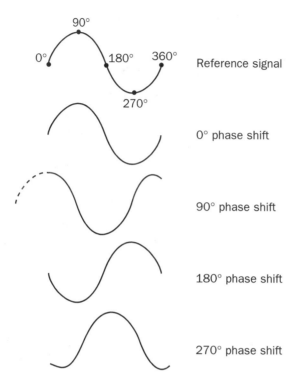

Reference signal

0° phase shift

90° phase shift

180° phase shift

270° phase shift

Figure 5–9
Visual depiction of phase shift.

There are many different types of PM used in digital wireless communications. The reason that so many exist is that the different modulation techniques evolved as the semiconductor technology evolved. The latest and greatest PM techniques utilized today just were not possible with the electronic components of 20 years ago. A sampling of some of the more popular PM techniques used in digital wireless communication are shown in Table 5–3.

The real power of phase shifting comes from the ability to modulate a digital bit stream onto an RF carrier by selectively phase shifting successive sine waves. And naturally there needs to be a way to retrieve the bit stream from the phase shifts after the RF signal reaches its destination.

How are these phase shifts imparted onto and then retrieved from the RF carrier? Recall from Chapter 4 the discussion on phase shifters and phase detectors. A phase shifter shifts a sine wave by a given amount. In digital phase modulation, the digital bit is used to select the desired phase shift. Once the RF signal

Table 5–3   Some Common Phase Modulation Types

Acronym	Phase Modulation
MSK	Minimum Shift Keying
BPSK	Bi-Phase Shift Keying
QPSK	Quadrature Phase Shift Keying
DQPSK	Differential QPSK
GMSK	Gaussian Minimum Shift Keying

reaches its destination, a phase detector is used to transform the signal's phase shifts into a voltage. The voltage is then easily converted to a digital bit stream. The two most popular phase modulations used in today's digital wireless communication are BPSK and QPSK, which are discussed below.

Bi-Phase Shift Keying (BPSK), as the name implies, has two different possible phase shifts: 0° and 180°. Since a digital bit also has two different possibilities (0 or 1), BPSK can be used to modulate one digital bit onto one sine wave. A 0° phase shift represents a 0 and a 180° phase shift represents a 1. The top of Figure 5–10 shows the result of modulating the digital bit stream 01101 onto an RF carrier using BPSK. Notice that whenever one sine wave "smoothly" follows another, there is no phase shift and therefore it represents a zero. However, whenever the next sine wave makes an abrupt transition, exemplified by the double hump, there is a 180° phase shift and it represents a one. BPSK modulates one digital bit onto one sine wave, which is pretty good. But there is something that is much better.

If you guessed that quadrature phase shift keying (QPSK) has four different possible phase shifts, give yourself a prize. They are 0°, 90°, 180°, and 270°. The four different possible phase shifts that comprise QPSK can be seen individually in Figure 5–9. Since QPSK has four possibilities but a digital bit (still) has only two, QPSK can be used to modulate two bits of information onto each sine wave (I told you there was something better). In this example, a 0° phase shift represents the bits 00. Likewise, 90° represents 01, 180° represents 10 and 270° represents 11. The bottom of Figure 5–10 shows the result of modulating the digital bit stream 0001101011 onto an RF carrier using QPSK. In effect, QPSK doubles the data carrying capability of an RF carrier (vs. BPSK). And since we are all wireless data hogs at heart, this is a good thing.

By now you have caught onto this phase modulation thing and you are probably wondering why not break up the sine wave into eight, 45° phase shifts or per-

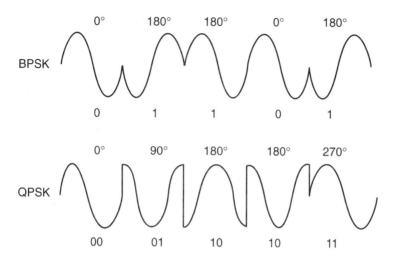

Figure 5–10
Examples of BPSK and QPSK modulation.

haps sixteen, 22.5° phase shifts? Wouldn't that increase the number of digital bits that could be modulated onto a single sine wave? The answer is yes, but. Yes, reducing the amount of phase shift absolutely enables the modulating of more bits of digital information onto a sine wave, and in more benign environments like cable TV distribution, it is actually done. But, as mentioned in Chapter 3, all RF signals pick up noise as they move around, and while most of the noise affects the signal's amplitude, there is also a type of noise that affects its phase. This phase noise manifests itself as unwanted phase shifts of the RF carrier. As long as these unwanted phase shifts are small compared to the modulated phase shifts, data integrity is maintained. As the modulated phase shifts get smaller (less than 90°), they run the risk of being confused with unwanted phase noise, which is why QPSK is about as far as it goes (today) for phase shifting in the wireless world.

Quadrature Amplitude Modulation

You know now that digital information can be modulated onto an RF carrier through the use of phase modulation (QPSK, BPSK) and amplitude modulation (BASK). So you have probably thought to yourself, if we are trying to get as much digital information as possible onto each sine wave, why not just combine the two? The newest form of modulation used in today's digital wireless systems is Quadrature Amplitude Modulation or QAM (pronounced kwäm), and that is exactly what it does. (QAM is just a contraction of QPSK and AM.)

To get an idea what a QAM signal might look like, refer to the example of QPSK on the bottom of Figure 5–10. Now picture that signal, where alternate sine waves can have one of two different amplitudes, like that in Figure 5–7. It is a rather complex signal to look at but the important thing to note is the additional information it contains. The QPSK by itself represents two digital bits per sine wave. If the AM portion of the signal has two different amplitudes, that represent one more digital bit. So in this example, the QAM signal can contain three bits of digital information. Now we're getting somewhere.

In theory, QAM can be modulated with smaller phase shifts and more than two possible amplitudes to cram even more digital information onto each sine wave. These QAM variants go by the name of QAM-16, QAM-64, etc. But as you have probably already figured out, these modulations are generally limited to wireline applications, where the effects of noise are greatly reduced.

Modulators and Demodulators

RF signals get modulated by modulators, which are fairly complex devices, but they can all be represented by a simple block diagram, as shown in Figure 5–11.

At their simplest, modulators have two inputs and one output. One input is the "information" input, which can be in analog or digital form. In Figure 5–11, the information is in digital form. The other input is the RF carrier (a perfect sine wave). When the modulator gets done doing its thing, out comes a signal that is a composite of the two signals. This is the modulated output signal, and in

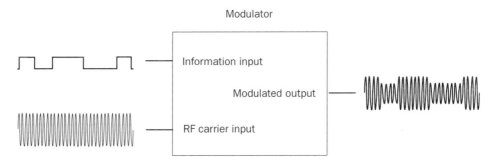

Figure 5–11
Block diagram of a modulator.

Figure 5–11, it is BASK modulation. *Demodulators* do the exact opposite: they take a modulated signal and break it down into an information signal and a carrier signal. After demodulation, the carrier is no longer needed and therefore it is disregarded while the information signal is sent somewhere else in the system for further use. Most times the modulator and demodulator are combined into one unit. What do you suppose they call this combination of MOdulator and DEModulator? Think about it.

What components are used to make modulators and demodulators? You can go ahead and assume that anytime two signals are combined or separated in the RF world, somewhere there is a mixer or two involved. In addition, there is usually an oscillator or synthesizer and, in the case of phase modulation, there are phase shifters and phase detectors, as mentioned previously. In terms of their location in an RF system, modulators come before the transmitter and demodulators come after the receiver (see Figures 3–1 and 3–2).

Did You Know?

Technically, saying "QAM modulation" is redundant, because QAM modulation literally means quadrature amplitude modulation modulation. The same goes for "AM modulation" and "FM modulation." But alas, it is spoken that way by convention, and because "QA modulation" just sounds too awkward.

GETTING AROUND ....

Once an RF signal enters an antenna and gets transformed into a current, it needs to get around, moving from component to component. I have called this thing that carries the current a conductor, but there are several media used in the RF world to get a signal from one point to another in a receiver or in a transmitter. These media, represented by the straight lines in any RF block diagram or schematic, fall into one of three categories: cables, waveguides, and circuit traces.

Cables

Cable Construction

One way RF signals move around is through cables. The cable hooked up to the back of a VCR is an example of an RF cable, albeit an inexpensive one. RF cables are known as *coaxial cables*, which is a fancy way of saying that there is an inner conductor surrounded by an outer conductor. To help you visualize it, picture an old-style wooden pencil (think kindergarten). If it were a coaxial cable, the lead would be the center conductor, the ugly yellow paint on the outside would be the outer conductor, and the wood, which separates the two conductors, would be referred to as the—brace yourself—*dielectric* material. Dielectric is just fancy engineering talk for *insulator*, which is any material that does not conduct electricity (or carry an RF signal).

The reason for the two conductors is a simple one. The inner conductor carries the RF signal and the outer conductor, which is really a shield, is there to keep the RF signal from escaping. The reason the outer shield is needed is because the center conductor thinks it is an antenna, and it tries to radiate the RF signal it is carrying out into space. The outer conductor prevents that from happening. (Think of it as the security guard of the coaxial prison.) A variety of coaxial cables is shown in Figure 5–12.

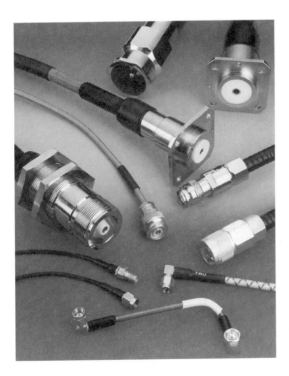

Figure 5–12
Coaxial cables. *Courtesy of Tru-Connector Corp.*

All RF coaxial cables try to accomplish the same objective: to get an RF signal from one point to another with the least amount of insertion loss possible. As you can imagine, in this no-free-lunch world there is always a tradeoff to be made. The bigger (and heavier) the coaxial cable, the lower the insertion loss, but the more it costs and the harder it is to deal with. Big heavy cables cannot be bent around small objects, which makes them difficult to work with, not to mention incredibly heavy. Therefore, RF engineers use the smallest possible cable that has an insertion loss they can live with.

Coaxial cables are most often used as interfaces between major building blocks within an RF system. For instance, cables are frequently attached to the bottom of antennas at basestations to carry the signal from the antenna, down the tower, and into a room where the low noise amplifier (LNA) awaits.

Cable Types and Designations

Not wanting to keep things too simple, RF engineers went out and developed several different types of coaxial cables for all different occasions. The three main types of coaxial cables are differentiated by their outer layer as detailed in Table 5–4.

Table 5–4   Coaxial Cable Types

Cable Type	Outer Layer	Description
Flexible	Rubber coating surrounding a very thin metal shield.	Very flexible, the rubber outer coating is used as protection for the thin outer shield.
Semi-flex	Thin metal (braided) shield.	Less flexible and less durable than flexible cable, often cheaper.
Semi-rigid	Thick solid metal shield.	Less flexible, but more durable, than semi-flex.

Cables of different sizes need to be specified as such. A flexible cable with a one-half inch diameter could be called a flexible cable with a one-half inch diameter, but by now you already know that RF engineers have a way of taking perfectly simple notions and complicating them. So the cable mentioned above is called

RG-58. In fact, most coaxial cables are referred to as RG something or other. There are dozens of different RG numbers and unless you plan on buying coaxial cables for a living, the only thing you need to know about a cable's RG number is that, with only a few exceptions, the smaller the number, the larger the cable's diameter. Therefore RG-58 is bigger (and more expensive) than RG-114.

Did You Know?

The "RG" designation for cables came from the military's old U.S. Army Signal Corp, which developed coaxial cables during World War II. RG stood for "Radio Grade," which perhaps helped to distinguish them from power cables (or a pastrami sandwich).

Connectors

Cables by themselves are of little use unless they are terminated with a *connector*, or more specifically, a coaxial connector. A coaxial connector is what allows one cable to be connected to another or to a component. Because of this, there are two different kinds of connectors: those intended to be attached to cables and those intended to be attached to components. Without both, it would be impossible to connect cables to components. The difference between a cable connector and a component connector can be seen in Figure 5–13. The component connectors are the ones with the four-hole flanges.

Connectors in Cable Assemblies

In the case of cables, connectors are firmly attached to the end of the cable mechanically, as well as electrically. Once connectors are attached to a cable, it becomes a *cable assembly*. Sometimes RF engineers purchase cable assemblies and sometimes they purchase plain (bulk) cable and individual cable connectors and attach the parts themselves. Why do they choose to make their own cable assemblies rather than purchase them ready-made? When only a few cable assemblies are required, then assembling them is cheaper and faster. However, when a lot of them are required, it is best to let the pros do it.

Figure 5–13
Cable connectors and component connectors. *Courtesy of Tru-Connector Corp.*

Connector Families

Just like with cables, the goal of every connector is the same: minimum insertion loss. Yes, connectors do have insertion loss, although it is tiny compared to the cable. If you think there are a lot of different cables, wait until you see how many RF connector types exist. A sampling, and I repeat a sampling, of RF coaxial connector types (called families) is shown in Table 5–5. Almost all of these connector families have connectors made for both cables and components. As a general rule, a connector of one family will NOT mate up with a connector of a different family.

Table 5–5   RF Coaxial Connector Families

SMA	SSMA
SMB	SMC
BNC	TNC
N	7–16

Table 5–5   RF Coaxial Connector Families (Continued)

SC	7mm
3mm	2.4mm
1.4mm	K
SMT	SSMT
SMP	SSMP
OSP	OSSP
OSX	Type 43

Why so many different connector families? There are two reasons. First, some connector families are physically large while others are small. As mentioned before, if an inexpensive cable assembly is desired, then a cable is chosen with a small diameter, which limits the choice of connector to the available small connector families. If the cable needs to carry a high-power RF signal, a large diameter cable is needed and therefore so is a large connector.

The second reason for all the connector families is one of evolution. Connector designers are constantly trying to improve connectors, either by lowering the insertion loss or making the connector easier to use. Each time they make a significant improvement to an existing connector type, a whole new family of connectors is born. All of these connector families just represent improvements in connector technology over time.

Did You Know?

One of the more popular RF connector types shown in Table 5–5 is the BNC. In the early 1940's, a group of three individuals (Bayonet, Neill, and Councelman) developed this connector with the express purpose of providing a secure interface and an easy-to-use locking mechanism. In recognition of the origin of its development, the new connector was called the BNC.

Adapters

An interesting thing happens as a result of all these different connector families. Sometimes RF engineers are forced to connect a cable with a connector from one

Figure 5–14
Coaxial adapters. *Courtesy of Amphenol Corp.*

family to another cable or component with a connector from a different family, which just cannot be done (without a crowbar). In steps the *adapter*. Adapters, which are also called coaxial adapters, are short, two-sided connectors with a connector from one family on one side and a connector from a different family on the other. Adapters facilitate connecting two RF "things" with connectors from different families. A variety of coaxial adapters is shown in Figure 5–14.

Did You Know?

It requires three adapters (3 male–female combinations) to accommodate every combination of connector family. That means it takes 3 × 231, or 693 different adapters to accommodate all the different connector families shown in Table 5–5. Now you know why there are some RF companies that spend most of their time manufacturing adapters.

Waveguides

Another way RF signals get around is by something called *waveguides*. Waveguides are older technology, they are very expensive (compared to cables), and are used either for military or very high power applications. Waveguides are rarely used in today's commercial wireless systems—they are too darn big and they cost too much. Nevertheless, waveguides are still used. Several pieces of waveguide are shown in Figure 5–15.

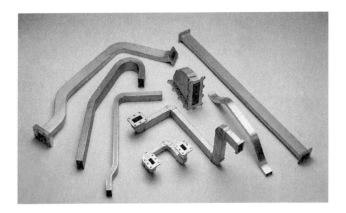

Figure 5–15
Waveguide. *Courtesy of A-Alpha Waveguide Co.*

Waveguides are essentially pipes, with a rectangular cross section, used to carry RF signals from one point to another. The interesting thing about waveguides is that, unlike cables, which carry RF signals on a conductor, waveguides transport RF signals around as invisible waves. The waveguide merely serves to contain the waves and control their direction of travel.

If waveguides are old technology and they are large and expensive, why or where would they ever be used? What I forgot to mention about waveguides is that they have almost no insertion loss, which is why they are used in very high power RF systems. (And you thought there couldn't be a good reason.)

Circuit Traces

Hybrids and Printed Circuit Boards

The final way a signal can get around in an RF system is on a metal trace, mounted on top of some sort of dielectric material (remember dielectric?). If the dielectric happens to be ceramic and the components are all unpackaged "chips," then the circuit is called a *hybrid* circuit or MIC (microwave integrated circuit). If the dielectric material happens to be some fancy plastic composite and the components are all packaged devices, then the circuit is called a *printed circuit*. A printed circuit is also called a *printed circuit board* (PCB) and a discrete circuit. For examples of both, see Figures 5–4a and 5–4b in the section on Circuit Technologies.

Stripline, Microstrip, and Coplanar Waveguide

RF circuits can have their metal traces laid out several different ways. There are three ways that are particularly popular: *stripline*, *microstrip*, and *coplanar waveguide.*

Stripline tries to mimic a coaxial cable, only in circuit form. Coplanar waveguide tries to mimic a waveguide, only in circuit form, and microstrip does not try to mimic anything, it is just an RF circuit. All three layout schemes have their advantages and specific uses. Figure 5–16 shows a cross-sectional view of all three layout schemes. The dark areas are the metal traces and the light areas are the dielectric material.

If you look closely at Figure 5–16, you can see that the cross section of stripline somewhat resembles the cross section of a coaxial cable (conductor in the middle, shield on the outside). And, if you look closely to the cross section of a coplanar waveguide (and you drink a fifth of whisky quickly), you still cannot see any resemblance to a real waveguide—because there isn't any. A coplanar waveguide may not look like a real waveguide, but it acts like it. Ask any RF engineer.

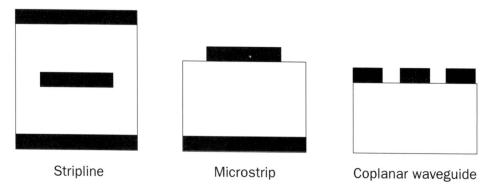

Stripline   Microstrip   Coplanar waveguide

Figure 5–16
Cross-sectional view of stripline, microstrip, and coplanar waveguide.

As a quick review, there are three ways that RF signals move around in an RF system: cables, waveguides, and metal traces on dielectric material. There are also two different types of RF circuits depending on the type of dielectric. If the dielectric is a ceramic, then the circuit is a hybrid (or a MIC). If the dielectric is a plastic composite, then the circuit is printed circuit (or PCB). There are three popular ways to lay out the circuit traces on RF circuits: stripline, microstrip, and coplanar waveguide. And finally, the goal of all the different media is the same: to move an RF signal from one point to another with the least amount of insertion loss.

Part 3

RF Systems

6 Older Technology

In this chapter...

- Broadcasting   143
- Radar   153
- Satellite Communications   162
- Point-to-Point Microwave   187

You might think with all the current excitement about wireless communications that the technology had been around for only a short time. Nothing could be further from the truth, which is the topic of this chapter: wireless technologies which have been around awhile. This chapter picks only four of these "older" technologies for discussion: broadcasting, radar, satellite communication, and point-to-point microwave. But even among these four there is a lot of variation in technology and system design. These three were chosen as they represent a good cross section of the various applications of RF technology.

AM radio, which has been around since the early 1920s, is an example of broadcast technology, as are FM radio and television. Broadcast technology is a unique RF application in that it conveys information—wirelessly—from one point to many points, with little concern for a response from the intended receivers. Broadcasting is a one-way technology (which does not keep people from screaming at their televisions). Recently, there has been an assault on the broadcasters by those using a different wireless technology, namely, satellite service (also discussed in this chapter).

Radar technology, which has been around since the late 1930s, is an interesting form of RF communication. Unlike other forms of wireless communication, radar does not work by superimposing an information signal onto an RF carrier (through modulation). Instead, the information is contained in slight changes in the RF carrier imposed on it by the environment. As you will soon learn, these small changes can contain a lot of information about an object that the radar is following.

Today, radar is used almost everywhere: on the ground, in the air, and out in space. The availability of low-cost RF electronics is enabling the use of radar technology in some surprising new places. The area experiencing the greatest effect from low-cost radar is the automobile industry. Some day in the not-so-distant future, all cars will come equipped with radar technology as a standard feature. (As far as I know, there is no plan to equip automobiles with missiles.)

Even satellite communication has been around since the early 1960s. It was first envisioned in the 1940s, but had to wait for technology to catch up to make it feasible. Satellites can be used for both one-way and two-way communications. If you have ever called someone in Hawaii (from outside the state), the call was probably routed by a satellite. And if you have ever watched a live sports event in a different time zone, that signal too was routed via satellite.

This chapter briefly touches on point-to-point microwave communication, including the fact that it was originally used for long distance telephone service, which eventually led to the breakup of AT&T. Also covered is a very important concept to all of wireless communication called multipath.

As you go through this chapter, you will see common themes among these four wireless systems. You will notice that the Federal Communications Commission (FCC) in the United States and the International Telecommunications Union (ITU) everywhere else are responsible for allocating frequency for each application. You will see how each of these wireless applications can be described simply by a combination of a few of the basic RF building blocks discussed earlier in this book. This chapter also discusses the role that frequency plays in each system. In every case, the system is designed to use the latest technology to take full advantage of each particular system's frequency allocation.

The goal of this chapter is to help you understand, at a very basic level, the workings of wireless systems you are already familiar with. In each instance you are given an opportunity to "follow the signal" as it travels and to see what changes, if any, it undergoes during its journey. Once you understand the fundamental principles of these four systems, you will have a general understanding of how all wireless systems work. Today's most sophisticated wireless technologies, like Doppler radar and low Earth orbit satellites, are merely refinements and improvements to these four basic systems.

BROADCASTING ....

What Is Broadcasting?

Characteristics

Broadcasting is nothing more than an RF system that transmits its signal over a "broad" geographic area and is intended for a "broad" audience. (You will never think of broadcasting the same way again.) Broadcasting is classified (in engineering speak) as a *one-to-many* system, which means there is one transmitter and many receivers. It also means there is no provision for the receiving party to communicate directly with the transmitting party. The three most recognizable broadcast applications are AM radio, FM radio, and television.

All forms of broadcasting in the United States have one thing in common: they have all been sanctioned, by the Federal Communications Commission (FCC), to operate within a very specific bandwidth. (Recall that a bandwidth is a frequency range uniquely defined by its upper and lower frequencies.) The FCC, being the kindhearted organization that it is, divides up these bandwidths into smaller bandwidths called *channels*, so that different broadcasters can transmit different things loosely considered entertainment.

Constraints

To comply with the FCC, broadcasters must operate within three constraints when transmitting their programs. Their first constraint is frequency. As mentioned above, each broadcaster is assigned a channel (frequency range) and can transmit RF energy only within that channel. To maintain order, everyone else is prohibited from broadcasting in that frequency range. Broadcasting is a perfect example of the need for filters in the output section of a transmitter.

The second constraint a broadcaster must obey is geography. Just because a radio station is granted the right to broadcast in San Francisco does not necessarily give it the right to broadcast in Oakland. In extreme cases, broadcasters have to "tailor" their radiated RF energy to conform to some agreed upon geographic boundary. If you recall from the discussion on antenna patterns, antennas can be designed to radiate RF energy in well-defined geometric patterns. Rarely, however, is there a need for such complex patterns (i.e., no clover leaves). A well-positioned circle or oval will frequently do the trick.

Broadcasters place their transmitting antenna at the highest elevation point in their allotted geographic region to ensure a "line of sight" to all the receivers. Suppose for a minute that the highest point (a hill) in a broadcaster's region happens to be at the northernmost point in the region. Further suppose that this northernmost point butts up against the southern edge of some other broadcaster's region (operating at the same frequency). In this situation, the first broadcaster is required to radiate RF energy strictly in the southerly direction (see Figure 6–1 for a visual depiction). By the way, it is entirely possible that the other region's broadcaster (broadcasting at the same frequency) will place their antenna on the same hill. Naturally they are required to transmit only in the northerly direction.

The final constraint a broadcaster must obey, closely related to geography, is power. There is a maximum limit to the amount of RF power a broadcaster can transmit. Two different RF behaviors serve to limit this power. First, as the transmitted power increases, the size of the antenna pattern grows (while the shape and direction stay the same). At some point, the antenna pattern will grow large enough to infringe on an adjacent broadcaster (operating at the same frequency).

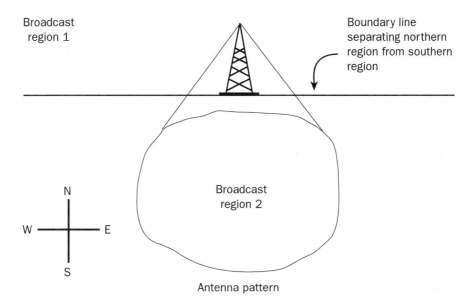

Figure 6–1
Antenna pattern of a broadcaster.

In Figure 6–1, if the antenna pattern grows too large, it will overlap the broadcast region to the south.

The other unwanted RF behavior, resulting from too much transmitted power, is due to the nature of the RF hardware. Because the output filter in a transmitter is not perfect, as the RF power coming out of the transmitter within the broadcaster's allotted frequency range increases, so does the power coming out of the transmitter *outside* of the broadcaster's allotted frequency range. Above a certain power output, this "out-of-band" power begins to interfere with channels in adjacent frequencies (operating in the same geographical region).

The Role of Frequency

Allocation

In the United States, the FCC has defined very specific frequency bands and channel allotments for AM radio, FM radio, and television (see Table 6–1).

Table 6–1   Broadcast Frequency Bands and Allotments

Service	Frequency Band(s)	Channel Allotment
AM radio	535–1605 kHz	10 kHz
FM radio	88–108 MHz	200 kHz
TV (VHF)	54–72 MHz	6 MHz
TV (VHF)	76–88 MHz	6 MHz
TV (VHF)	174–216 MHz	6 MHz
TV (UHF)	470–890 MHz	6 MHz

Your intuition should tell you that the greater the channel allotment (in frequency), the more information that can be broadcast, which is why AM radio, with its 10 kHz allotment, can only broadcast in mono, while FM radio, with its 200 kHz allotment, can broadcast in stereo, and TV, with its 6 MHz allotment, can broadcast video.

A quick look at the AM radio frequency allotment might lead you to the conclusion that, with a total frequency allocation of 1070 kHz (1605–535 kHz) and a channel allotment of 10 kHz, there will be 107 (1070 kHz ÷ 10 kHz) different channels in the AM band, which is not the case. In practice, radio channels are not mathematically adjacent to one another, but are separated by a small frequency "buffer" to ensure that consecutive channels do not interfere with each other.

Referring again to Table 6–1, the first TV frequency band (54–72 MHz) includes channels 2, 3, and 4. Since each channel is allocated 6 MHz and the total frequency range is only 18 MHz, it appears as though TV channels butt up against one another. In reality, each 6 MHz channel allotment contains a frequency buffer within it. You now have the ability to calculate the 6 MHz frequency allocation of any channel, since the channels are listed in order (by frequency) in Table 6–1. For instance, 76–82 MHz is channel 5, 82–88 MHz is channel 6, and so on. For those of you with too much free time, what frequency range corresponds to channel 51? (I should be mean and not tell you, but I won't.) It's 692–698 MHz, for whatever it's worth.

Did You Know?

You can probably figure out by now why high definition television (HDTV) has taken so long to become reality. All the television sets in the

United States are designed to receive an entire program's information in only 6 MHz. HDTV signals contain more information than can be crammed into 6 MHz. (More bandwidth equals more information.) Of course, there is also the infighting among all of the various manufacturers over standards, but that's another story.

Propagation

The way a broadcast signal behaves in the environment has a lot to do with its frequency. As mentioned in Chapter 2, when an RF signal, traveling in the air, encounters a solid object, the signal either gets reflected or absorbed (or both). This behavior makes RF signals what is known as *line-of-sight* (LOS) signals, which means that the transmitting antenna must be able to "see" the receiving antenna, without obstruction, for a wireless connection to be made. (There are exceptions to this line-of-sight rule but they are beyond the scope of this book.)

Line-of-sight behavior has four implications for anyone trying to receive a television signal over the air. First, there must not be any major obstructions between the transmitting antenna and the television's antenna. Second, the television's antenna must be constantly readjusted as all of the TV stations have their transmitting antennas located in different places. Third, trying to receive an over-the-air television signal in an area with tall buildings will probably result in a signal reception phenomenon called a *ghost*. A ghost is a double image in a TV's picture and it is very easy to understand. It is simply the result of a television receiving the same signal twice, at slightly different times. What causes a TV to receive the same signal twice? Signal reflections. One signal goes directly from the transmitting antenna to the television. The other signal reflects off of one or more large objects and then makes its way to the television. And since the second signal has farther to travel, it arrives later. (This phenomenon is called multipath and is discussed later in the chapter.)

The final implication for line-of-sight signals, and probably the most significant for RF communications, is that to receive an RF signal the receiver must be within a certain number of miles of the (ground-based) transmitter or else the curvature of the Earth will make reception impossible. (Refer to Figure 6–7 to see a visual depiction of this.) There are some exceptions to this line-of-sight limitation, however. For instance, at lower frequencies (less than 30 MHz), signals can travel farther than line of sight by reflecting off the ionosphere (a layer of the Earth's atmosphere). This behavior explains why an AM radio station can occasionally be picked up at night from hundreds of miles away.

Tuning In

The Tuner

The following discussion pertains to television broadcasting, but it applies to AM and FM radio as well. Since all TV signals are only 6 MHz wide, the electronics within the television can only process signals between 0 and 6 MHz. This 6 MHz signal is what I have referred to as the "information" signal in earlier chapters. It contains all of the audio and video information necessary.

This presents a dilemma. The television's internal electronics can only accommodate signals between 0 and 6 MHz, but none of the transmitted signals are between 0 and 6 MHz. They are all at some higher frequency (see Table 6–1). How does the television get these higher frequency transmitted signals down to the frequency (called *baseband*) that the television's internal electronics can accommodate? It uses a device called a *tuner*.

Now a tuner is a pretty sophisticated piece of electronics with all kinds of mixers, filters, and other components. But it can be understood, from a functional standpoint, with a very simple block diagram as shown in Figure 6–2. Keep in mind this is not exactly how tuners work, but this is functionally what tuners accomplish.

In this block diagram, the tuner works in a two-step process. First, it selects the desired 6 MHz channel from all of the channels that are out there by adjusting the frequency of the variable bandpass filter to reject all of the unwanted signals, letting only the desired one pass. After which the mixer takes the one signal remaining and downconverts it to the baseband frequency (0–6 MHz). Note that for this block diagram to work properly, the oscillator needs to change its frequency for each different channel.

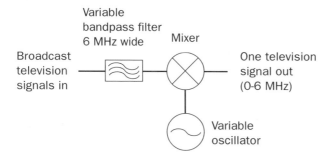

Figure 6–2
Block diagram representing a TV tuner's functionality.

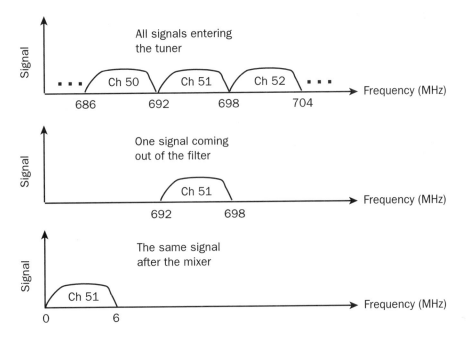

Figure 6–3
The steps in the tuning process.

To help you visualize the workings of this tuner, refer to Figure 6–3. The upper graph is a frequency diagram showing all the channels that enter the tuner. After the variable filter, the only channel still remaining is the desired one, channel 51. (I figured you already knew the frequency band.) At this point the signal is at a frequency that is of no use to the television's electronics. After the mixer, however, channel 51 gets downconverted to baseband, where it is useful. It is at this point where the television's internal electronics take over, process the signal, and produce Seinfeld reruns.

Television Delivery

Three Ways

There are basically three (legal) ways to receive a television signal today: over the air, by cable, or via satellite. While they use completely different methods to relay the signals, all three try to accomplish the same objective: to get as many different 6 MHz channels to your television set as possible. With over-the-air television, the number of 6 MHz channels is limited by the amount of *spectrum* (frequency bands) allocated by the FCC. This gives both cable and satellite a distinct advantage.

In the case of cable delivery, the cable itself carries signals between the frequencies of zero and approximately 1000 MHz. At 6 MHz per channel, this gives the cable the theoretical ability to carry 166 different channels. The reason it can transmit this many signals is because the signals are trapped within the cable and therefore do not interfere with over-the-air signals.

Keep in mind that this 6 MHz bandwidth requirement is for analog TV, meaning the signal that gets modulated onto the RF carrier is analog. With the newer digital TV systems, the same information can be crammed into less than 6 MHz, which translates to more TV channels (hello Golf Channel).

As expected, satellites have the ability to deliver a tremendous number of television channels because they use digital signals and because they use something called *digital signal processing*, which is covered in the section on satellites.

There is actually a fourth method of television delivery, which is a hybrid of the other three, called Multichannel Multipoint Distribution Service (MMDS). MMDS is covered in the section "Broadband Fixed Wireless" in Chapter 8.

Did You Know?

Cable TV providers do not deliver all 166 channels that they theoretically can. The reason they do not is because they have set aside a portion of the cable's frequency band (0–1000 MHz) for receiving signals. Part of the cable's frequency band is now used for two-way communications, which makes it ideal for connecting to the Internet.

Breaking News

I thought it might be interesting to show the path a television signal travels during a breaking news event—from the event to your TV. In this example, you will be exposed to all of the different roles that wireless communications play in an ordinary, everyday event.

Assume you are in your living room somewhere in Montana and you decide you need some entertainment and so you turn on the television. When you turn it on you discover that you are watching a high-speed police pursuit happening in

Los Angeles (a daily occurrence). How has the signal reached your TV (refer to Figure 6–4)?

In this particular example, the news event is being filmed by a camera crew out in the field represented by the news van. The news van needs to get the live feed back to the local television station for processing and retransmission. The news van has the ability to transmit the signal wirelessly back to the TV station. However, it cannot send the signal directly back to the station because, more often than not, there are tall buildings and other obstructions interfering with the line of sight. So the news van sends the signal to the station indirectly, by way of a microwave relay tower (paths A and B in the figure) located at some high point in the city. This form of wireless communication is called point-to-point microwave communication and is covered at the end of this chapter.

After the signal reaches the local television station, the program manager decides that the news story is exciting enough even for people in Montana to see. So the local news station transmits the signal up to a satellite (path C) hovering over the United States, and the satellite in turn retransmits the signal back down to the

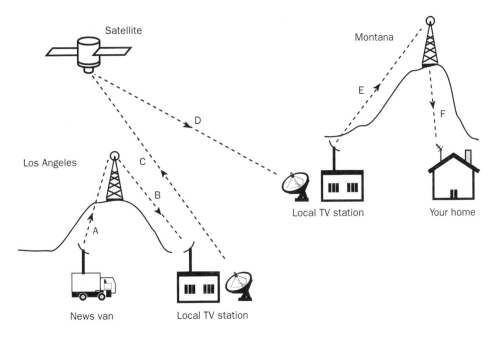

Figure 6–4
The signal path of a news event.

local TV station in Montana (path D). (The satellite does not just retransmit the signal to Montana, it retransmits it to every place in the United States, but you will learn more about that in the forthcoming section on Satellite Communications.)

Finally, the local television station in Montana needs to get the signal to you, and since you live way out on a farm, you do not have cable TV. So the local station in Montana uses point-to-point microwave communication to get the signal to a high point in your area (path E). It is at this point where the signal becomes a "broadcast" signal for the first time and gets transmitted to you (path F) and all of your neighbors, too. The signal you received used six different wireless paths and traveled over 45,000 miles just so you could laugh at some crazy person in Los Angeles. (Where would you be without wireless communications?)

New Uses for an Old Technology

Not too long ago, the FCC allocated some additional spectrum to each broadcaster to enable them to deliver HDTV. However, they gave the broadcasters some flexibility in how they used the spectrum, in return for a piece of any non-HDTV revenue generated, such as pay-per-view (every little bit helps). While most of the new allocation will undoubtedly be used to distribute HDTV programming, the broadcasters see this as an opportunity to distribute other content and increase their revenue.

To take advantage of this forthcoming service, you will connect a special antenna to your PC. You will then be able to download video games, software, or theoretically anything in digital form. (You will also be able to watch TV on your PC.) The broadcasters will utilize much of their existing infrastructure to deliver this additional content so little new investment will be required. This will present the first opportunity to purchase downloadable software, for instance, without going to the Internet. Of course you need to ask yourself if you want your local broadcaster to be your retailer of choice, but that's a separate issue.

RADAR ....

What Is Radar?

Definition

Probably the most famous acronym in all of wireless communications, *radar* stands for RAdio Detecting And Ranging, which is a real big hint as to what it does. It uses radio waves to detect things. More specifically, today's advanced radars can measure four distinct characteristics about an object. Radar can detect if an object is present, how far away it is, where it is, and, most impressively, how fast it is moving. (Anyone who has ever gotten a speeding ticket can attest to that.)

Radar is used in many places, including on the ground (called ground-based), on a ship (called shipboard), in the air (called airborne), and out in space (called space-based).

The Role of Frequency

Like every other wireless application in the United States, the FCC has allocated specific frequency bands for radar. Some of the allocated radar frequency bands are shown in Table 6–2.

Table 6–2   Some Radar Frequency Bands

Radar Band	Frequency Range(s)	Some Uses
UHF	220–225 MHz	Early warning, satellite surveillance.
VHF	420–450 MHz	Early warning, satellite surveillance.
L-band	960–1215 MHz	Air traffic control.
S-band	2.3–2.5 GHz 2.7–3.0 GHz	Shipboard military, early warning.
C-band	5.25 -5.925 GHz	Altimeters, weather.
X-band	8.5–10.55 GHz	Airborne fighter, weather, police.
Ku-band	13.4–14 GHz 15.7–17.7 GHz	Airborne fighter, police.

There are four main factors that dictate what frequency is selected for a particular application. All four, which are highlighted in Table 6–3, must be taken into account when making the frequency decision. Notice in Table 6–3 that several of the words are surrounded by quotes, which is because each of these is a relative measure. For instance, a "large" radar system for airborne applications will probably be considered a "small" radar system for ground-based applications.

Table 6–3   Factors Affecting Frequency Selection in Radar Systems

Factors	Implication
As the frequency goes up, the atmospheric absorption (attenuation) goes up.	If the radar needs to detect something "far" away, a "low" frequency is required.
As the frequency goes up, the size of the system's components gets smaller.	If space is limited (as on an airplane), the frequency must be "high."
For a given frequency, as the antenna size gets bigger, the beamwidth gets smaller.	If radar accuracy is important, a "large" antenna is needed.
As the output power goes up, the system size and weight goes up.	If "high" power is required, a "large" space is needed to house the radar.

Table 6–3 contains a word you may not have seen before called *beamwidth*. The beamwidth of a radiated RF signal describes how wide the antenna pattern is from an antenna that is *not* omnidirectional. (See Figure 3–6 for a review of antenna patterns.) RF energy can be radiated in a wide pattern or a narrow pattern (see Figure 6–5). Antenna beamwidths are measured in degrees (of a circle). With respect to the antenna patterns in Figure 6–5, the antenna on the left has a narrow beamwidth (perhaps 10 degrees out of 360) while the antenna on the right has a wide beamwidth (perhaps 45 degrees out of 360).

It should be intuitive that the narrower the beamwidth, the more accurately a radar's antenna can locate an object. As with all aspects of the RF world, there is a price to be paid for this accuracy. As you can see in Table 6–3, a narrow beamwidth (i.e., more accuracy) requires a large antenna, which is heavy and difficult to move.

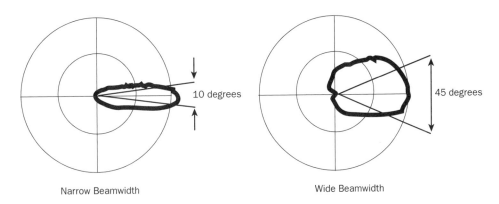

Figure 6–5
A comparison of antenna beamwidths.

How Radar Works

The Role of Reflection

Radar works off the simple principle, covered back in Chapter 2, that when an RF signal encounters a solid object, at least some of the RF energy is reflected. The key concept to this RF "reflection" is something called *radar cross section*. Every solid object has a radar cross section. Radar cross section can be visualized by viewing the two-dimensional silhouette of any three-dimensional object. To help you envision this, imagine looking at a football straight on at the pointy end. Even though the football is oblong and comes to a point, when viewed from its end the radar cross section of a football is a perfect circle. It is like looking into a football that has been cut in half.

The fundamental principle of radar is this: the greater the area of the cross section, the more RF energy that gets reflected, and the more RF energy that gets reflected, the easier it is to find the object. As a consequence, it is not the size of the object which matters, but the area of its radar cross section (silhouette). In that respect, a football is easier for radar to find than a fishing rod.

Did You Know?

The B-2 bomber in the United States Air Force is almost invisible to radar. It accomplishes this feat in two ways. First, the entire outside of the plane is covered with an RF absorbing material. Almost all of the

RF energy (radar from an enemy) that hits the plane gets absorbed (converted to heat) rather than reflected. Second, the unique design of the plane gives it an incredibly small radar cross section when viewed from the front. It is almost like looking at a pencil, which also has a small radar cross section.

How Radar Determines Distance

To determine an object's distance—and consequently its presence—the radar simply invokes the easiest equation you ever learned back in Algebra: distance equals rate times time ($D = R \times T$). The key to using this equation is that the radar system already knows the rate (at which the RF signal is traveling). RF waves travel at the speed of light, which just happens to be 186,000 miles per second. To put it in perspective, light can race around the equator of the Earth almost eight times in one second. (And you thought Ferraris were fast.)

In determining distance, the radar's transmitter sends out a signal and the super-fast electronics within the radar counts the time until the reflected signal reaches the receiver. Dividing this count by two (because the RF energy has to travel there and back), gives the time required for the signal to reach the object. This time, multiplied by the speed of light, determines the distance to the object. Radar systems that only determine distance are known as pulsed radars, because it "pulses" the transmitter off and on. During its brief "on" period, the transmitter sends out RF energy at a particular frequency. During its off period, the receiver "listens" for the reflected signal. Since the reflected signal is at the same frequency as the original (transmitted) signal, the transmitter must be off while the receiver listens for the reflected signal. (Otherwise, all the receiver hears is the transmitted signal.)

Did You Know?

Back in the 17th century, Sir Isaac Newton—the genius that discovered gravity—tried to measure the speed of light. He did so by standing on top of a mountain with a lantern and he had a colleague stand on another mountain, not far away, with another lantern. Newton's intention was to uncover his lantern and, upon seeing the light, have his partner uncover his lantern. All Newton needed to do was to count the time between uncovering his own lantern and seeing the other light, divide by two and he had the speed of light, or so he thought. Needless to say, this did not work very well, given the infinitesimal time it took for the light to make the trip. However, rumor has it that it did cause Newton to ponder his dilemma by sitting under an apple tree.

How Radar Determines Direction

Radar determines an object's location by moving the antenna in a process called *scanning*. Scanning involves pointing the antenna in a single direction, transmitting a signal in that direction, and waiting for the reflected signal. If a reflected signal is received, the radar knows which way the antenna is pointing and therefore it knows in what direction the object is located.

After a short period of time, the antenna moves a small amount and repeats the process. The radar repeats this three step process (move antenna, transmit a signal, wait for a reflection) until it has covered the entire area of interest and then points the antenna back to the first position and starts the process all over again.

This is where beamwidth size comes in. Smaller beamwidths require more of these "antenna moves" in the scanning process but allow the radar to pinpoint the object more exactly. Obviously there is a trade-off. Narrower beamwidths take longer to find the object, but once it is found its location is known more precisely. When airborne radar is used in combat, a wide beamwidth is initially used to scan, just to know if there is something out there. Once an object is detected, a narrower beamwidth is used to pinpoint the actual location of the target.

Think about all of the different trade-offs that need to be made in designing a radar system. If you are the pilot of a fighter aircraft and you are hunting down enemy aircraft, you want a radar that can produce a very narrow beamwidth so that you can locate the target precisely before you fire your missile. A narrow beamwidth requires one of two things: either a big antenna or a high frequency of transmission. A big antenna is an excellent choice if it does not keep the aircraft from taking off in the first place. As expected, there is a limitation. On the other hand, a high frequency is a good choice to produce a narrow beamwidth, except for one thing: high frequencies suffer from extreme atmospheric attenuation, which means that the radar can only locate the closest of targets. If I were flying a fighter aircraft, I would want to see *all* of the targets (near and far). Today's radars are a combination of constant technological innovation and performance trade-offs.

One of the drawbacks to conventional radar is that it requires the antenna to physically move to scan the area of interest. Not only does it require expensive motors to move the (heavy) antenna, but it is impossible for the antenna to move from one position to another, non-adjacent position instantaneously. As a result of this limitation, a new technology has been developed called *electronically scanned arrays*, in which the antenna pattern in the radar moves without anything physically moving. To understand the details of this would truly require a degree in engineering, so you will just have to take my word for it.

How Radar Determines Velocity

Back in the 1800s, a clever Austrian physicist named Christian Doppler made an amazing discovery. He observed that the frequency of sound waves emanating from a moving object changed as the object moved by. And as things turned out, it is not just true for sound waves but all waves including RF. In fact, this observed "frequency shift" (called a Doppler shift) is proportional to the velocity of the moving object. This is the fundamental principle underlying what is known as *Doppler radar*. Doppler radar is used to determine an object's velocity. It is Doppler radar that is responsible for all the "false" readings the police use to give out speeding tickets.

Doppler radar is somewhat different from conventional radar in that the transmitter is always on. This type of radar is known as *continuous wave* or CW radar. The transmitter must stay on continuously because, unlike conventional radar, which counts the time between transmission and reception, Doppler radar is looking for a change in frequency. Since this change in frequency may not last long, the transmitter must stay on continuously.

You may be wondering why the transmitter does not interfere with the receiver if it is always on. It would, if the receiver were listening for the same frequency that the transmitter is transmitting, but it isn't. It is looking for a signal which is frequency *shifted* from the transmitted signal. In fact, the receiver filters out any reflected signals at the transmitter's frequency. Reflected signals at the transmitter's frequency are, by definition, not moving (there is no frequency shift). Doppler radar does not care about stationary objects.

Perhaps you are thinking that in certain circumstances it would be advantageous to combine the capabilities of conventional radar (distance and location) with the capability of Doppler radar (velocity). In fact, today's most sophisticated radar systems, called pulsed Doppler radar, do just that. It not only counts the time lapse of the received signal (to determine distance), but it also looks for frequency shifts (to determine velocity).

Did You Know?

If you have ever heard a train whistle's tone change as it passed by you, you have experienced a Doppler shift. What you heard, as the train came toward you, was the frequency of the train's whistle "shifted" by the velocity of the train. Since the train was coming toward you, the frequency was shifted up. As the train passed by you, the tone dropped, shifted downward by the velocity of the train going away from you.

Different Radar Systems

Pulsed Radar Systems

As mentioned before, pulsed radar systems are used to calculate distance and, as a consequence, presence. Two common systems using pulsed radar are automatic door openers (found at many supermarkets) and automatic toilet flushers (found in many airports). The systems' operations are simple to understand. In both cases the system continuously transmits a radar pulse and waits for a response. The systems expect to receive a response at one of two time intervals. In the case when no person is present, the signal reflects off of the ground (for the door opener) or off the lavatory door (for the flusher), which result in a "long" time delay. With this long time delay, the system knows to do nothing. When a person is present, the signal in both cases reflects off of the person, which is closer to the system, resulting in a shorter time interval. When the system senses this shorter time interval, it knows to do its thing (open the door or flush the toilet).

A new application for pulsed radar is called *near object detection system* or NODS. NODS is nothing more than an inexpensive pulsed radar on the rear bumper of an automobile. When the car is put in reverse, the radar turns on and begins pulsing and timing the response. While backing up, if the car gets too close to an object (the time delay gets too short), it signals a warning—which should make parallel parking easier.

Did you ever wonder how commercial airline pilots know what altitude the airplane is at? They know because they use a neat little device called an *altimeter*.

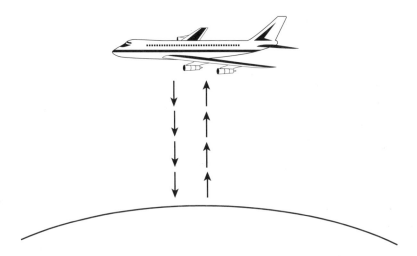

Figure 6–6
The signal path of a radar altimeter.

You have probably heard the word before but did not know what it was or how it worked. Well, now you do. An altimeter is nothing more than pulsed radar in an airplane, pointing down at the ground. It sends out a signal, waits for a response, and converts the time delay into a distance (see Figure 6–6), which is the airplane's altitude.

Now for the fun part. If an airplane is cruising at 33,000 feet, how long does it take for the round trip of the altimeter's signal? That is 66,000 feet (the length of the signal's round trip) divided by 984 million feet per second (the speed of light), or about 67 millionths of a second. (I guess that's what they mean by how time flies.)

Another useful pulsed radar system is weather radar. It works simply by detecting the RF energy reflected off of raindrops. No rain, no reflection; a little rain, a little reflection; a lot of rain, a lot of reflection. These differences in reflected RF power show up as different colors on the weather maps shown on the evening news. And taking several of these (radar) weather readings periodically results in the "moving cloud" display, which captures everyone's attention during hurricane season.

Doppler Radar Systems

The most common use of Doppler radar is the radar gun used by your local law enforcement to punish you for running late. The radar gun simply detects the change in frequency from the signal reflected off the automobile and converts it to a speed in miles per hour. (I understand that the next generation of radar guns will be able to convert a car's speed measurement directly into a debit in a checking account.)

A more interesting use of Doppler radar, used in fighter aircraft, is called *fire control radar*. (It is called fire control radar because it "controls" the "firing" of the aircraft's missiles.) In today's modern aircraft, pulsed Doppler radar is used to determine both location and velocity.

In the nose of every fighter aircraft is a pulsed Doppler radar. In air combat, fighter pilots only care about situations (called threats) in which an enemy aircraft is coming toward them. The pulsed Doppler radar uses a wide beamwidth in the pulsed mode to scan the sky for any threats. Once it detects a threat, the radar locks onto the target with a narrow beam. The receiver then analyzes the return signal for one of three conditions: no change in frequency, a lower frequency, or a higher frequency.

When the receiver senses no change in frequency, it is implied that there is no relative difference in the velocities of the two airplanes, which means the enemy plane is traveling away from the pilot's plane at exactly the same speed. Interpretation: the enemy pilot is prudent.

When the receiver senses a drop in frequency, it means that the enemy plane is traveling away at a greater velocity and thereby increasing the distance from the pilot's plane. Interpretation: the enemy pilot is chicken. Finally, if the receiver senses an increase in frequency, it means that the enemy aircraft is heading right for the pilot, and the greater the frequency shift, the faster the enemy is closing in. Interpretation: the enemy pilot is crazy.

Did You Know?

Police radar jammers—which may be illegal—work by transmitting an RF signal at a constantly varying frequency within the frequency band of the radar gun. The radar gun is expecting to receive a single frequency (which reflects the speed of the car). Instead, it receives a whole bunch of different frequencies, which drives the display crazy. Oh well.

The police are not the only ones having fun with Doppler radar. Weather forecasters are also taking advantage of it. As strange as it sounds, Doppler radar can be made to measure the velocity of wind. How it does this depends on the RF energy's ability to reflect off moving air differently than static air. With this capability, Doppler radar is used to detect things such as wind shear, which is a strong and sudden change in the wind's direction near the ground (usually near airports).

The last radar I will mention, only briefly, is a relatively new system called *collision avoidance*. Collision avoidance—also called *adaptive cruise control*—is similar to NODS, only for the front of an automobile. It has the ability to detect distance and velocity of objects in front of the car. With both of these pieces of information, an onboard computer determines whether the car in front is too close for the speed it is traveling. If the car is too close, the system either gently applies the brakes or berates the driver incessantly about their overly aggressive driving behavior.

The reason that you may not have seen collision avoidance systems on automobiles yet (*circa* 2001) is that car manufacturers in the U.S., Europe, and Asia cannot agree on which frequency band to use. Stay tuned.

SATELLITE COMMUNICATIONS................................

Why Satellites?

Satellite technology evolved from a limitation of RF behavior: line-of-sight transmission. If the earth were flat, this line-of-sight behavior would not be an issue (which is *one* of the reasons there were no satellites before Columbus). A signal transmitted in any direction that has sufficient power will get to its intended receiver, and over (relatively) short distances, this is exactly what happens. The problem arises when an RF signal is transmitted over long distances and the receiver is obscured by the curvature of the Earth (see Figure 6–7).

The left side of Figure 6–7 demonstrates what happens to RF signals that have sufficient power to travel long distances. They head toward outer space. This behavior, while a limitation, is also a benefit. Because of this behavior, the FCC can allocate the same frequency to different parties in different geographical locations. After a certain number of miles, the signal is no longer earthbound and it therefore no longer interferes with other signals that are at the same frequency.

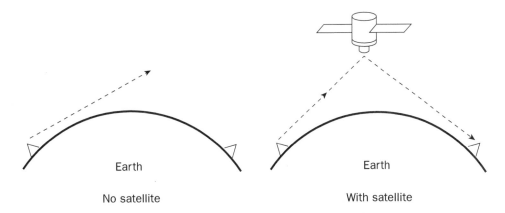

Figure 6–7
Line-of-sight behavior and the satellite solution.

An interesting thing to note is that there is an exception to the behavior depicted on the left side of Figure 6–7. As previously mentioned in the section on broadcasting, at low RF frequencies (less than 30 MHz), the RF energy gets reflected off the ionosphere and "bent" around the earth. Satellites are not needed for signals at these frequencies.

Did You Know?

Arthur C. Clarke, the author who wrote *2001: A Space Odyssey*, among other things, first conceived of the idea of communication satellites back in 1945. This is a pretty insightful observation, given the fact that space travel did not even exist yet. Maybe he got the idea from his buddy Hal.

The right side of Figure 6–7 shows all you need to know about the utility of satellites. Satellites allow RF signals to overcome the curvature of the Earth and still obey their line-of-sight behavior.

Given the tremendous expense involved in launching and maintaining satellites, they are only used for long distance communications. You will probably never see people using satellite communications to call their next door neighbor.

How Satellites Work

Geosynchronous Orbit

The satellite systems used for intercontinental telecommunications and television re-transmission work for only one reason: the satellite does not move with respect to the Earth. This is a pretty good trick since the Earth is rotating at about 1,000 miles per hour at the equator.

It just so happens that there is one specific orbit around the Earth, located 22,000 miles up from the equator, called *geosynchronous Earth orbit* (GEO). It is also called a *geostationary Earth orbit*. (Technically, geosynchronous and geostationary do not mean the same exact thing. However, in this book, for the sake of simplicity, we'll assume they do.) It is in this orbit where a satellite can rotate around the Earth at the same rotational speed as the Earth. A satellite rotating around the Earth in geosynchronous orbit appears to remain stationary when viewed from a point on the equator. (If the satellite did not remain fixed, the direction of the transmitted signal from the ground would have to be continually altered.)

How does a geosynchronous orbit work? Without going back to Physics 101, there are two forces pulling the satellite in different directions, and at the GEO these two forces cancel each other out. One of these forces is the result of constant angular velocity. You can envision this force by picturing yourself whipping a ball on a string around your head. If you let go, the ball goes flying outward. The other force acting on the satellite is gravity, which tries to pull the satellite inward (toward Earth). At 22,000 miles above the equator, these two forces cancel each other out and the satellite does not move with respect to the Earth.

As a visual appreciation for how high up 22,000 miles is, Figure 6–8 is an approximate scale of the Earth and the satellite's distance above it. Because the satellite is so high above the Earth, it is a good news/bad news situation. The bad news is that because the satellite is so high up, it takes a lot of RF power to reach it from the Earth. The good news is that signals transmitted down from the satellite can reach almost an entire hemisphere. Therefore, a satellite used to forward telephone calls from the United States to Great Britain is located halfway across the Atlantic Ocean, at the equator.

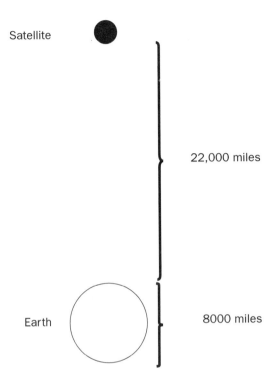

Satellite

22,000 miles

Earth

8000 miles

Figure 6–8
The relative height of a GEO satellite.

Did You Know?

When a GEO satellite is launched from onboard the space shuttle, it is only about 300 miles up when it is jettisoned from the craft. It still has another 21,700 miles to go before it reaches GEO. Why bother launching from the shuttle, you ask? It just so happens that the first 300 miles is where all the gravity is.

Uplink/Downlink

Once the satellite is comfortably situated in GEO, the next areas of concern are the *uplink* and the *downlink*. The uplink describes the signal that travels from the ground transmitter (called the *Earth station*) up to the satellite receiver, while the downlink describes the signal that travels from the satellite transmitter to the ground receiver.

The uplink and downlink frequency bands for satellite systems are allocated by the FCC in the United States (just like every other form of wireless communication). Since some satellites are used for international communications, the downlink frequencies affect countries other than the United States. The responsibility for allocating these "international" frequencies falls on the International Telecommunications Union (ITU). Think of the ITU as the FCC for the rest of the world.

A really ingenious feature of satellite communications is that the uplink frequency band and the downlink frequency band (in a given system) are never the same. When signals traveling in different directions use different frequency bands, it is called *duplex* communication. (If they travel at the same time, it is called full duplex communication.) A satellite used for telecommunications is an example of duplex communication. The implication of duplex communication is that when you call somebody in another country, halfway around the world, using satellite communications, both of you can speak at the same time. (This advantage is somewhat diminished if you do not speak the other person's language.)

However, when talking to someone using satellite communications there is another issue to be considered called propagation delay. Remember that RF energy travels at the speed of light. The time it takes a signal to travel across town, using a cellular phone, is inconsequential and cannot be detected by human beings (or any other beings). Satellite communication is different. With a round trip of 44,000 miles, there is a one-quarter-second delay between the originating transmitter and the ending receiver. But this delay is only in one direction. When trying to hold a conversation in which the other person also gets to speak, the round trip delay is half of one second. (Two round trips are made to the satellite.) This one-half second delay is very noticeable when making an intercontinental telephone call. Today, most intercontinental phone calls are made using undersea fiber optic cable and so the delay is no longer an issue.

The one-quarter-second delay is also present when viewing a sports event from another continent. In the case of broadcasting, the one-quarter-second delay is of little consequence, unless finding out the result of the World Cup final 250 milliseconds after the people in the stadium bothers you.

Satellite Dishes

Earth stations and satellites transmit and receive signals using dish antennas. (See Figure 6–9 for an example of an Earth station dish antenna.) They are used be-

Figure 6–9
A satellite dish antenna. *Courtesy of Andrew Corp.*

cause they are highly directional (they have a narrow beamwidth). The size of the dish antenna used depends on the frequency and power of the uplink and downlink signals. High uplink power requires a large Earth station dish for transmission. On the other hand, high downlink power only requires a small Earth station dish (like that used for DTH TV) for receiving.

When receiving the downlink signal, dish antennas act as funnel reflectors. First, they funnel as much of the RF energy (from the satellite) as possible into the dish, which is made of an RF reflecting material. The bigger the dish, the more RF energy it can funnel, which is why high-power satellites, like the ones used in DTH TV, only require a small dish. Once the RF energy enters the dish, it all gets reflected to a single "focal" point, slightly elevated from the surface of the dish (see Figure 6–9). This focal point contains the actual antenna element and the low noise amplifier (LNA).

Footprints

The antenna on a satellite projects an antenna pattern just like every other antenna. (An antenna pattern is a visual display of the direction that RF energy is radiating out from an antenna.) Because the antenna pattern generated from a satellite is projected onto the surface of the Earth, it is called an antenna *footprint*. The power radiated inside this footprint takes the antenna gain into consideration and is called the *effective isotropic radiated power*, or EIRP. (I guess just plain "radiated power" was already taken.) A graphical depiction of an antenna footprint covering the United States is shown in Figure 6–10.

Notice from Figure 6–10 that the antenna pattern approximately covers the land area of the continental United States. This is not by accident. There is only a finite amount of RF energy being transmitted from the satellite, and while the satellite is high enough in GEO to transmit a signal that covers half the globe, why bother? (Other than television-watching whales, who would know the difference?) Covering half the globe results in less power reaching the United States. This leads to an interesting aspect of satellite footprints. They can be contoured, somewhat, to approximate the shape of the area they are designed to cover to make maximum use of the available RF power.

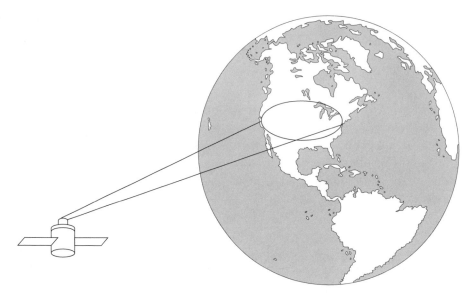

Figure 6–10
A satellite footprint covering the United States.

Satellite footprints are predominantly in the shape of a circle or oval. With respect to Figure 6–10, it might appear that certain parts of the United States receive no signal at all (those outside the footprint), which is not the case. Recall that an antenna pattern is a silhouette of an area that receives half the amount of RF energy leaving the transmitter. In this figure, the area outside of the oval still receives RF energy; it just receives less than the area inside. There are some ramifications to a footprint not covering the entire United States. Under certain adverse conditions (e.g., heavy rain), it is entirely possible that those areas that lie outside the footprint will receive a degraded (or no) signal.

The footprint shown in Figure 6–10 is for a broadcast signal. It is meant to be received by many different points in the United States. More than likely this is some kind of television broadcast. But what if the satellite carries intercontinental telephone calls? What will the footprint look like then? It will still be a circle or oval, only much smaller and focused only on the long distance telephone carrier's Earth station.

The size of a satellite's footprint is not without limitations, however. There is a direct relationship between the size of the antenna (on the satellite), the frequency being used, and the size of the footprint. Like most things in the world of RF, when one thing gets larger, other things tend to get smaller. For instance, at a given frequency, the larger the antenna, the smaller the footprint that is possible. Likewise, for a given antenna size, the higher the frequency, the smaller the footprint that is possible. As you will soon learn, the ability to make small footprints can dramatically increase a satellite's usefulness.

Did You Know?

When a satellite's footprint covers the entire continental United States it is called a "CONUS" footprint, which is just a contraction of continental and U.S.

RF Electronics

By now you are probably wondering what the RF electronics on board a satellite consist of. (Even if you're not, that's what you're about to read.) At its most basic, the RF electronics on board a satellite, called a *transponder*, is just a simple combination of a few RF devices (see Figure 6–11).

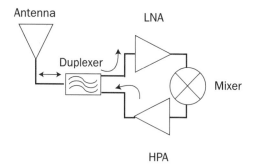

Figure 6–11
Block diagram of a satellite transponder.

Referring to Figure 6–11, the satellite antenna receives the uplink signal (at the uplink frequency) and sends it on to the duplexer. (Recall that a duplexer is nothing more than two bandpass filters in one box.) The duplexer then routes the signal to the low noise amplifier (LNA), which amplifies the signal. Next, the mixer frequency shifts the signal to the downlink frequency (source not shown) and, finally, the signal gets boosted by the high power amplifier (HPA) and sent through the duplexer on its way out the antenna. Figure 6–11 is a block diagram that describes the basic RF function of every satellite that has ever had the good fortune to make it all the way to GEO.

Did You Know?

When a satellite's RF section is simple like that shown in Figure 6–11, it is called a "bent pipe" architecture. In essence the RF acts like a bent pipe (in the shape of a "U"). It receives the uplink signal and without any real signal processing, shifts the frequency and routes it back down to Earth. Today, the newer generation of satellites is beginning to add some smarts to the electronics section of the satellite, which is called a "process payload."

About the Spacecraft

GEO satellites do not last forever, but it is not because the RF electronics fail. (If nothing else, RF engineers build reliable satellites.) In fact, the RF electronics on board a satellite can last almost indefinitely. Because it gets its power from the sun (via solar panels), there should be no reason why a satellite does not last forever.

Except for one thing. For GEO satellites to work properly, they need to stay fixed in GEO and, unfortunately, over time, satellites tend to drift a little. (Okay, so GEO isn't perfect.) To counteract this natural tendency to drift, satellites are equipped with something called *station-keeping*.

Station-keeping is nothing more than an onboard propulsion system that periodically releases small bursts of fuel. The momentum shift from these small bursts serves to reposition the satellite in its proper place. A satellite only carries a limited amount of this fuel, so when it runs out, the satellite can no longer be repositioned and quickly becomes useless. Just prior to using up the last of the fuel, the onboard propulsion system gives one big burst and sends the satellite to a different, out-of-the-way orbit, where it spends the remainder of its existence in the lonely, dark void of space.

Satellite Systems

Three Topologies

There are three basic topologies used in satellite communications: point-to-point, point-to-multipoint, and multipoint-to-point. Which topology is used is dictated by the application.

One example of point-to-point topology is intercontinental telecommunications. When a bunch of people in Great Britain want to call a bunch of people in the United States, their calls first go to an Earth station in Great Britain. All of the calls are combined into one signal and transmitted to a telecommunications satellite hanging out somewhere over the Atlantic Ocean. The signal is then retransmitted (by the satellite) to an Earth station in the United States (owned by one of the long distance carriers). The calls are then separated and routed along their way to their final destinations. In this example, the satellite is used to connect a single point (the Earth station in Great Britain) to a single point (the Earth station in the United States). In point-to-point topology, only two large satellite dishes are required and both are used to transmit and receive.

Point-to-multipoint topology is used in DTH satellite television (also referred to as DBS for *direct broadcast satellite*). For broadcasts in the United States, a single Earth station, owned by the broadcast company, transmits its "entertainment" up to a satellite (situated somewhere over Kansas). The satellite then retransmits the signal in a footprint that covers the whole country, like the one shown in Figure 6–10. Anybody with a small dish antenna, located within (or near) the footprint, will be able to—for $39.99/month—receive the broadcast signal. In point-to-multipoint topology, there is one large dish for transmitting and many small dishes for receiving (only).

The most frequent use of multipoint-to-point topology is something called VSAT, which stands for *very small aperture terminal*. In this topology, many Earth stations with small to medium size dishes are used to relay information from a point of sale back to a single location, typically the central office. One of the big users of VSATs are gasoline companies. Quite often you will see gasoline stations with small satellite dishes on their roofs. This is a VSAT system. The system periodically relays sales information from the station, via satellite, back to the main office. In this way, the main office has an up-to-the-minute status on the sale of gasoline all over the country. In multipoint-to-point topology, there are many small dishes transmitting and only one dish receiving.

The Role of Frequency

Satellite systems fall into one of two main categories: fixed satellite services (FSS) or mobile satellite services (MSS). In FSS systems, the Earth-bound receiver does not move. An example of an FSS system is the DTH TV. It follows that in MSS systems the Earth-bound receiver does move. Unlike FSS systems, MSS systems come in three different varieties: aeronautical, land, and maritime. If you are rich enough to make a telephone call from one of those built-in phones on a commercial airliner, you are using an aeronautical mobile satellite system. From the user's standpoint, whether you are using an FSS system or a MSS system is irrelevant. However, from the satellite owner's viewpoint it is very important because the different service types are allocated different frequency bands.

The FCC has allocated many different frequency bands for FSS. By far the two most popular to date have been C-band and Ku-band. In the next generation of satellites, Ka-band will play an increasingly important role, which is discussed in a later section. The specifics of C-band, Ku-band, and Ka-band are shown in Table 6–4.

Wherever there is a home outfitted with a large dish antenna, it is probably receiving a C-band downlink (originally intended just for reception by the broadcast stations). If they have a small dish antenna, chances are it is Ku-band (DTH TV).

Table 6–4 C-Band, Ku-Band, and Ka-Band Frequency Allocations

Band	Frequency Allocation
C-band downlink	3.7–4.2 GHz
C-band uplink	5.925–6.425 GHz
Ku-band downlink	11.7–12.2 GHz
Ku-band uplink	14.0–14.5 GHz
Ka-band downlink	27.5–29.5 GHz
Ka-band uplink	29.5–31.0 GHz

Did You Know?

For a given satellite system, the uplink signal is always at a higher frequency than the downlink signal. Do you know why? It is because RF electronics are less efficient at higher frequencies, which translates to more wasted power. Now where do you suppose RF engineers would rather locate the more wasteful electronics—on the ground, where power is plentiful, or in space, where power is at a premium? Take your time.

If you recall, the RF section of a satellite, called a transponder, is used to frequency shift the uplink signal to the frequency of the downlink signal. In today's satellites, there is more than one transponder in a given frequency band. For instance, C-band, with a downlink bandwidth of 500 MHz (3.7 GHz–4.2 GHz) has 12 transponders to cover the entire bandwidth. The 500 MHz bandwidth is divided into 12, equally sized bandwidths (42 MHz each) called *channels*. Each transponder is assigned a channel. There are many reasons for breaking up the total bandwidth into channels, but by far the most important is redundancy. If there are 12 transponders and one fails, there are still 11 left, but if there is only one transponder and it fails, you get the picture. (Besides, do you have any idea how hard it is to get an RF technician into GEO?)

The main goal of every satellite user is to make maximum use of the available bandwidth on the satellite. Transponder bandwidth, called *capacity*, is leased out at a very expensive hourly rate. Satellite users try to cram as much information as possible into every MHz of every transponder. Take the case of standard broadcast television. As pointed out earlier in the chapter, a standard broadcast television signal requires 6 MHz of bandwidth. But transponders have 42 MHz of bandwidth. What do you suppose the TV stations do? If you guessed that they cram seven different channels into each transponder, you are on the right track, but you forgot about polarization. (You are forgiven if you didn't read that section.) Polarization allows TV broadcasters to cram 14 (7 horizontally polarized and 7 vertically polarized) different television channels into one transponder.

In more sophisticated satellite systems today, the 6 MHz television signal is digitized before it is transmitted up to the satellite. Why digitize it? Once a signal is digitized, it can be compressed in a process called *digital compression* (what else?) with the use of digital signal processors (DSP). Digital compression involves removing redundant information in the TV signal, resulting in less bandwidth required to transmit the signal. After compression, a 6 MHz signal may take up as little as 1.5 MHz, and you know what that means: more television channels into the same transponder (and more money into the satellite owner's pocket).

Did You Know?

(Digital) data compression is very simple to understand. Picture a 50-page book in which the first twenty-five pages say the same exact words, "good morning." (A pretty boring book, I admit.) For you to know exactly what is in the book, you could read each of the first 25 pages. Or, I could compress the book by writing on the first page, "good morning, the next 24 pages say the same exact thing." Now you can skip 24 pages and not miss a single thing because I got rid of the redundant information. That is data compression.

To give you an appreciation for the capacity of a 42 MHz transponder channel, an (uncompressed) telephone call requires 4 kHz of bandwidth, which means each transponder channel can carry over 10,000 different voice calls simultaneously (ignoring polarization).

A Special Satellite System—GPS

What Is GPS?

GPS, or global positioning system, is a satellite system developed by the U.S. government, which consists of 24 satellites that do nothing but continuously transmit a strange, but useful, signal. GPS satellites offer no provision for receiving signals from its users. The signals transmitted from the GPS satellites are used for two things: navigation and timing. The signals allow anyone with a GPS receiver to know approximately where they are on the surface of the Earth. (I say approximately because there is always some error in the measurement, which ranges from inches to miles, depending on many things.) The GPS signals can also be used to tell what time it is, but then again so can a wristwatch.

Since the GPS system was originally intended for military use, there are a couple of different signals being transmitted that produce different grades of location accuracy. A military GPS receiver, which utilizes an encrypted signal from the satellites, can pinpoint a location to within a meter or two. Civilian grade GPS receivers typically produce accuracies of 20–30 meters. However, in times of war, the government can institute what they call *selective availability*, and purposely degrade the signals from the satellites. In these instances, the position accuracy will be greater than 100 meters.

When a GPS receiver is used to determine present location, it does not respond with something like "the corner of 5th and Market in downtown Pittsburgh." Instead, what it gives is a measurement in degrees of longitude and latitude, and while knowing your present location by longitude and latitude is interesting, by itself it is not particularly useful (unless you happen to be Gilligan). Conveniently, today's GPS receivers come with a trip function, which enables it to remember your starting point and give you relative distance and direction measurements from that point as you travel. As an example, if you are hiking in a densely wooded area that you are unfamiliar with, at your launching point you can command the GPS receiver to store that location in memory. Then, at any point in the trip, if you ask the GPS receiver how to get back, it will relay how far and in what direction you need to go to get there. Now that is useful.

An interesting thing about the GPS satellites is that they are *not* in geosynchronous orbit, which means they are not stationary with respect to the rotation of the Earth. If you could see them from Earth (you would be Superman), you would see GPS satellites cruising by overhead periodically from one horizon to the other. Since each of the 24 satellites more or less transmits the same signal, and since there is no need for them to *receive* any signals, as long as some of the satellites are overhead at any moment in time—even though they are moving—the system works just fine.

Did You Know?

The GPS satellite system, deployed by the Department of Defense, was originally intended solely for the purpose of enabling soldiers in the battlefield to know their exact position. Today it has many more uses. One of the most exciting is a service called E911, in which a cellular phone is equipped with a GPS receiver. In the event you break down, not only can you use your cellular phone to call for help, but the GPS receiver relays your location to the emergency service so they know where to find you.

Theory of Operation

GPS operates on the same distance-rate-time relationship as radar: if the time it takes for a signal to reach a certain point is known, then its distance can also be calculated. A GPS receiver receives specially encoded signals from the GPS satellites, which enables it to determine how long it took for the signal to arrive. The GPS receiver then takes this time and converts it into a distance.

GPS is also based on another concept called *triangulation*. In overly simplified terms, triangulation is used to determine where you are if you know how far you are from three different points. For reasons that you will soon learn, if a GPS receiver receives signals from at least four different GPS satellites, it can determine its location precisely.

Figure 6–12 is a graphical explanation of the GPS position determination process. The top of Figure 6–12 depicts a sphere with a GPS satellite at the center. If a GPS receiver knows its distance from a single satellite, then it must be somewhere on the surface of a sphere (with the distance from the satellite equaling the radius of the sphere). The middle of Figure 6–12 depicts the situation when a GPS receiver knows how far it is from two satellites. If the receiver knows how far it is from two satellites, then it must be on the surface of both spheres (one for each satellite). Since the (3D) intersection of these two spheres is a circle, the receiver must be located somewhere on it.

When the distance from a third satellite is known, a third sphere comes into play. This third sphere intersects the circle at only two points, as shown in the bottom of Figure 6–12. Therefore, the GPS receiver must be located at one of these two points. Technically a fourth satellite is needed to eliminate one of the two points. However, since one of the two points is usually an absurd location, like inside the mountain with the mole people, it can be eliminated and the location of the receiver is known with certainty.

Since there are only 24 satellites in the GPS system, they are concentrated around the equator, which means there are places on Earth, near the north and south poles, where less than four satellites are visible at all times. The result is that GPS does not work very well at the ends of the hemispheres (which is why you never hear about Santa Claus using it).

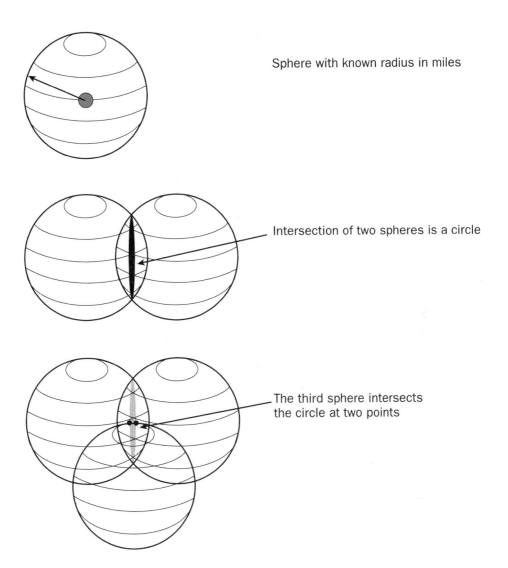

Sphere with known radius in miles

Intersection of two spheres is a circle

The third sphere intersects
the circle at two points

Figure 6–12
Graphical depiction of the GPS location determination process.

Uses for GPS

There are many uses for GPS, some of which are being used today while others
have yet to be implemented. For instance, GPS has been used for some time now
by dispatchers wanting to track fleets of eighteen wheelers delivering their cargo.

More and more you are starting to see electronic maps in automobiles to aid in navigation (called *telematics*). It also makes sense that delivery and emergency vehicles use GPS to more quickly locate their destinations.

One of the newer markets for GPS is in the aviation industry. Very accurate GPS can be used to help planes land in near zero visibility (which is important when it absolutely, positively has to be there). An even more important use of GPS in the future may be to help avoid collisions between airplanes while in flight.

An application that uses GPS today, and one which you may not have thought of, is cellular telephony. As mentioned briefly above, GPS can also be used to tell time. Why use GPS to tell time? Because it is really accurate. We are talking one nanosecond accuracy. That is one billionth of a second (it ain't no Timex). CDMA, one of the more important cellular technologies today (which you will learn about in the next chapter), works because all of the signals in the systems are perfectly synchronized, thanks to GPS.

GPS is also used in precision farming and construction grading to help farmers and builders more accurately control the use of their land. There are even insurance companies threatening to use GPS to track your automobile's every move. Their motivation? To base your insurance premium on your actual driving behavior. In theory, those that drive only during the day (when it is safer), will get lower rates (yeah right).

Eventually, some people hypothesize that every square meter on the planet will have its own GPS address, along with its physical address. The physical address will be for us humans and the GPS address will be for those ubiquitous computers. So when you are looking for the nearest McDonalds and you cannot find it, your car can.

Did You Know?

There are companies out there today delivering something called *Indirect GPS*. Suppose you want GPS in your office building but do not have access to the roof to put up a GPS antenna. You can now get the same GPS signals from a nearby CDMA basestation, by using its signals as a timing reference. Recall that CDMA gets its timing from GPS in the first place. Seems a little fishy to me.

The Next Generation Satellites—LEO

Up until now, I have assumed that all communication satellites are in geosynchronous orbit, which was true until very recently. Today, there are several consortia (which is a fancy word for a group of rich people) working on a new kind of satellite system based on *low Earth orbit* satellites or LEOs. Low Earth orbit satellite systems (called *constellations*) use many small satellites, only a few hundred miles up, to relay RF information.

Why LEO?

There are several ramifications to using satellites in low Earth orbit. First, the satellites are not stationary with respect to a fixed point on Earth. (If you could see them, they would fly by overhead very quickly.) These non-stationary satellites make communicating with them more complicated than with GEOs. First, RF contact must be made with a moving satellite (which is a challenge in itself). Then, after the RF link is established with the first satellite, it is only a short time before that same satellite is no longer visible and an RF connection is no longer possible.

The second ramification of LEO satellites is that because they are so low, they can only project a small antenna footprint (covering a small area), which means that many LEOs are required to fully cover a land area the size of the United States. People on opposite ends of the country, wishing to use LEOs to make contact, will not be able to use the same satellite to connect. All of these ramifications result in a satellite system that is much more complex than a standard, off-the-shelf GEO system.

If LEOs are so complex and require many satellites, why bother? The answers are surprisingly simple: power and time delay. First, LEOs require less RF power to reach than GEOs (which makes sense since they are closer). In fact, some LEOs are low enough to reach with the power in a handheld phone. Second, unlike GEOs, LEOs do not suffer from the one-half second round trip time delay when speaking on a phone. As a result, the initial motivation for deploying LEOs was only to provide mobile telephony. It does not make sense to use LEOs to broadcast your favorite television show.

Did You Know?

There is another Earth orbit used in satellite communications and it is referred to as medium Earth orbit or MEO. The GPS satellites discussed earlier in this chapter are situated in MEO, which is why they are not stationary (like GEOs). Where do you suppose MEO is located above the Earth? If I told you between LEO and GEO, would you believe me?

Since telephony by LEO is very expensive, it is only meant to be used in places where no other form of mobile telephony (e.g., cellular phones) exists, like out in a desert or in the middle of the ocean. This niche use of an expensive technology has fueled a long-running controversy over the soundness of the LEO business. There is one question that everybody is trying to answer: Are there enough customers out in the desert or in the middle of the ocean to pay for the expensive LEO satellite system? Stay tuned.

Did You Know?

The first, and probably most (in)famous LEO satellite system was the Motorola-sponsored Iridium system. Iridium was originally designed to use 77 low Earth orbit satellites and it got its name from Iridium, which is the 77th element in the periodic chart of basic elements. Sometime into the program however, some bright engineer discovered that the system would work just as well with only 66 satellites, but chose to keep the name Iridium. I guess they figured nobody would ever make a phone call using something called Dysprosium. As it turned out, nobody used something called Iridium to make a phone call either.

How LEOs Work

LEOs work by continuously relaying signals among each other as they move. Figure 6–13 shows generally how a LEO system works. In this example, the satellites are moving counterclockwise. The left side of the figure (Time = 0) shows how a person (located at point 1) on one side of the planet can talk to someone on the other side of the planet (located at point 2) using a LEO system. The phone call, using the LEO's frequency, is transmitted to whichever LEO satellite is closest overhead at that given moment (satellite A on the left side of the figure). That satellite (A) then relays the call to the next closest satellite (B) in the direction of the final destination. This relay process repeats itself until the call reaches the satellite (D) that is over the intended receiver. At that point, the signal is transmitted down with an antenna footprint that encircles the intended receiver. How the system knows which satellites to use at any moment is what makes LEO systems so complex.

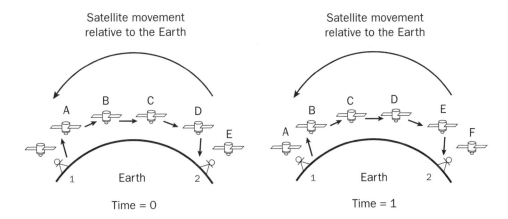

Figure 6–13
Graphical depiction of the workings of a LEO satellite system.

After a short period of time (Time = 1 on the right side of Figure 6–13), satellite A will no longer be over the person originating the call (1). It is at this point when satellite A "hands off" the call to satellite B and the process continues as before, only this time the last satellite utilized is no longer D but E. (All of the satellites have rotated counterclockwise.)

The other thing to know about LEOs is the satellite-power tradeoff. If the LEO satellite system is used with very low-powered handheld phones, then the satellites must be close to Earth (but not so close that they fall on you). The closer to Earth they are, the smaller their footprints will be and, therefore, the more satellites that are required to blanket the whole Earth. And a lot of satellites—even small ones—translates into an expensive system. LEO system designers are constantly trading off between the fewest possible satellites (higher up) and the most user-friendly (low-powered) handheld phones.

The Internet from Above

You knew it would not take long for the satellite people to get involved in this maelstrom we call the Internet. The original story was that these satellites would deliver Internet access to under-served and rural communities, who have no other way to gain access. But when you see the dollars required to put one of these systems in place, you have to believe they are going after more than a couple of farmers in Montana.

Why not take advantage of satellite technology? On the one hand, there are already satellites in orbit that can receive and transmit digital data. On the other hand, new satellite systems can be put in place especially designed for TCP/IP (the communication protocols of the Internet) to provide even better connectivity. What you see today (*circa* 2001) is a plethora of different approaches from companies wanting to be the next generation ISP (Internet "satellite" provider).

There are as many different approaches to Internet access via satellite as there are satellite systems, but they all have one thing in common: they all use satellite downlinks (in one form or another) to provide access from the Internet (called the *downstream*). Where they differ is in their approach to making connection to the Internet (called the *upstream*).

Downstream Technologies

The downstream technologies can be divided into two categories: GEO and LEO. The first generation of Internet access via satellite utilizes existing (GEO) Ku-band satellites. Some of these are the same ones delivering DTH TV (DBS), while others were originally designed as VSAT systems. (Ku-band is in the 12–14 GHz range.) It is not that these Ku Band satellites are ideal for providing access to the Internet, it is that they are already there (it's a first mover advantage thing).

Ku-band satellites in GEO are far from a perfect Internet solution however. First, given their frequency and the spacecraft's antenna size, Ku-band satellites are limited to producing only large footprints. They typically cover the continental U.S. (CONUS). This is fine when you are broadcasting TV direct to the home and the goal is to reach as many people as possible with the same programming. But the Internet is different. Everyone wants their own unique information. Since only a finite amount of digital data can be transmitted at any given time within the footprint, the number of simultaneous users seeking unique, Internet-type data is severely restricted.

Another problem for any GEO satellite is the one-quarter second round trip time delay needed to make a connection. Without going into too much detail, TCP/IP expects information sent using its protocol to reach its final destination in a given time frame. If it does not, it can really mess things up, and as it turns out, a one-quarter second delay is long enough to really mess things up. On top of that, the one-quarter second delay seriously affects the quality of any real-time Internet application like telephony or videoconferencing.

So what is the answer? One of the answers is Ka-band. (Ka-band is around 30 GHz.) Ka-band satellites offer many advantages compared to the existing Ku-band ones. First, there is much more bandwidth (3.5 GHz compared to 1 GHz), and as you know by now, more bandwidth equals more information. Also, there are a lot less RF things going on at Ka-band so there is less signal interference.

More importantly, for the same size spacecraft antenna, Ka-band satellites can produce much smaller footprints than corresponding Ku-band satellites. Instead of one single footprint covering the U.S. (like that shown in Figure 6–10), Ka-band satellites are able to use multiple, smaller footprints to cover the same area (like that shown in Figure 6–14). This allows the same Ka-band frequency to be used by different Web surfers in different locations. This frequency reuse effectively multiplies the number of users who can access the Internet simultaneously by the number of footprints (called *spot beams*). Because of these spot beams, information can also be tailored for delivery on a local or regional basis. The bottom line is Ka-band delivers a lot more information than Ku-band. In fact, one of the most exciting aspects of using Ka-band satellites is the possibility of combining Internet access and DTH TV programming, all delivered to a single 18" dish antenna.

Did You Know?

In the old days of RF, there was no Ku-band or Ka-band, just plain old K-band. Unfortunately, K-band covers a very large frequency range. RF engineers wanted more precision when speaking about K-band and so they divided the old K-band into three sections: Ku, K, and Ka. Ku stands for "under K" while Ka stands for "above K." How many people do you suppose know that?

One of the implications of these smaller Ka-band spot beams is that the "dumb" bent pipe architecture typically used in the Ku-band satellites will no longer work. Since a Ku-band footprint covers the whole U.S., whatever signal it receives just gets re-transmitted everywhere. Whomever is looking for the signal will certainly receive it. This is not so with Ka-band spot beams. Referring to Figure 6–14, if a person in a location covered by spot beam A wants to access a Web site in a location covered by spot beam C, the satellite needs to know that and route the request accordingly. In essence, these Ka-band satellites become Internet routers in the sky. As a consequence, these Ka-band satellites become costly to manufacture.

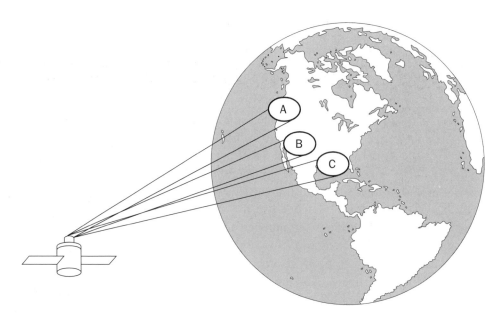

Figure 6–14
A Ka-band satellite with 3 spot beams.

Note: It is possible to use Ka-band without spot beams. However, this approach would lose the benefits of frequency reuse, but it would make the system much simpler. Why use such an approach? To take advantage of Ka-band's extra bandwidth.

Another hurdle for Ka-band satellites is rain fade. The higher frequency (and smaller wavelength) is more susceptible to absorption by rain than either Ku-band or C-band. In short, Ka-band satellites are a good news/bad news proposition. They are good because they offer a much higher data carrying capacity (compared to Ku-band). But they are bad because they are more costly and complex to build, while suffering worse from the effects of rain fade. A comparison of all the satellite approaches can be seen in Table 6–5.

Okay, so maybe Ka-band satellites address the broadband requirements of the Internet, but what about the time delay? There are two approaches to solving the time delay problem: one expensive and one inexpensive. The inexpensive one simply requires some software magic to convince TCP/IP to ignore the one-quarter second delay. Unfortunately, this approach will not help applications like telephony and videoconferencing. The expensive approach avoids the time delay altogether by using LEO satellites.

Table 6–5   A Comparison of Different Satellite Internet Connectivity Approaches

Connection	Data Rate	Advantage(s)	Disadvantage(s)
Downstream			
GEO Ku	400 Kbps	Already in orbit.	Limited users; time delay.
GEO Ka	100 Mbps	Many users; high data rates.	Expensive; rain fade; time delay.
LEO	64 Mbps	Many users; high data rates; no time delay.	Expensive; complicated to build and maintain.
Upstream			
GEO Ku	64 Kbps	Already in orbit.	Low data rate; expensive end-user equipment; time delay.
GEO Ka	2 Mbps	High data rate.	Expensive end-user equipment; rain fade; time delay.
LEO	2 Mbps	Many users; high data rates; no time delay.	Expensive; complicated to build and maintain.
POTS	64 Kbps	Already there; low cost.	Low data rate; may tie up phone line; requires two ISPs.
Cable	128 Kbps	Moderate data rate; doesn't tie up phone line; already there.	Not available everywhere; requires two ISPs.

LEO satellites, which are only several hundred miles up, can have a time delay as little as tens of milliseconds, which makes them ideal for real-time Internet applications. Also recall that a LEOs footprint only covers a small area, which makes frequency reuse possible. So what is the downside of Internet delivery utilizing LEOs? As mentioned previously, LEOs require the manufacture, launch, and maintenance of as many as several hundred satellites (and we all know what happened to the first LEO system). There are some ambitious LEO systems on the drawing board for Internet access. Stay tuned.

Upstream Approaches

While Internet delivery via satellite always uses the satellite's downlink for the downstream data flow, it is not the case for the upstream data flow. There are two approaches to upstream data flow: wired and wireless. Because of the asymmetrical nature of data flow in the Internet, the real high-speed requirements are for the downstream data. With the exception of real-time applications like videoconferencing, the upstream data flow requirements are typically pretty meager. Since the data flow requirements are not as great, it opens up a whole host of possibilities for the upstream data.

Generally speaking, satellites in GEO are difficult to reach in the uplink. It requires some combination of a large dish antenna and/or a very high-power RF amplifier, making it an expensive (and perhaps complex) consumer purchase. As a result, Internet satellite providers have chosen initially to provide upstream connectivity via something other than the satellite. When they do this it is considered a one-way satellite service.

The first Internet satellite systems utilize(d) the plain old telephone systems (POTS) for the upstream. You can imagine that it will not be long before the cable companies get into the act. These wired upstream approaches have some drawbacks though. Their upstream bandwidth is usually pretty limited, which in most instances is not a problem. In the case of dial-up service, it still requires tying up a phone line. Perhaps most important, this wired-wireless approach to Internet connectivity requires signing up (and paying) two Internet service providers (ISP).

Ultimately what these satellite providers want to offer is two-way satellite service. There are many two-way satellite systems on the drawing board as of this writing. Some are based on GEO systems, while others are based on LEO systems. There is even one system in the works that requires the use of a rooftop antenna to wirelessly connect to the Earth station located some distance from the premises.

The great challenge for the two-way GEO satellite systems is developing uplink hardware that is affordable and consumer-friendly. Recall that VSAT systems are already two-way GEO satellite systems, so they may have a head start in this area. As for the two-way LEO satellite systems, they already have the advantage of requiring lower uplink power. Which systems and approaches will win out? It is hard to say. But what is certain is that there are a lot of systems in the works (perhaps as many as 50 worldwide) and not all of them will come to fruition.

POINT-TO-POINT MICROWAVE ....

What Is Point-to-Point Microwave?

Point-to-point microwave, sometimes called *microwave relay*, has been around since the mid 1940s. Back then, microwave relay was analog, meaning it used modulation to combine an analog information signal with an RF carrier. Nowadays most point-to-point microwave systems are digital in nature.

Point-to-point microwave, as the name implies, is used to communicate, wirelessly, between a single transmitter and a single receiver, both owned by the same entity. This point is important, because when someone is given the right (by the FCC) to communicate using point-to-point microwaves at a certain frequency and in a certain geographical location, everyone else is prohibited from using that frequency in that location. In this respect, it is similar to broadcasting.

The tremendous advantage of point-to-point microwave is the user's ability to get information from one point to another without owning the underlying real estate.

Uses for Point-to-Point Microwave

The FCC has allocated many frequency bands for this application, and for many different uses, but there are three uses which dominate all others by far. The first of these uses is *private operational fixed microwave*. Most often, the owner of the transmitter and receiver is a private company. In these cases, the wireless systems are used to control (an unattended piece of equipment), to monitor (temperature, pressure, voltage, etc.), or to relay (voice, data, fax, etc.). These systems are especially useful along right-of-ways like highways and railroads.

A second use for point-to-point is relaying large volumes of voice traffic called *common carrier microwave*. This is one of the ways in which long distance telephone companies get calls from here to there. As will be discussed in the next chapter, this application is also used by mobile telephony providers to get the phone call from the basestation back to the home office. Common carrier microwave is often used when the terrain over which the signal must travel is severe and laying copper wire (or optical fibers) is impractical.

The third main use for point-to-point microwave is video relay and is referred to as *broadcast auxiliary microwav*e. This is the way in which mobile TV news vans get their signals back to the station. It is also the way the television stations get their signals up to their broadcast antennas, as previously discussed and detailed in Figure 6–4.

> **Did You Know?**
>
> Private microwave relay is how the long distance carrier MCI came into being. Back in the early 1960s, a man named Jack Goeken set up a series of microwave relays between Chicago and St. Louis to help his customers keep track of their merchandise on the way to market. One day he had a brainstorm. Those same relays could be used to provide long distance telephony. That insight led to a 20-year battle that ended with the breakup of AT&T.

When the FCC gives permission to a single operator to use a specific frequency in a certain area, it is called *licensed* point-to-point microwave. As you will see in Chapter 8, there is a whole new category of point-to-point communications in which many operators share the same frequency. This "unlicensed" application of point-to-point communications comes under the heading of broadband fixed wireless.

Point-to-Point Operations

As mentioned above, microwave relay is used in places where laying copper or optical fibers makes no sense or is impossible, but there is a limit. Our old friend, line-of-sight, ensures that microwave relays are spaced no more than about 25 miles apart, which means if a signal is to be transmitted from Los Angeles to San Diego (about 120 miles) using point-to-point microwave communications, at least four microwave relay stations are required. A microwave relay tower with directional antennas is shown in Figure 6–15.

The first thing to notice in Figure 6–15 is that microwave relays use dish antennas, which are covered in this picture by something called a *radome*. (Radome is the general term given to anything that covers an antenna to protect it from the environment while allowing the RF to pass through.) Recall that dish antennas are highly directional (their antenna pattern has a narrow beamwidth). This makes sense as the microwave relay wants as much RF energy as possible going in only one direction (toward the next receiver). In some instances, microwave relays use horn antennas (shaped like square funnels) to cover wider bandwidths. Most point-to-point communication takes place at high enough frequencies to allow the use of small dish antennas.

Figure 6–15
A point-to-point microwave tower. *Courtesy of Andrew Corp.*

As much as the RF system designers desire that *all* of the RF energy go from one relay to the next, it does not. Instead, as the RF energy leaves one relay, the energy spreads out, like water coming out of a hose (remember free space loss?). Some of the RF energy goes directly to the next relay, some goes off into space, and some bounces off the ground. If that were the end of the story, everything would be fine. Unfortunately, some of the RF energy which bounces off of the ground also makes its way to the next relay, as shown in Figure 6–16.

Since the reflected signal has further to travel, it arrives at the next relay later than the direct signal. This situation is called *multipath*. In some cases multipath signals add together in phase and cause no problems. In other cases, they add together out of phase, or destructively, rendering the received signal almost worthless. Multipath is responsible for the ghost images you see on over-the-air television reception. It is caused by the broadcast signal bouncing off of nearby buildings. But what can be done about multipath, which occurs in almost every wireless system to some degree, especially those indoors?

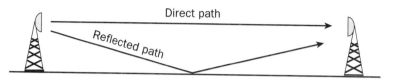

Figure 6–16
Graphical depiction of the multipath effect.

While many sophisticated signal processing techniques have evolved over the years to deal with multipath, there is a very simple technique that has been around awhile called *antenna diversity*. Antenna diversity is a fancy term meaning adding a second antenna. What does adding a second antenna do for us? As you can imagine, multipath is a very location-specific phenomenon. If two signals add destructively at one location, they probably will not add destructively at a second, nearby location. If there are two nearby antennas, both capable of receiving the intended signal, then at any moment at least one of them should be receiving a usable signal, even if the other one is receiving garbage. Antenna diversity explains why you see three antennas (in each 120° sector) on the top of most cellular base-station towers: one is for transmitting and the other two are for receiving with antenna diversity.

Did You Know?

Antenna diversity is a very special case of the more general *spatial diversity*, which just means having redundant things and putting some space between them. In fact there are other types of diversity like temporal diversity (time) and frequency diversity. In each case it means the same thing: redundancy with something (space, time, frequency) in between.

As mentioned, most of today's high-volume point-to-point microwave communications, which is used primarily for long distance voice traffic, use digital modulation. The reasons are twofold. First, the RF electronics have become sophisticated enough to implement digital microwave communication. And second, digital modulation allows for cramming more information (more simultaneous telephone conversations) into a given bandwidth. Microwave point-to-point frequency allocations run as low as a few Megahertz up to and beyond 38 GHz.

7 Mobile Telephony

In this chapter...

- A World of Choices   193

- The Cellular Concept   195

- Underlying Technology   201

- CDMA Explained   209

- Cellular Evolution   218

Is there any artifact more indicative of the wireless revolution than the mobile phone? I think not. Which is why I have devoted an entire chapter to it. (Heck, you'll probably get interrupted by a call on one while you are reading this chapter. Wouldn't that be ironic?)

There are many different mobile telephone systems worldwide. There are different generations, different technologies, and different frequency bands. If you live in the U.S. and think it is the only place with cellular phone service, you are in for a big surprise. Not only is there mobile phone service outside the United States, but a case could be made that the U.S. trails the other two leading regions (Japan and Europe) in technology deployed and services available. The reason why will soon become apparent.

In any event, it is good to understand the underlying technology of this life-style-altering wireless service. This chapter gives you a top-down view of mobile telephony, which includes a discussion of basestations, mobile switching centers, and what makes it mobile. But you will not be spared the details. You will also learn about frequency reuse, air interfaces, and the specific inner workings of an actual cellular phone.

CDMA, which is a popular air interface (and getting more popular all the time), is a mystery to most people. You may know what CDMA stands for, but it is doubtful that you understand how it works. Well all that is about to change. In recognition of its growing importance in the world of mobile telephony, an entire section of this chapter is devoted to explaining how CDMA (and spread spectrum) can cram more phone calls into a given bandwidth than any other air interface.

Finally, this chapter concludes with an abbreviated discussion of the migration paths to 3G (third generation cellular service). As much as I would like to tell you that this chapter will clear up the mess that is 3G, I'm just not that good. The reality is that the paths to 3G nirvana (*circa* 2001) are a free-for-all. Different technologies using different frequencies (some not yet allocated) in different parts of the world are all trying to accomplish the same thing: make a lot of money for the service providers. Because of all these incompatible approaches, the one truly noble goal of 3G—international uniformity—is not likely to happen any time soon. What will be the outcome? If I knew that, I'd have to charge a lot more for the book. Stay tuned.

A WORLD OF CHOICES..

Differentiators

There are many choices for mobile telephone service in the United States. Each of these systems has one or more distinguishing characteristics that differentiate it from the others.

One of the most prominent ways that these mobile telephone services differentiate themselves is by frequency. Each service is allocated a different frequency band in which to operate. The first mobile service offered in the U.S., and the one that is most commonly referred to as "cellular," operates in the 900 MHz band. The newer mobile service in the U.S., dubbed *Personal Communications Service* (or PCS), operates in the 1900 MHz band. In some cases, the only thing that separates "cellular" from PCS is the frequency band of operation. All other aspects of the technology are identical. (Of course the marketing people at the PCS companies don't want you to know that.) Table 7–1 is a summary of the frequency band allocations for some mobile services in the United States.

Table 7–1   Allocated Frequency Bands in the U.S.

System	Mobile to Basestation	Basestation to Mobile
Cellular	824–849 MHz	869–894 MHz
PCS	1850–1910 MHz	1930–1990 MHz
SMR	806–824 MHz	851–869 MHz

Another way these services differentiate themselves is by the technology used to transport the voice signal. The earliest mobile phone systems used analog voice signals, while the newer ones use digital. (In the not-too-distant future, I predict there will be no more analog systems.)

In the case of the first cellular systems, the upgrade to digital technology used much of the existing infrastructure, including the assigned frequency bands. These new digital systems differentiate themselves by the modulation they use to encode the digital information onto the RF carrier. Most use a form of phase modulation or QAM (discussed in Chapter 5). Mobile telephone services also differentiate themselves by something called air interface, which you will learn about shortly.

Some of these services differentiate themselves by offering additional features compared to "standard" mobile service. One of the lesser known mobile services available is something called *Specialized Mobile Radio* or SMR. SMR, which operates in two different frequency bands in the 800 MHz range in the U.S., was originally intended for use as a wireless dispatch service (think taxi cabs). Today, it has evolved into a combination dispatch and mobile phone service. This combination service distinguishes SMR from all the other mobile phone services available. Not only can the service be used to make "ordinary" mobile calls in the interconnected mode, it can also be used to conduct wireless teleconferencing in dispatch mode. In this mode, several people using the service can hold a conversation simultaneously. As such, SMR is popular with teams of mobile salespeople who need to conduct spontaneous sales meetings.

Worldwide Systems

Just so you do not get the wrong idea, the United States is far from being the only place with mobile telephony. Table 7–2 shows some of the world's major mobile telephone systems. The first thing to notice is that there are a lot of different analog and digital technologies that have evolved over the years and none of them talk to each other.

Table 7–2 Worldwide Mobile Telephone Systems

Acronym	System	Where First Deployed	Technology
AMPS	Advanced Mobile Telephone Service	United States	Analog
CDMA	Code Division Multiple Access	United States	Digital
D-AMPS	Digital Advanced Mobile Telephone Service	United States	Digital
DCS1800	Digital Communication Service	Germany & England	Digital
GSM	Group Special Mobile	80 European countries	Digital

Table 7–2   Worldwide Mobile Telephone Systems (Continued)

Acronym	System	Where First Deployed	Technology
JTACS	Japan Total Access Communications System	Japan	Analog
NADC	North American Digital Cellular	United States	Digital
NMT	Nordic Mobile Telephone	Scandinavian countries	Analog
PCS1900	Personal Communications Services	United States	Digital
PDC	Personal Digital Cellular	Japan	Digital
SMR	Specialized Mobile Radio	United States	Both
TACS	Total Access Communications System	England	Analog

THE CELLULAR CONCEPT ....

Topology

Cellular technology requires large geographical regions to be identified and as-signed to the various service providers. In the United States, these large geograph-ical regions are identified as Metropolitan Statistical Areas or MSAs (think city) and Rural Statistical Areas or RSAs (think country) in the cellular frequency bands. In the PCS frequency bands, they are identified as Metropolitan Trading Areas or MTAs (large regions) and Basic Trading Areas or BTAs (small regions). While MTAs overlap BTAs, MSAs and RSAs have exclusive territories.

There are two service providers authorized to provide mobile telephony in each of the MSAs, RSAs, and MTAs, and four providers authorized in each of the BTAs. All of these service providers distinguish themselves by being allotted different fre-quency sub-bands within the overall frequency allotment. Within their assigned re-gion, each service provider breaks up the region into smaller sub-regions called *cells*.

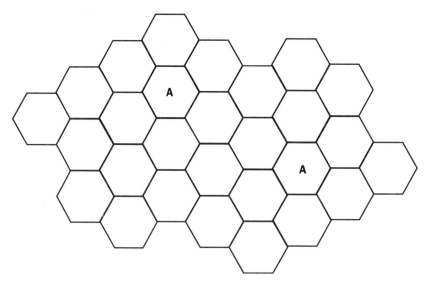

Figure 7–1
Cell pattern covering a geographic area.

Each of these cells has an antenna (or antennas) at the center of the cell that projects an antenna pattern, or footprint, covering the entire cell. These antenna patterns provide transmitting and receiving coverage for users within it. Because of the nature of RF, these antenna footprints are circular in shape. However, when RF engineers display a cell pattern on a map, they ordinarily use hexagons to describe the antenna footprints. It is not that hexagons more accurately reflect the antenna patterns, it is that hexagons fit together very nicely into an orderly pattern (see Figure 7–1).

In the world of mobile telephony, there is one major tradeoff constantly taking place. Ideally, the system has a large number of very small hexagons. The greater the number of hexagons, the more simultaneous calls the system can handle (think revenue). However, the greater the number of hexagons, the more infrastructure that is required to implement the system (think expenses). As a result, cell coverage is a dynamic activity that is constantly changing in response to increases in capacity requirements.

Did You Know?

Cells come in three basic sizes: macrocells, microcells, and picocells. There are no exact definitions for each of these except to say that macros are bigger than micros, which are bigger than picos. Macrocells are representative of the first-generation cellular systems. Microcells and picocells are new developments that have resulted from the subdivision of macrocells to add capacity.

Infrastructure

At the center of every cell is a *cell site* or *basestation*. The cell site contains all of the electronics that enable wireless communication, including all of the RF hardware. At a minimum, cell sites consist of one or more antennas, cables, a transmitter and receiver, a power source, and other control electronics. If the capacity requirements of the cell are small, the cell may employ a single omnidirectional antenna to provide coverage. In situations where more capacity is required, the cell is usually broken down into three sectors (120° each) and one or more antennas are used to provide coverage for each sector. This is the familiar triangular-top tower often seen by the side of the road and shown previously in Figure 3–5.

At their very simplest, all cell sites provide three functions. Cell sites talk to each other (think mobile-to-mobile calls), they connect to the public switched telephone network or PSTN (think mobile-to-landline calls), and they count how many minutes you talk (think money). All three of these functions take place at something called a *mobile switching center* or MSC, also called a *mobile telephone switching office* or MTSO.

The MSC is the quarterback for a cellular system. It acts as a hub through which all cellular calls are routed. Figure 7–2 shows the cellular system infrastructure and the role of the MSC.

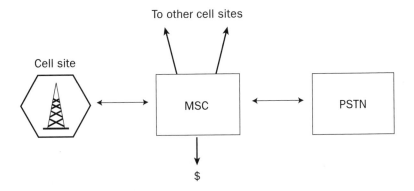

Figure 7–2
Cellular system infrastructure.

As can be seen in Figure 7–2, the MSC is directly connected to each cell site and to the PSTN. When a call is made, it gets routed from the current cell to the MSC and then onto the PSTN (if the other person is on a landline phone) or to another cell (if the other person is on a mobile phone)—and all the while the cash register at the MSC is ringing away.

The MSC is connected to the PSTN by a very high-capacity telephone connection. The MSC is connected to each cell site by one of three methods. It uses either a high-capacity copper telephone line (called a T1 line), a fiber-optic cable, or a point-to-point microwave relay (as discussed in the previous chapter). The choice of which method is used depends on several things, including the particular cell site's traffic level, how far away the cell is from the MSC, and the terrain between them.

Mobility

The feature that separates mobile telephony from most other wireless applications is the notion that the mobile unit must be able to change what it communicates with dynamically. In fixed wireless communications, there are two transceivers used to establish a single communication and they remain unchanged during the entire event. In mobile telephony, the mobile transceiver must be constantly changing between transceivers (located at different cell sites) it communicates with as it moves.

Cell sites continuously transmit a control signal to all the mobile units within their cell. When a mobile phone is first turned on, it shortly receives this control signal and responds by transmitting one of its own. Several cell sites within the area receive this response from the mobile, not just the cell it is in. The key to mobile telephony is power level discrimination. All of the cell sites receive the mobile unit's response, but they all receive different power levels. The cell that receives the highest power response is the cell that the mobile is in. Step one is complete: the MSC knows where the mobile unit is.

When the mobile attempts to make a call, it is allocated a small frequency band within the cell to conduct the call. During the call, the signal level (power) is constantly monitored by the MSC by way of the cell site. As the signal level drops, the MSC knows that the mobile is getting ready to leave that cell and enter another cell. Keep in mind that the control signal is still being received by multiple cell sites. It is at this point that the MSC looks to see which adjacent cell site is receiving the most powerful control signal. That cell site is the one that is going to get the call next. How does it make the transition?

At the appropriate time, the MSC conducts an operation called *handoff*. The handoff process is what is known as a make-before-break connection. In essence, the mobile phone is communicating with two different cell sites for a brief period of time during the handoff. (Otherwise parts of conversations go missing.) This type of handoff process has its advantages and disadvantages. On the one hand, it provides true mobility. On the other hand, it ties up two cell sites for one call (think lower profits). Transferring the connection from one cell to another is called a hard handoff, while transferring the connection from one sector to another within the same cell is called a soft handoff.

Adding Capacity

Within a Cell

Because people have fallen in love with mobile phones, macrocells have run out of call capacity. The service providers like this because it means their cellular infrastructure is being utilized to its fullest. Consumers, on the other hand, get frustrated when they try to make a mobile call and they are greeted with a busy signal. When macrocells run out of call carrying capacity, the only thing the service providers can do—if they want to keep their customers—is to subdivide the macrocell into smaller microcells, as shown in Figure 7–3.

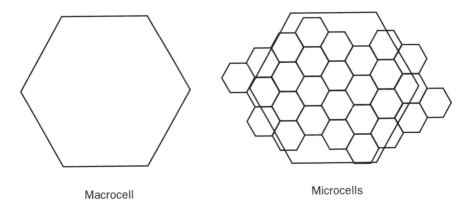

Macrocell

Microcells

Figure 7–3
Dividing up a macrocell into microcells.

When subdividing a macrocell into microcells, each microcell must be capable of communicating directly with the MSC, which means laying copper wire or fiber-optic cable or, more frequently, setting up a point-to-point microwave connection. In any event, replacing a macrocell with several microcells is an expensive proposition and the expense must be justified. As a result, microcells only appear in well-traveled corridors, like along a busy freeway.

Occasionally, it even makes sense to further subdivide a microcell into smaller picocells, where mobile traffic is highly concentrated, like a common area in a large city (think Times Square).

Uncovered Areas

When mobile telephone service providers began to roll out their systems, they naturally placed the first macrocells in the highest traffic areas, which meant that even after the service was up and running, there were still areas within the service provider's territory that did not have service. The two places that got call coverage last were the outer fringes of the service provider's territory and places within the territory that suffer from some sort of obstruction. The latter is comprised of tunnels, subways, and the insides of buildings.

The general category of product used to extend a macrocell's coverage is called a *repeater*. Repeaters come in many shapes and sizes but they all perform one basic function: they extend the wireless range of a macrocell. In that vein, they communicate directly with the macrocell either via copper, fiber optics, or a wireless link. Figure 7–4 shows the layout of a system using a macrocell and a repeater to reach automobiles within a tunnel.

Functionally, there is a very significant difference between using a repeater to extend capacity and breaking down macrocells into microcells to increase capacity. Microcells add capacity because each microcell communicates directly with the MSC. Repeaters, because they communicate with the macrocell itself, actually take away capacity from the macrocell. Every person using the repeater's capacity inside the tunnel in Figure 7–4 means that one less person outside the tunnel can use the macrocell's capacity.

One of the fastest growing uses for repeaters is for in-building applications. In this situation, an antenna is placed on the roof of the building to transmit and receive mobile calls. The signal is then routed from the rooftop antenna, down through the building, to a small repeater on every floor. The signals from the repeater are transmitted and received through an antenna no bigger than a smoke

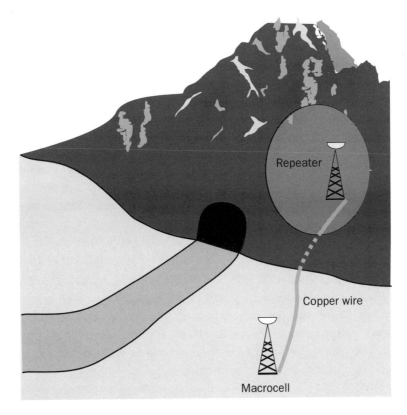

Figure 7–4
Graphical depiction of a repeater inside a tunnel.

alarm. With in-building repeaters, you can begin a cellular phone call in your car, continue it while you enter the building—even in the elevator—and finish it after you arrive at your desk. (There goes your last excuse to hang up on your mother-in-law.)

UNDERLYING TECHNOLOGY................................

Frequency Reuse

The goal of every mobile telephone service provider is to conduct as many simultaneous calls as possible (think greed). In most wireless technologies, only one party is permitted to transmit a signal at a given frequency in a defined geographical location, which works fine for applications like broadcasting. (Having two different stations simultaneously transmitting Channel 6 would really cause a headache.) But cellular technology is different.

In the United States, each cellular provider is allocated 25 MHz of spectrum, 12.5 MHz for transmitting (called the *downstream*) and 12.5 MHz for receiving (called the *upstream*). Cellular telephony is a *full duplex* system—both parties can talk at the same time (think husband and wife) because transmitting and receiving are allocated their own frequencies.

In first-generation cellular systems, each phone conversation is allocated 30 kHz of spectrum. Therefore, each 12.5 MHz of bandwidth can handle 416 simultaneous phone calls as shown in Figure 7–5. If the cellular service providers were to follow the broadcast model, only 416 total calls could be conducted simultaneously in a given geographical area (an MSA or RSA). Letting only 416 people talk at once in, say, Southern California, would not even satisfy the demands of Beverly Hills.

The good news is that there is no need for cellular service to follow the broadcast model. Since a person on a mobile call only needs their allocated frequency *within* the cell they are currently in, there is no reason somebody else on the other end of town cannot be using that same exact frequency in an entirely different cell. The concept of multiple users operating at the same frequency, at the same time, and in the same geographic area, is called *frequency reuse*, and it is what separates mobile telephony from non-cellular wireless communications.

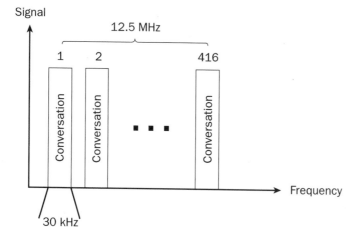

Figure 7–5
Frequency division multiple access.

For frequency reuse to work properly, it is imperative that each mobile phone only put out enough power to reach the cell site of the cell it is in. If it puts out too much power, it will not only reach the intended cell site, it will reach unintended cell sites, which others may be using at the same frequency for a totally different conversation. This strict limitation on transmitted power, called *power management*, however, is an advantage in that low power transmission means that the cellular phone's battery will last longer and therefore people can talk longer (always a good thing) between charges.

Referring back to Figure 7–1, users located in the cells marked with the letter A can both be using the same exact frequency to conduct their own separate conversations. Here is a challenging question: how come adjacent cells cannot conduct different conversations at the same frequency (and the same time)? Imagine that you are a cellular caller on the border between cells and you are communicating with one cell site, but the power level received at the other cell site is almost as great, causing interference to anyone using that frequency in that cell. Because of this potential interference, identical frequencies in adjacent cells cannot be used simultaneously.

Once again there is a tradeoff to be made. To avoid the possibility of interference, cells using the same frequency at the same time must be as far away as possible. Conversely, if the cellular provider wants to make as much money as possible (and they do), the cells must be as close together as possible, so more people can talk simultaneously. In practice, the number of cells of separation, which depends on many things, ranges anywhere from 4 to 21.

Air Interface

FDMA

As mentioned above, each 12.5 MHz of bandwidth is broken down by frequency into 416 different channels, with one conversation per channel. This dividing up of the frequency band is known as *frequency division multiple access* or FDMA. FDMA is a type of *air interface*. Think of air interface as a way of manipulating signals to maximize the capacity of the allocated bandwidth. In the case of FDMA, the manipulation breaks up the allotted frequency band into smaller frequency sub-bands. Is FDMA the only air interface? Just wait.

Having 416 different possible conversations at one time (in a given cell) is fine, but what if there were a way to get more than 416 possible simultaneous conversations at one time out of the same 12.5 MHz frequency allocation? With the new digital technologies available, there are.

TDMA

The first of these new digital technologies, or air interfaces, is known as *time division multiple access* or TDMA. TDMA takes the same 30 kHz bandwidth discussed above and breaks it down into time slots, as shown in Figure 7–6. Notice that the horizontal axis is labeled with "Time." Several conversations can take place simultaneously in the same frequency band because each conversation is periodically allocated a short time slot in which to transmit its message. As you can imagine this requires some sophisticated signal processing, but it does result in higher cell site capacity. Some systems break up the channel into as many as eight different time slots, which theoretically increases the call-carrying capacity of the system eightfold.

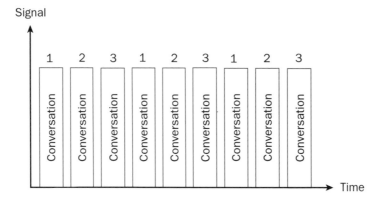

Figure 7–6
Time division multiple access.

CDMA

Another way to increase call capacity is with an air interface known as *code division multiple access* or CDMA. CDMA uses a technology (explained in detail shortly) called *spread spectrum*. In essence, spread spectrum stamps each RF signal with a unique destination address. As a result, many signals can coexist in the

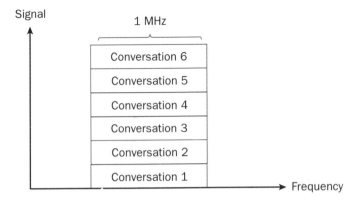

Figure 7–7
Code division multiple access.

same frequency band at the same time since each receiver can only decipher the intended signal (by its address). And because of the miracle of digital technology, more conversations can be crammed into a given bandwidth with CDMA than any other currently employed air interface. Figure 7–7 is a graphical depiction of CDMA.

Referring to Figure 7–7, when the RF signal in a CDMA system gets the "address" imprinted on it, the spectrum it occupies gets bigger. For instance, a signal that occupies 30 kHz before the address is applied might occupy 1 MHz after the address is applied. This "spreading" of the occupied frequency is why it is called spread spectrum. At first thought, it might seem that having a signal occupy more frequency than it does in its original form is a mistake. However, even though it does occupy a greater frequency band than in its original form, the system can now pile many signals on top of each other because they can all be distinguished by their "addresses." In this manner, more *total* signals can fit into a given frequency band, and that is, after all, the goal of every service provider.

CDPD

Another air interface, and one that has been around for awhile, is called *cellular digital packet data* or CDPD. Unlike the other air interfaces that try and increase the amount of voice traffic, CDPD is only concerned with data. In fact, CDPD is a packetized data service, which works well for short, bursty data like e-mail. It is meant to enable computers (and not people) to talk to each other.

In a typical configuration, a laptop computer is outfited with a special CDPD modem (usually installed in the PCMCIA expansion slot). The CDPD air interface uses the same infrastructure (see Figure 7–2) and frequency bands as regular cellular phones, with the PSTN interface essentially replaced by an Internet router. The unique feature of CDPD is that it only occupies unused channels to send the data.

CDPD was originally meant as an overlay to first-generation analog systems in the United States. (When I hear the word "overlay," I think same hardware, new software.) As mentioned above, these first-generation systems have 416 30-kHz channels within a given cell. Rarely are all 416 channels in use at any instant in time (except Friday afternoon rush hour). CDPD uses a special scanning receiver to constantly monitor which, if any, of the 416 channels are available for sending data. In general, voice traffic has priority, so whenever there is a conflict over a channel, the talker wins. This probably stems from the fact that conversations are more time-critical than bursty data. (Who cares if you get an e-mail to your laptop five seconds later?)

With CDPD, because it can only use unallocated channels, the data being sent is constantly hopping from channel to channel. One of the consequences of this is the potential for interference with voice calls. One way around this is to avoid the channel hopping altogether and assign specific channels (among the 416) just for CDPD. The downside with this approach is that it takes away from the voice capacity of the cell. For a service provider to do this, it must make economic sense in terms of increased revenue from the service.

Another interesting thing about CDPD is that it is an always-on connection. There is no need to "dial up" from your laptop. Unfortunately for users of CDPD, the maximum data transfer rate is only 19.2 Kbps. At the time it came out that was pretty fast, but in light of all the recent increases in data throughput, it is hard to know what the future holds for this air interface. The good news is that CDPD can coexist with the newer air interfaces like TDMA and CDMA. And there are companies working with advanced modulation techniques that claim to increase the CDPD data rates up to 400 Kbps, which is screaming fast. Stay tuned.

Cellular Phone Block Diagram

At this point you are probably wondering how a cellular phone works and so I have included a block diagram of one in Figure 7–8. It is a block diagram of a generic digital cellular phone. Because of all the possible variations, it is not meant

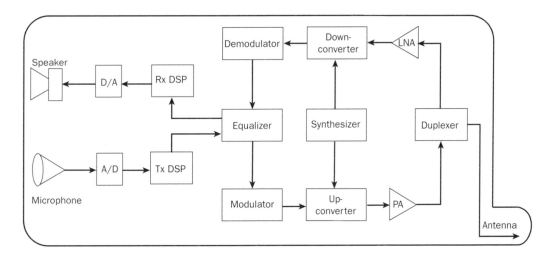

Figure 7–8
Block diagram of a digital cellular phone.

to be an exact functional diagram of any particular digital phone, but rather it shows the main functions contained within most digital phones. Keep in mind that some of these "generic" blocks will differ in function and location within the system depending on things like the air interface used.

Referring to the lower left portion of Figure 7–8, you will see a microphone. This is where the whole process starts. The microphone just converts sound (air movement) into an analog voltage. Being a digital phone, it cannot remain an analog voltage very long and so one of the first things the analog signal does is get converted to a digital signal by an analog to digital (A/D) converter. A/D converters change the constantly varying analog voltage into a corresponding string of 1s and 0s. Without going into too much detail, let's just say that the higher the (analog) voltage, the more 1s there are and the lower the analog voltage, the more 0s there are.

After the A/D converter, comes the transmitter (Tx) digital signal processor (DSP). The DSP is the real brains of the mobile phone and performs many operations to the digital bit stream. One of the operations it performs is speech encoding. Speech encoding is concerned with speech quality and compression. Recall that compression is used to eliminate redundant information.

Another function of the DSP is channel encoding, which modifies the bit stream to compensate for any errors that might occur during its transmission through the air. The DSP may also be involved in encrypting the bit stream so that no one else can overhear the conversation.

Finally the DSP almost always performs some sort of *interleaving*. As you will soon learn, when a signal is sent from the mobile unit to the basestation, more than just the conversation information is sent. The interleaving function of the DSP interleaves the voice information with any other information sent.

After the DSP, the bit stream enters the *equalizer*. The purpose of the equalizer is to compensate for any frequency-dependent impairments that occur during transmission through the air such as phase and amplitude distortion.

After the equalizer, the signal is ready to enter the world of RF. Here the digital bit stream is combined with an RF signal by a modulator. (In this block diagram, you don't see the source of the RF because it is assumed to be contained within the modulator.) In a digital system, the modulation can be frequency modulation or more typically phase modulation. So what comes out of the modulator is just a sine wave with its phase modulated all over the place. However, the frequency of this sine wave is not yet at the frequency of transmission so it gets sent to an upconverter.

The upconverter is really just a mixer that is used to change the frequency of the signal. The "intermediate frequency" RF signal (coming out of the modulator) is combined in the upconverter with another sine wave coming from the synthesizer. The synthesizer generates a frequency such that the output of the upconverter is at the exact frequency of transmission.

Why do cellular phones use a synthesizer? Because they are required to transmit at multiple carrier frequencies. Recall that one way or another, all cellular systems break up their allotted frequency range into multiple sub-bands (using FDMA). Each of these sub-bands requires their own, different RF carrier frequency. The synthesizer must be able to generate all these different frequencies at a moment's notice for the system to work properly.

After the upconverter, the signal is in the exact form it needs to be to be sent wirelessly (it is at the right frequency and the digital information has been modulated onto it). The only problem now is that the signal is too small and so it is sent through a power amplifier which increases the signal to the appropriate power level. Remember that in cellular systems power management is used to ensure the signal is at just the right power level. It is not shown in Figure 7–8, but the power amplifier is in reality a variable gain amplifier whose gain is controlled by the DSP from information it receives from the basestation. This is how power management is realized in a mobile phone.

Now the signal is ready to be sent wirelessly, but one more thing must be done first. The signal needs to be filtered so that no unwanted frequencies are transmitted. The signal is sent to a duplexer, which is just a double filter (one for the transmit band and one for the receive band). Finally the signal is sent out the antenna to find its way in the wireless world.

On the return path, the signal does many of the things it did on the transmit path only in reverse. The signal first enters the antenna, and because it is quite small by this time, the very next thing it does is get amplified by a low noise amplifier. Then the downconverter lowers the carrier frequency and the demodulator strips away the RF leaving only a digital bit stream.

Once in digital form, the signal goes through the equalizer again and then on to the DSP, where many of the previous DSP functions are done in reverse. Finally the bit stream is sent to a digital to analog (D/A) converter and then to a speaker where you get to hear those magic words: "I'm not here right now, so please leave a message."

CDMA EXPLAINED ....

Spread Spectrum

Signal and Noise Spectrums

CDMA technology either does or will play an important role in current and future cellular systems, so I figured it might be nice to understand how it works.

To understand how CDMA works, you will need to understand how spread spectrum works. Before you can understand how spread spectrum works though, you will need to be able to visualize what the spectrum of a signal and the spectrum of noise look like. Figure 7–9a is a graphical depiction of a signal's spectrum. The horizontal axis represents the frequency and the vertical axis is the signal's strength or power. Where the signal comes to its peak is the location of the carrier frequency (on the horizontal axis, represented by the f_c). This is representative of a single conversation in the old analog cellular systems. In such a case, the signal is about 30 kHz wide and the location of the carrier is in the 900 MHz range.

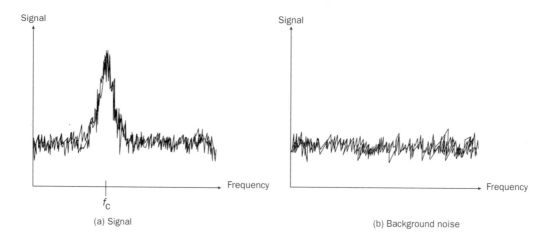

Figure 7–9
Signal spectrum and noise spectrum.

Did You Know?

Spread spectrum technology has really been around since World War II, where it was used to avoid signal detection and jamming by the enemy. The reason it is just now beginning to appear in the commercial arena is more a result of the improvements in and cost reduction of integrated circuits.

Figure 7–9b is the spectrum of noise. In this case there is no signal present and all you see is a low-level, fairly flat but randomly varying noise signal. This low-level, random signal exists everywhere and is the result of all the various RF and non-RF signals floating around in the air. The way an RF engineer views a signal or noise spectrum is with a piece of equipment called a *spectrum analyzer.*

Think back to the analogy of wireless communications being like mailing a letter. In this analogy, the letter is the information signal and the envelope is the RF carrier signal. Modulation is used to combine the letter (information) and the envelope (the carrier). In the previous discussions of wireless communications, I assumed that only one party could transmit and receive at a given frequency within a given geographical location. In that version of the analogy, there was no need to address the envelope because there was only one party who could receive it. (Maybe there was only one other house in the neighborhood.) This is not the case with spread spectrum. With spread spectrum, many parties can transmit and receive at a given frequency within a given geographical location. (There are a lot of houses in the neighborhood and they can all mail letters to each other.)

Direct Sequence

Spread spectrum is analogous to imprinting an address onto the wireless signal. How does spread spectrum pull off this little magic trick? It modulates the signal *again*. The type of spread spectrum used in CDMA is called *direct sequence spread spectrum* or DSSS. In DSSS, the spread spectrum modulation takes place before the "RF modulation" (that is the one that puts the information signal onto the RF carrier). By the way, did I neglect to mention that spread spectrum only works with a digital information signal?

Did You Know?

> There are other types of spread spectrum in addition to DSSS. There is frequency hopping spread spectrum or FHSS (which you will learn more about shortly), and time hopping spread spectrum or THSS. So far nobody's invented bunny hopping spread spectrum (BHSS?), but give them time.

DSSS imprints the address by logically multiplying the digital information signal by another, higher frequency digital signal. This other digital signal is known as a *pseudo random noise* or PN signal. The reason it is called random is that the 1s and 0s appear to have no discernible pattern. More importantly, if the PN signal were modulated onto an RF carrier, its signal spectrum would look just like that of noise (Figure 7–9b). The reason the PN signal is called pseudo is because as random as the bit stream appears, in reality it repeats itself over and over. Of course quite a few random-appearing 1s and 0s go by before the pattern repeats itself. The 1s and 0s in the PN signal are called *chips* and the frequency of the PN signal is called the *chipping rate*. This PN code is generated thanks to the magic of digital signal processing.

The other aspect mentioned above is that the PN signal is at a much higher frequency than the information signal. For instance, in the case of voice over CDMA, the digital bit stream for voice is on the order of 64 Kbps and the chipping rate of the PN signal is on the order of 1.25 million chips (bits) per second.

Spreading

Figure 7–10 depicts graphically the result of logically multiplying a digital voice signal by a PN signal. The top of Figure 7–10 is just the digital bit sequence 101101, which is part of a digital signal that represents a telephone conversation.

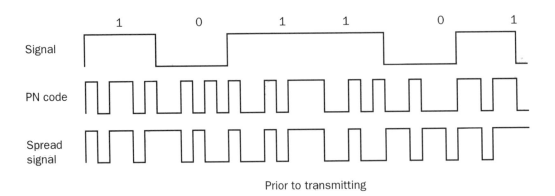

Figure 7–10
Spreading of an information signal by a PN signal.

The middle of Figure 7–10 is the PN signal. Notice that the 1s and 0s appear to be random and that the frequency is much higher (in this case about six times) than the voice signal. The bottom of Figure 7–10 is the result of "multiplying" the top two signals. In fact this multiplying is really just an exclusive OR function, which is very easy to understand because there are only two rules. In places where both of the signals above it are the same (either both high or both low), the bottom signal is high. In places where both of the signals above it are different (one high, one low), the bottom signal is low.

There are three very important things about this new "spread" signal. First, it is at a much higher frequency than the original voice signal. Second, it is random-like, which means that in a plot of its spectrum, it would look just like noise. And third, all of the information contained in the original voice signal (101101) is still contained within it.

Why is this new signal considered a spread signal? Because the original signal occupied perhaps only 30 kHz of bandwidth. This new signal occupies on the order of 1.25 MHz of bandwidth (it is at a much higher frequency). The signal has been spread over a larger bandwidth. The real trick, however, is not this spreading of the original signal over a wider bandwidth. The real trick is that as the signal is spread over a wider bandwidth, its power level drops.

The top of Figure 7–11 is a graphical simplification of this phenomenon. Figure 7–11a shows a signal 30 kHz wide, located somewhere in the 900 MHz range with some amount of energy represented by the gray area under the rectangle. (This is representative of the signal shown in Figure 7–9a.) Since spreading the signal does not add any energy to the signal (only an amplifier can do that), the

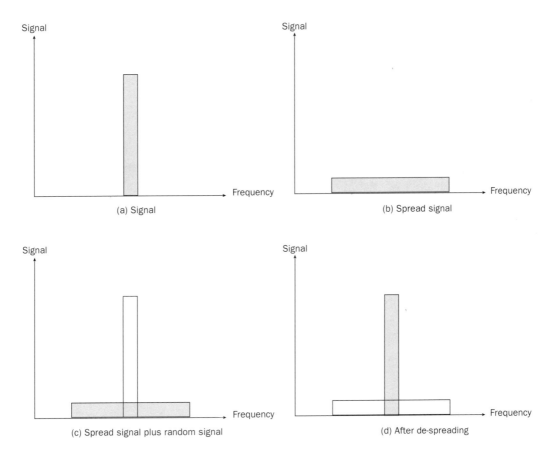

Figure 7–11
Spreading and de-spreading of signals.

gray area under the spread signal must be the same, and therefore, as the signal gets wider, the power drops lower as shown in Figure 7–11b.

In reality, this new lower spread signal appears to be noise, just like that in Figure 7–9b. In fact this new signal is noise, with one notable exception. It still contains the original voice information. And because it is noise, up to a certain limit, a whole bunch of these noise signals can be piled on top of one another. The result is just more noise, and noise is noise, assuming you can still retrieve the original information signal. How does one retrieve the original voice information? I'm glad you asked.

De-spreading

The original signal is retrieved from the noise the same exact way it was spread: by logically multiplying it by the same exact PN signal. This restoring of the information signal is referred to as *de-spreading*.

The top of Figure 7–12 is the same exact spread signal as the one at the bottom of Figure 7–10 (take my word for it). The only difference is that the signal in Figure 7–10 is coming out of the sending transmitter and the one in Figure 7–12 is going into the receiving receiver. Assuming for the moment that the same exact PN signal that was used to spread the signal in the transmitter also exists in the receiver, it can be used to de-spread the signal.

The middle of Figure 7–12 is the same exact PN signal as the one in Figure 7–10. By applying the same exclusive OR function to the top two signals in Figure 7–12 a miracle happens: the original voice signal (101101) reappears. Isn't this stuff amazing?

This may be all well and good, but since all of the signals in a CDMA system occupy the same bandwidth at the same time, what happens to the other, unwanted signals that just happen to make their way into our handset?

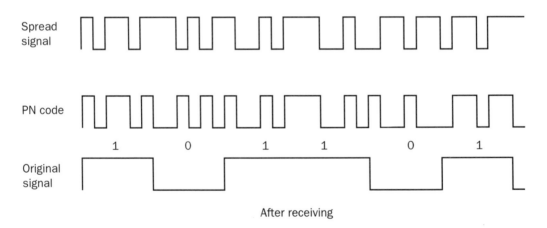

Figure 7–12
De-spreading of an information signal.

Unwanted Signals

Let us see what happens when someone else's signal makes it into our handset. There are two possibilities here. We can receive someone else's CDMA (spread) signal or we can receive someone else's narrowband (unspread) signal from a non-CDMA system. In either case, we will attempt to de-spread it with our PN signal.

The top of Figure 7–13 shows a CDMA voice signal spread with someone else's PN signal. When we attempt to de-spread this signal with our PN signal (middle of Figure 7–13), what results is the signal at the bottom of Figure 7–13. While it may not be totally evident from the figure, the bottom signal is still a high-frequency, random signal, which means it is not de-spread. This signal appears as noise to our receiver and so it gets ignored.

When a narrow band signal enters our mobile unit, the attempt to de-spread it just ends up spreading it because the two processes are identical. Once again this spread signal appears as noise and is ignored by our receiver. This phenomenon is depicted in Figure 7–11c and Figure 7–11d. Figure 7–11c shows two signals entering our receiver: the wanted spread signal (in gray) and the unwanted narrowband signal (clear). After the de-spreading (Figure 7–11d), the wanted signal becomes narrow band and the unwanted signal become spread. The bottom line is that any unwanted signal that enters our receiver, spread or not, will ultimately be ignored by our receiver.

For a CDMA system to work properly, everybody has to use a different PN signal. But in reality, everybody uses the same PN signal (which just repeats itself over and over). How is that possible? Everyone uses the same PN signal but they all start at a different bit (chip). Refer back to the middle of Figure 7–13. Suppose that very first bit (a high) is labeled bit number 1. The second bit (a low) is bit

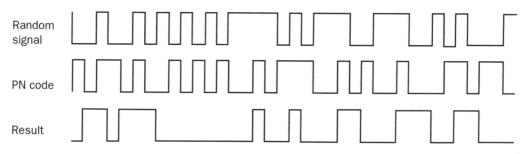

Figure 7–13
Attempting to de-spread someone else's signal.

number 2 and so on. Would you believe me if I told you that two, otherwise identical PN signals that start at different bits are completely different PN signals? I'll prove it.

The top of Figure 7–14 is our original spread signal, which was spread with our very own PN signal. The middle of Figure 7–14 is our PN signal shifted by one bit. It now starts at bit number two rather than bit number one. Attempting to de-spread our signal with this one-bit shifted PN signal results in the signal shown at the bottom of Figure 7–14, which clearly is not our original 101101 bit stream. This signal is still a high-frequency, random noise-like signal, which is ignored by our receiver. In fact, this noise signal is just the result of our spread signal entering someone else's receiver and being multiplied by their PN signal (one-bit shifted from ours). And their receiver ignores this "noise" signal.

So in a CDMA system, there is just one long, continuously looping PN signal, which is used by all the basestations and all the mobile phones and the only difference is that each conversation starts at a different bit. It follows that all of the basestations need to have their PN signals synchronized to a master clock. What facilitates the synchronization of all basestations to a master clock? Go back and read the section on GPS.

Not only do all the basestations need to be synchronized, but the sender and receiver in a particular call need to be synchronized to each other. How is this accomplished? Through the use of a synchronization channel.

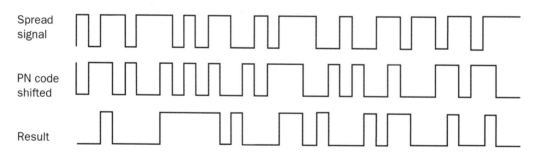

Figure 7–14
De-spreading a signal by a one-bit shifted PN signal.

Channels

When a conversation is sent wirelessly in a CDMA system, more than just the voice data is sent wirelessly. In fact, the wireless information sent is broken up into different channels, or packets of information. From the basestation to the mobile unit there are four of these unique packets of information. From the mobile to the basestation, there are two.

The top of Figure 7–15 shows how the information sent from the basestation to the mobile unit in a CDMA system is broken down into channels. The pilot channel, which is continuously transmitted by the basestation, is used for several things including power management and to aid in handoff. As mentioned previously, all cellular telephony requires power management. It is even more important in CDMA because for the system to work properly, the received power level from every cellular phone must be the same. (If not, signals received from close-in phones will swamp out those received from far away ones by raising the combined noise level too high.) The pilot signal from each basestation has a different time offset (from the master clock), which uniquely identifies each basestation and therefore helps the mobile switching center know where each mobile unit is located.

The sync (or synchronization) channel helps synchronize the basestation's PN signal to that of the mobile unit, among other things. The paging channel is used to page the mobile unit. Recall that when a cellular phone first turns on, it listens for a signal from the basestation. The paging channel is what it listens for and it contains overhead and subscriber-specific information. Finally, the downstream information contains one or more traffic channels, which contain the voice signal.

The bottom of Figure 7–15 shows how information is sent from the mobile unit to the basestation. The access channel is used by the mobile to initiate a call, respond to a paging channel, and to update location information. Just like the downstream, there are also traffic channels to carry the voice and data information.

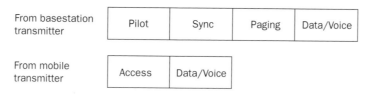

Figure 7–15
Downstream and upstream CDMA channels.

There you have it. A general understanding of direct sequence spread spectrum and a specific understanding of how CDMA systems uses it to cram a lot of users into a fixed amount of bandwidth.

CELLULAR EVOLUTION......................................

Different Generations

Mobile telephony has evolved over the years reflecting the improvements in technology, specifically microelectronics and digital signal processing. The first generation of mobile telephony, dubbed 1G, modulated an analog signal onto an RF carrier and utilized something called *circuit switched* technology. Circuit switched technology establishes a persistent connection between the two communicators. (It is the same technology that is used in plain old telephone service [POTS].) Circuit switched technology makes for a good quality of service but an inefficient use of the equipment. For example, when two people establish a phone connection but nobody says anything for a prolonged period of time (think husband and wife fighting), the telephone line is still tied up. No one else can use it.

Analog modulation was used in 1G because it was easy to implement, given the state of the art at the time. Also, the supply of bandwidth exceeded the demand for bandwidth (back in the days of $500 cellular phones) and so efficient use of spectrum was not a priority. As mentioned previously, the only available air interface for analog is FDMA, in which the entire allotted bandwidth is divided into smaller frequency bands. When all 416 slots are in use, the next one in gets a busy signal. The 1G mobile phone service in the U.S. is called *Advanced Mobile Phone Service* or AMPS.

The best feature of first-generation cellular service was that every service provider throughout the United States used the same modulation and air interface. This uniformity led to the concept of *roaming*: using a cellular phone outside its home area. In effect, one cellular phone could be used everywhere. Unfortunately, analog technology quickly ran out of capacity. The identifying characteristics of all the mobile phone generations are summarized in Table 7–3.

Table 7–3 *Characteristics of the Various Cellular Generations*

	1G	2G	2.5G	3G
Signal Type	Analog	Digital	Digital	Digital
Switching	Circuit	Circuit	Packet	Packet
Offerings	Voice	Messaging	Internet	Multimedia
Data Rate	—	14 Kbps	144 Kbps	384 Kbs–2 Mbps

The growing demand for cellular telephony, combined with advances in digital technology, led to the second generation of cellular telephony (2G). In 2G, a digital signal is modulated onto an RF carrier, but circuit switched technology is still employed. Even though the channels are still tied up, digital modulation allows for the use of novel new air interfaces (like TDMA and CDMA) and power management. In addition to longer talk time and accommodating more users, 2G offers other first-time mobile features such as conference calling and voice mail.

In 2G systems, FDMA is still used to divide the total bandwidth into smaller frequency chunks, but it is also combined with other air interfaces: either TDMA or CDMA. Second-generation data rates approach 14 Kbps (kilobits per second). In upgrading to the new 2G systems, service providers tried to use as much of their existing hardware and software as possible. Unfortunately, little could be used. Much of the RF and signal processing equipment needed to be upgraded. In the case of the RF hardware, it was mostly the result of the new digital signals requiring much higher linearity performance. And since all of the upgrades could not be done instantaneously, the result was a geographical area with part digital and part analog coverage. This led to the creation of the *dual mode* phone. These (expensive) dual mode phones communicate with both analog and digital signals (and switch between the two). They typically attempt to communicate digitally first, and, if that does not work, they switch to analog. Of course, to take advantage of the new digital technology, somebody (you) has to go out and buy a new mobile phone.

By far the biggest problem with upgrading to digital technology stems from the fact that there is more than one scheme from which to choose. Many of the service providers chose different technologies for different reasons. You may have already guessed the problem. The roaming feature that was so universal in analog cellular systems is not quite so universal in the 2G systems.

Another aspect of 2G (both in the U.S. and Europe) is the allocation of another frequency band. While 1G only offered service in the 900 MHz band (U.S), 2G offers service in both the 900 MHz and 1900 MHz bands (U.S.). This 2G 1900 MHz service is referred to as PCS (DCS in Europe), or more specifically wideband PCS. Wideband PCS is nothing more than 2G cellular technology at a slightly higher frequency. (Don't you believe any of that marketing stuff.)

Did You Know?

After realizing the error of their ways in the cellular lottery, the FCC began auctioning off bandwidth for wireless services. The auction for PCS alone netted over ten billion (that is with a "b") dollars. The fact that many of the "winners" did not actually have the money to pay up is another story altogether. You live and learn.

Just when everyone was getting comfortable with 2G features and performance, along comes this thing called the wireless Internet. This led to what has become known as 2.5G. While 2.5G does utilize some more advanced modulation techniques (compared to 2G), the real change is in the use of *packet switching* technology, which is the same one used to access the Internet (using IP or Internet Protocol). Unlike circuit switching with its persistent connection, packet switching assigns a channel (i.e., frequency band) only as long as the user needs it and no longer. When the user is done transmitting or receiving information, they relinquish the channel so that someone else might use it. When the user needs a channel again, they get another one, but not necessarily the one they just gave up.

Packet switching is a much more efficient use of bandwidth than circuit switching. And besides, all data transferred to and from the Internet is done in (non-continuous) packets, so it is a perfect fit. What about telephone conversations? As things turn out, transferring voice information in packets is okay too (remember TDMA?).

The inherent efficiency of packet switching leads to more users (per bandwidth) and higher data rates, up to 144 Kbps for 2.5G. And while other features are available with 2.5G, the best new feature is the ability to surf the Internet from a mobile unit. In most cases, changes to the infrastructure for 2.5G are just bolted on to existing 2G networks. As a result, these 2.5G systems are not pure packet switched networks. In reality, data is being sent as packets over circuit switched networks. Pure packet switched wireless networks will not be available until the so-called third-generation networks or 3G.

The vision for 3G began in 1992. The vision was of a single global standard (at a single global frequency), which included using digital, packet-based networks to deliver bandwidth on demand and variable data rates up to 2 Mbps. With these lofty goals, it is envisioned that multimedia content could be delivered to the mobile unit (although who is going to watch a movie on a cellular phone is beyond me). This vision for 3G requires new packet switched networks and new frequency allocations.

Alas, the vision is not meant to be, at least not in its entirety. First, the United States refuses to allocate the agreed upon spectrum (2000 MHz) for 3G services. Second, because incumbent service providers want to take advantage of their existing infrastructure and incumbent equipment providers want to take advantage of their existing product lines, there are at least three different paths to 3G utopia being pursued. All this will end up doing is making the semiconductor companies, which manufacture dual band and tri-mode devices, rich.

Paths of Migration to 3G

For many reasons, the world of cellular telephony evolved along three different paths in three different places: Europe, the United States, and Japan. All three started with their own analog standard, which at the time was fine since no one expected their cellular phone to work in some other country. But from those first-generation analog systems, as the world turned digital, things became really complicated.

Somebody got the idea that it would be really nice if there were a single digital technology deployed worldwide that allowed the use of a single mobile phone anywhere in the world (which has service). In steps the International Telecommunications Union or ITU. The ITU is the FCC of the world, with responsibility for allocating "international" frequencies. The ITU, along with all the member nations, started a program called IMT-2000 (International Mobile Telephone). The goal of the program is to develop a single, digital standard that will work all over the world. The IMT-2000 frequency allocation is situated between 1885 and 2200 MHz. Unfortunately, the fracturing that resulted from the switch to digital technology in 2G remains an obstacle in the way to 3G.

The 2000 in IMT-2000 originally had three meanings. It stood for the year the program was to start, the frequency band of operation, and the maximum data rate in Kbps. To this point, they've missed the starting date and only time will tell whether the other two are ever realized.

Europe

Europe started with several first-generation analog systems like TACS in England and NMT in the Scandinavian countries. These systems did not even operate at the same frequencies, so there was no use trying to get them to talk to each other.

Fortunately, when it came to upgrading to second-generation digital technology, Europe got it right and decided on a single technology for every country. That technology is GSM (Group Special Mobile), which uses a type of TDMA air interface and operates in just two bands: 800 MHz and 1800 MHz.

Not wanting to wait for a true 3G system to take hold (it could take years), Europe has more or less fashioned a path to 3G that consists of several intermediate steps. The first of these intermediate steps (2.5G) is something called *General Packet Radio Services* or GPRS. In oversimplified terms, GRPS just overlays packet switching on the existing GSM system. Recall that packet switching is more efficient than circuit switching and therefore allows more simultaneous users. Additionally, packet switching is more similar to the way data is transferred to and from the Internet, which makes this technology better for doing that.

The next intermediate step is called *Enhanced Data GSM Environment* or EDGE. (It can also stand for *Enhanced Data Rates for Global Evolution*.) Among other things, EDGE incorporates a modulation improvement to GRPS. Where GPRS uses GMSK modulation, EDGE uses 8 PSK modulation that delivers three times the data rate, which is a good thing when you are trying to watch a *Lethal Weapon* rerun on your mobile phone.

The "official" 3G system for Europe is *Universal Mobile Telecommunications System* or UMTS. The good news about UMTS is that it is a true packet switched network (none of this overlay stuff). The bad news is that it is at a different frequency (2000 MHz) than either 1G or 2G, which means big bucks to upgrade the system. Strangely, UMTS is not based on a TDMA air interface (like GSM), but rather on a CDMA air interface called *Wideband CDMA* or WCDMA.

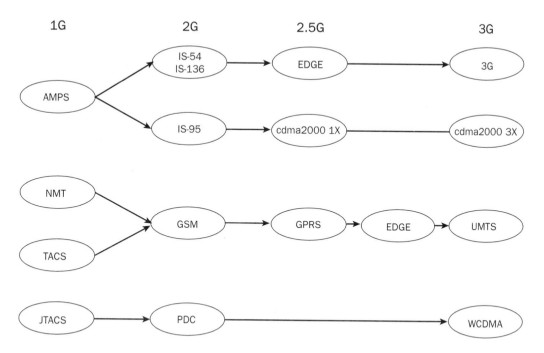

Figure 7–16
Migration paths to 3G.

WCDMA uses the same spread spectrum technology used by the North American CDMA, but has a 5 MHz bandwidth as opposed to a 1.25 MHz bandwidth, ergo the wideband. All of the 3G migration paths are summarized in Figure 7–16.

The United States

Unlike Europe, the U.S. started with a single analog cellular standard (AMPS) in one frequency band (900 MHz). Ironically though, when it came to upgrading to 2G, the United States took a completely different tack and splintered into three different technological approaches. The three systems are IS-95 (also called cdma-One and based on a CDMA air interface), IS-54 (based on a GSM TDMA air interface), and IS-136 (also called D-AMPS and based on a different TDMA air interface). These three approaches are spread across two different frequency bands: 900 MHz and 1900 MHz.

As much as I would like to tell you that 2.5G or 3G will reunite the U.S into one uniform cellular technology, it will not. There will be two distinct migration paths to 3G in the United States. And to make matters worse, they will not be compatible with those in Europe.

The TDMA path will unite in 2.5G under the EDGE technology, which is the same one being used in Europe. So these 2.5G system will interoperate with those in Europe, albeit at slightly different frequencies. Unfortunately, as it migrates to 3G, it will not go to UMTS and it will not be in the 2 GHz band.

The CDMA path will go through a series of CDMA upgrades. The 2.5G version is called cdma2000 1x while the 3G version is called cdma2000 3x. Each of these represents an increase or improvement in signal processing, bandwidth, and/or modulation. If you guessed that this version of CDMA is incompatible with the WCDMA used in Europe, you are right. What a mess!

Japan

For the first two generations, Japan pretty much worked in isolation with their 1G analog system (JTACS) and their 2G digital system (PDC based on a TDMA air interface). Because of all this uniformity, it was possible for Japan to essentially jump over 2.5G and go right to a 3G system. As a result, Japan is the first country to deploy a system with 3G capabilities. The system is based on a WCDMA air interface similar to that in UMTS.

Ultimately, the goal for the ITU is to somehow harmonize one or more of these 3G systems to try and achieve their original vision: a single universal standard. Good luck.

Did You Know?

With all the talk of 3G, unbelievably there are already companies out there discussing 4G systems. These 4G systems, which will include new technologies such as improved modulation and smart antennas, should be able to deliver multimegabit per second data rates for true, full motion video delivered to a mobile environment. Get the *Lethal Weapon* video out.

8 The New World of Wireless

In this chapter...

- Broadband Fixed Wireless   227

- Wireless Networks   240

- The Mobile Internet   252

- The Bleeding Edge   256

If the technology of wireless has been around for such a long time, then what is so new about it? What is new are the myriad of applications that lend themselves to wireless communications as a result of the tremendous advances made in RF and digital electronics. It took 30 years for the cellular phone to go from concept to serious market penetration, and most of that time was spent waiting for the advent of low-cost semiconductor technology to make it financially feasible.

This chapter is a snapshot of the wireless world today (*circa* 2001), a world which is in constant transition. Newer technologies continue to replace older, less efficient ones while new applications for existing technology pop up every day. New markets are evolving for this technology as developing countries seek basic local telephone service and turn to wireless to provide it. The regulatory landscape is in flux as regulators seek to address the many challenges—from efficient use of the available spectrum to the coordination of wireless emergency services.

This chapter is divided into four sections. The first section covers broadband fixed wireless systems. Broadband fixed wireless, as the name implies, describes a family of high data rate wireless systems in which all of the parties communicating are stationary. More specifically, these systems are designed to compete with all the other wired systems that bring communication services to where you live and work. There are several different realizations of broadband fixed wireless, but only the four most prominent ones are covered here.

The second section deals with wireless networks, which is any network of things communicating wirelessly, not just computers. Networks can be built around the office, around the home, and surprisingly, around the human being. There are more wireless networking applications than there are different wireless technologies. In other words, most new wireless networking applications are just modifications or enhancements to a few core, existing wireless technologies. That should not be surprising as wireless manufacturers try and use their products in as many places as possible.

The next section covers the mobile Internet. Undoubtedly this is the application for wireless technology that has gotten the most attention in the last few years. Of all the challenges facing the mobile Internet—like 3G compatibility and sufficiently high data rates—perhaps the greatest challenge is figuring out how the wireless service providers charge for their services.

The real technology challenges of the mobile Internet are not wireless ones. Instead they are political (3G compatible), they are electrical (extending battery life), and they are human factors (small screen, voice recognition, etc.). The mobile Internet is here to stay and just like the personal computer, it will evolve over time, so be prepared to be constantly upgrading your toys.

The last section in this chapter is entitled The Bleeding Edge. Here you will be introduced to a handful of leading edge technologies that have not found their way into the mainstream yet (and one technology that has). They go by the acronyms TM-UWB, MEMS, and BLAST. These may or may not be the technologies that lead to the next great wireless breakthrough.

Finally, the chapter concludes with a brief discussion of things that keep us up at night: security and health. Wireless security is an ever-evolving story in response to what seems like an unending series of threats. Unfortunately, wireless technology will not fully penetrate the business world until we are convinced it is safe to use.

Speaking of safe to use, there has been a lot written lately about the adverse health effects of using a cellular phone. Nobody today can say definitively whether using a cellular phone poses any danger or not. This section merely points out all of the different health threats from being exposed to RF radiation.

BROADBAND FIXED WIRELESS ....

Wireless Local Loop

In the United States, when you pick up your telephone to make a call, you hear a dial tone, which means you are connected to a Class 5 switching center, also called the central office. You are now connected to your local telephone company. The electrical circuit between you, the end office, and back again is affectionately referred to as the *local loop*. And today the local loop no longer means just telephone service. It now includes everything that connects you to the outside world including the Internet, television and movie programming, and a plethora of other digital services soon to appear on the horizon. Whether you know it or not, today there is a battle being waged over control of the local loop.

Basically there are only four ways to implement the local loop: copper wire, coaxial cable, fiber-optic cable, and wireless communications. The copper wire is owned by the local phone company and they try to cram as much information down that poor little piece of wire as is technologically possible using something called *digital subscriber line* or DSL. The coaxial cable is owned by the local cable company (if you are lucky enough to have one). They too are trying to cram as much information as is technologically possible down the cable. Today, running fiber-optic cable to individual homes is considered infeasible. And then there is wireless.

In the battle for local loop supremacy, *wireless local loop* (WLL) is proving to be a very formidable competitor. Wireless local loop technology is simultaneously addressing two very different markets. One market that WLL is addressing is local telephone service in developing nations who do not yet have it, like China and Vietnam. In places such as these, wireless technology is much less expensive and far faster to deploy than laying copper wires in the ground. All of the major wireless infrastructure manufacturers are aggressively pursuing WLL business in developing countries.

The other market being addressed by WLL is in the United States. Why would anyone need WLL in a country where almost everyone has hard-wired local loop service? Two reasons. First, long distance telephone companies want more than anything else to be local telephone companies too. And they can be, immediately, if they want, but they have to use the local telephone companies' equipment and pay them a fee, which sort of defeats the purpose. Wireless local loop technology allows long distance telephone companies to deploy telephone equipment at a fraction of the cost of laying copper wire, and compete directly with the local telephone companies for local phone business. And with the growth of the Internet, an increasing amount of phone time is considered "local." WLL will some day soon offer most people an alternative to local phone service, probably from their long distance provider.

The other reason for WLL in the United States is increased bandwidth. Everyone wants high-speed access to the Internet, and high speed means more bandwidth. There is only so much information that can be stuffed down a copper wire or a coaxial cable, and if more bandwidth is desired than either of them can supply, it must come from somewhere else. And until someone figures out how to lay fiber-optic cable inexpensively, the only other solution is wireless, and more specifically, WLL. High-bandwidth WLL is called *broadband fixed wireless* service.

Did You Know?

Believe it or not, there is at least one company out there today that has trained a stable of robots to lay fiber-optic cable under the ground in an effort to deploy it more cost effectively. Now before you start thinking that one of these precious strands of silica is coming to your home soon, you can forget it. Apparently these robots have only been trained to run fiber to big (and rich) corporations that are hungry for bandwidth.

A broadband fixed wireless system can use one of two layouts. It either uses the "supercell," which attempts to serve everybody in a geographic region from a single, high-power basestation (like the TV broadcasters), or it breaks up the region into smaller cells (just like mobile telephony).

Regardless of the layout, each cell is serviced by a basestation, which communicates with all of the wireless local loop customers within the cell. In the smaller cells, the basestation may be as simple as an omnidirectional antenna and control box hanging from the overhead electrical lines. Each customer is equipped with a transceiver and a small antenna. The transceiver may have several outputs: one for a telephone, one for a PC, and maybe even one for a television. The small antenna, which may be inside or outside the house, is positioned to communicate with the basestation.

What equipment, technologies, and frequencies are used? It depends. If the system is meant to provide basic local telephone service in a developing nation, then the bandwidth requirements will be modest, and almost any equipment at any frequency will do. The major wireless infrastructure manufacturers, who provide the systems for mobile telephony, are naturally trying to use that same equipment for WLL to avoid having to develop anything new. Most of the WLL in developing countries will ultimately be at the same frequencies as the mobile telephony in developed countries and will utilize the same basic equipment, only slimmed down to provide fixed service only.

In the U.S., the battle for broadband fixed wireless is being waged among four major contenders: MMDS, LMDS, unlicensed, and wireless fiber. (All four are discussed below and compared in Table 8–1.) Regardless of which one is selected, they all must deal with two fundamental trade-offs. First, the area covered by the cell is inversely related to capacity. Translation: big cells mean low data rates and little cells mean high data rates. Second, the number of users is inversely proportional to the data rate. Translation: a few users all get high data rates or many users (which must share) get lower data rates.

MMDS (Multichannel Multipoint Distribution Service)

This frequency band (2600 MHz) was originally set aside in the U.S. for over-the-air cable television (think broadcast). To use the service, the consumer only needs a small antenna and a TV set top box (and to pay the monthly fee). The hope was to foster competition to the cable providers, resulting in lower prices for the consumer. Unfortunately, right around the time MMDS was coming into being, direct-to-home (DTH) satellite began to take off and those consumers who were motivated to change typically went that route.

The good news for MMDS is that the United States is only part of the equation. In developing countries (those without direct broadcast satellite), MMDS has found a receptive audience. But in the United States, there sat this unused bandwidth for a period of time. And then all of a sudden, along came this thing called the Internet. In 1998, the FCC made it okay to use the spectrum for two-way wireless services and MMDS was reborn as a viable fixed broadband wireless alternative.

MMDS is a point-to-multipoint topology and as such is ideal for residential service. And even though MMDS requires line of sight (LOS) to work properly (i.e., the transmitting antenna must be able to see the receiving antenna), its relatively low frequency and high transmit power means it has a usable working distance of up to 35 miles. That means the cells can be relatively large and therefore less basestations are required to cover a given area. And the 200 MHz of available spectrum translates to data rates of up to 2 Mbps for customers in the cell. All this adds up to a pretty good solution for fixed broadband wireless connectivity to the home.

LMDS (Local Multipoint Distribution Service)

This frequency band (31 GHz) was not specifically allocated for WLL. The owner of the frequency band (in a given geographic area) can use it for almost any application. However, there is something very special about the A Block frequency allocation. (LMDS is divided into two different frequency bands: A Block and B Block.) The A Block frequency allocation for LMDS is 1150 MHz wide, which makes it the widest allocated frequency band (by the FCC) in the history of the United States. And since frequency is like real estate (they ain't makin' any more of it), the LMDS A Block is one of the most valuable commodities in the wireless world today.

Did You Know?

The LMDS frequency allocations, like every other frequency allocation today, was auctioned off by the FCC to the highest bidders in early 1999. The auctions raised about $45 million, which is not very much when you consider it gives the winners the ability to compete with the local telephone company, the local cable company, and Internet service providers. This is probably the result of price shock from previous wireless auctions in which the bidders, getting caught up in all the excitement, bid exorbitant amounts of money. You gotta pay to play.

To get an appreciation for how substantial 1150 MHz of wireless spectrum is, a telephone conversation requires 4 kHz of bandwidth (uncompressed), which means the LMDS A Block can simultaneously transmit over a quarter of a million phone calls. Now you know why most owners are opting to use it for WLL.

Just so you don't think that LMDS is a perfect solution for WLL, it is not without its hurdles to overcome. First, RF electronics at 31 GHz is still relatively expensive, both on the system side and the consumer side. Second, if you recall something from a previous chapter called absorption, you will remember that it limits the distance an RF wave can travel and that the higher the frequency, the worse it gets. Well, at 31 GHz (LMDS's frequency), it is pretty bad. Signal attenu-

Table 8–1   Comparison of Broadband Fixed Wireless Alternatives

	MMDS	**LMDS**	**Unlicensed**	**Wireless Fiber**
Frequency	2.6 GHz	31 GHz	2.4 GHz 5.8 GHz	10,000 GHz
Primary Topology	Point-to-Multipoint	Point-to-Point	Point-to-Multipoint	Point-to-Point
Coverage	35 miles	3 miles	10 miles	1 mile
Data Rate	2 Mbps	155 Mbps	1 Mbps	622 Mbps
Advantages	Large coverage area.	High data rates.	No license required.	No license required; very high data rates.
Disadvantages	License required.	License required; rain/foliage problems; expensive equipment.	Must share spectrum; limited output power.	Limited range; fog problems.
First Market(s)	Home (rural); small offices.	Medium and large businesses.	Homes (urban).	Building to building (campus).

ation from absorption at 31 GHz requires the receiver to be relatively close to the basestation's transmitter. To make matters worse, at LMDS frequencies, rain and foliage from trees also causes havoc with the signals

The bottom line with LMDS is that the signals do not travel very far so there needs to be a lot of basestations to cover a given geographical area. And a lot of basestations translates to an expensive system.

Like MMDS, LMDS requires line of sight, but unlike MMDS, it is a point-to-point system and, given its constraints on distance combined with its massive bandwidth, it is most suited for service to medium and large businesses, typically located in business parks (in the middle of the desert).

Note: Point-to-multipoint systems can use omnidirectional antennas to simultaneously communicate with multiple receivers. Point-to-point systems are limited to using directional antennas to communicate with a single receiver. However, several point-to-point systems could be co-located at a single place to produce a point-to-multipoint system.

Unlicensed

The FCC has allocated several frequency bands that require no license and can be used for broadband fixed wireless service (among other things). The FCC's intent was to enable small, entrepreneurial companies to quickly and inexpensively offer wireless services in these frequency bands.

These unlicensed frequency bands (shown in Table 8–2), which are referred to collectively as ISM (*industrial, scientific, and medical*) bands, were not originally intended to be used for wireless communications. In fact, just the opposite is true. As the acronym implies, the ISM bands were originally intended to allow various electrical and mechanical industrial equipment to radiate unintentional RF energy (at the specified frequencies), without interfering with other wireless communications. The thinking was, as long as the industrial applications and the wireless applications are operating in their own frequency bands, they cannot interfere with one another. ISM applications include everything from industrial heating equipment to microwave ovens. What ISM did not include—until recently—was wireless communications.

Table 8–2   ISM Frequency Bands

Frequency Band	Frequency Allocation
UHF	902–928 MHz
S-band	2.40–2.4835 GHz
C-band	5.725–5.875 GHz

Surprisingly enough, the ISM bands now provide an opportunity for wireless communications (including broadband fixed wireless). If nothing else, wireless communications operating in an ISM band certainly will not have to worry that their signals interfere with existing applications. (Microwave ovens don't mind listening in on wireless conversations.) The only problem is, how is it possible to communicate wirelessly in a frequency band with so much unintentional RF energy being radiated? You may have already guessed the answer: spread spectrum. Recall from the discussion of CDMA that many signals can coexist in the same frequency band using spread spectrum.

As spread spectrum technology became widely available, the FCC recognized an opportunity to make more spectrum available by opening up the ISM bands to wireless communications. And because the FCC is so generous, they decided that as long as their rules are obeyed, no license is needed to operate a wireless system there. This lack of license requirement has made the ISM bands incredibly attractive to those companies wanting to roll out broadband fixed wireless service quickly and inexpensively.

Using spread spectrum in an ISM band is called *unlicensed spread spectrum* (what else they gonna call it?). The FCC imposes many rules for using unlicensed spread spectrum in these bands, including limiting the transmitted power to one watt and specifying exactly which spread spectrum technology can be used. There are several ISM bands (see Table 8–2) for unlicensed spread spectrum, but the two most popular ones being used for broadband fixed wireless (for now) are at 2.4 GHz and 5.8 GHz.

Did You Know?

Recently the FCC has allocated a sub-band of the 5.8 GHz band for non-spread spectrum communications. Like all of the others, since it is an unlicensed band, precautions still need to be taken to keep multiple service providers from interfering with one another. This sub-band in the 5.8 GHz band is known as the *Unlicensed National Information Infrastructure* or UNII band.

There are two substantial challenges that need to be overcome to successfully deliver broadband fixed wireless service in one of these unlicensed bands. First, the power limit of one watt severely restricts the range of the RF signal. Limited signal range generally means more cells (and therefore higher costs) to cover a given area. Second, because it is unlicensed, not only are there a lot of unwanted industrial signals floating around, there may also be a lot of wireless signals floating around from all the companies wanting to offer communication services in these frequency bands. Your intuition should tell you that a frequency band cannot accommodate an unlimited number of activities (even spread spectrum) before it has an adverse affect on something. The bottom line is that these unlicensed bands are free to use for broadband fixed wireless, but using them does not come without its challenges. To overcome these challenges, companies are using a combination of sophisticated antenna and signal processing technology. Will they succeed? Stay tuned.

Wireless Fiber

If ever there was an oxymoron, wireless fiber is it. Another term for wireless fiber is free space optics. Whatever it is called, it uses lasers or light emitting diodes (LED) to send data wirelessly by encoding it onto light pulses sent through the air. Although it uses light pulses, wireless fiber does not use visible light. Its signals are typically in the terahertz (THz = 1000 GHz) range, which is technically infrared.

Free space optics is not new. It has been around since the 1980s. Unfortunately it did not work very well back then and it is just now beginning to gain acceptance as a broadband fixed wireless option.

Wireless fiber uses a point-to-point topology that works by installing transceiver terminals (called *nodes*) on rooftops or inside windows and pointing them at each other. Like the other broadband fixed wireless alternatives, wireless fiber has line-of-sight restrictions, but much more severe. The optical transceivers must be more or less perfectly aligned for the system to work properly. An example of one of these terminals is shown in Figure 8–1.

There are many advantages to wireless fiber. For starters, it requires no license (for now) and is relatively inexpensive to deploy (compared with real fiber optics). It also provides excellent security because the signal can only be intercepted by being in the exact line of sight between two transceivers. But the best part of wireless fiber is that there is a ton of bandwidth, which translates to very

Figure 8–1
A wireless fiber transceiver. *Courtesy of Plaintree Systems.*

high data rates. As of this writing, wireless fiber providers are talking about 622 Mbps data rates, a number that is certain to grow over time.

Because of the extremely high data rates, wireless fiber is meant as a replacement for real fiber optics. (Nobody needs 622 Mbps data rate coming into their home.) This high capacity though is also a limitation. To be able to deliver the high data rates wirelessly, the system deployments must be near the big telecommunications hubs that are capable of processing those high data rates. As a consequence, wireless fiber is currently limited to dense urban environments, with the ideal application being building-to-building communications in a campus setting.

Wireless fiber is not without its disadvantages. The two major ones are its limitation on signal range and environmental interference. Recall from the discussion on free space loss that no wireless signal maintains a perfectly tight signal path as it travels, but rather it spreads out as it goes. Naturally the longer the signal travels, the more it spreads. In the case of wireless fiber, after a certain distance, the signal is spread so much it cannot be properly received. This spreading problem limits the range of wireless fiber communications to at most one mile, with some claiming an upper limit of only 500 meters.

How does this distance limitation manifest itself? With something called a *bit error rate* (BER). All digital wireless signals—not just wireless fiber—have a BER associated with them. BER is simply the number of incorrectly received digital bits per million. As you can guess, if one or two bits per million are received incorrectly, the system can take steps to correct it (like requesting the data be resent) and it is no big deal. However, as the BER rises, the data rate drops and the system becomes useless. As the signal spreading in the wireless fiber system increases (due to increased distance), there is less signal to receive (at the receiver), which results in more bit errors. Translation: longer distance equals a higher BER.

Environmental interference is also a big problem for wireless fiber, with perhaps fog as the number one culprit. The tiny water particles that make up fog act like prisms and break up the signal. Other sources of environmental problems include snow, birds (yes birds), and even building sway (a big problem in earthquake country).

Air Link Transmission Technologies

FDD versus TDD

Unlike the cellular frequency bands in which specific sub-bands are identified for upstream and downstream, the broadband fixed wireless systems discussed above have only been allocated one lump of frequency. How the service providers partition it is up to them. As things turn out, there are two ways to break up the allocated spectrum in an attempt to utilize it as fully as possible.

The first way is to utilize the cellular approach and break up the total spectrum into separate frequency sub-bands (called channels). Then, some of the channels are identified as upstream and some as downstream. This approach is called *frequency division duplexing* or FDD.

The other way to fully utilize the frequency spectrum is to break it up into separate time slots, alternating between the upstream and the downstream. This approach is called *time division duplexing* or TDD. TDD can still break up the total allotted frequency band into sub-bands. In this case, each of these channels is used for both upstream and downstream communications. Both of these approaches are depicted visually in Figure 8–2.

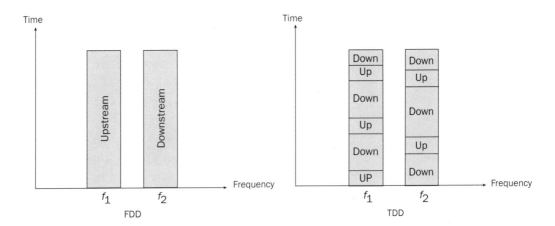

Figure 8–2
FDD and TDD.

Which approach is better? Remember we are talking about broadband fixed wireless applications. In most cases, this involves people surfing the Internet. And if that is true, there is usually a lot more downstream data than upstream. So using FDD requires dedicating more of the channels for downstream than upstream. Still, since no one knows in advance exactly what the downstream and upstream data loads will be. Some portion of some channels (either upstream or downstream) may not be fully utilized.

As an example, suppose you have a water system with ten pipes identified as downstream and one pipe identified as upstream. If the ratio of downstream water flow to upstream water flow is exactly ten to one, then all the pipes can work at full capacity all of the time. But if the ratio is different, either the upstream pipe or one of the downstream pipes will need to be turned off momentarily to let the whole system catch up. This unused pipe time—or in the case of wireless communications, unused bandwidth—is a waste when all the providers are trying to use their capacity to its fullest.

What people are beginning to find is that TDD has better *spectral efficiency* (more bps per Hertz). There is very little waste. Every pipe can be used for both upstream and downstream. When a pipe (bandwidth) has some available capacity, whatever is waiting to move, either upstream data or downstream data, that is what gets access.

OFDM

One of the biggest problems in a broadband fixed wireless system is multipath. Recall from a previous chapter that the multipath phenomenon occurs when a receiver receives the identical signal from the transmitter more than once, usually offset in time. Multipath occurs because the transmitted signal can take several paths to the receiver including bouncing off buildings, trees, etc. Receiving multiple signals can really cause havoc in the system.

You already learned that one of the ways to combat multipath is through antenna diversity. There is another way, which involves sophisticated signal processing, called *frequency division multiplexing*. From the previous section you have probably deduced that if frequency division duplexing breaks up the transmission into two (frequency) channels, then frequency division multiplexing must break it up into multiple (frequency) channels, and you are right.

Referring to Figure 8–3, the left side shows a single, 1 GHz wide signal with a carrier in the center. This is a typical spectrum for a single carrier signal. The right side of Figure 8–3 shows what happens to the same signal when it is frequency division multiplexed. That is, the signal is divided into ten smaller, equal frequency sub-bands. In this case, each of these narrower band signals has their own (RF) carrier, all at slightly different frequencies.

Now you must be asking yourself, what does all this buy you? Nothing appears to have changed as there is still 1 GHz worth of information. Actually it is worse than that. Because each of the sub-bands must be separated by a frequency guard band, in reality there is less information in the multiplexed case. So why bother? Simple. Frequency division multiplexing breaks up a single high-speed signal into many lower-speed signals. And these lower-speed signals greatly reduce the effects of multipath. Allow me to demonstrate.

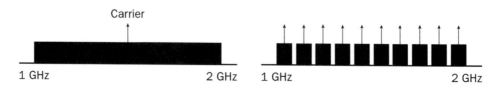

Figure 8–3
Frequency division multiplexing.

Multipath can be simulated by combining identical signals slightly offset in time. Refer to the top half of Figure 8–4. The top signal is the primary (direct) received signal at the receiver. In this example it is shown after demodulation as a digital signal. Just below it is the same signal, slightly offset in time by the delay shown. This is the (indirect) multipath signal. In this particular example, the delay is about as long as one bit length. In reality, the delay is on the order of a few microseconds.

When the two signals are received at the receiver, they are combined in a logical "OR," which is very easy to understand. If either of the two signals is a high ("1") when ORed, the result is a high. When the two signals are combined in this manner, what results is the third signal down. Even after a crazy weekend in Mexico, you could never confuse this resultant signal with the original (top) signal. Multipath has destroyed it.

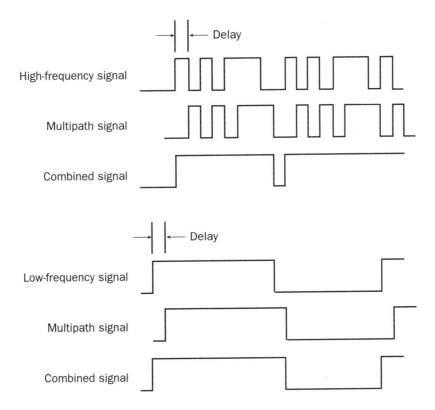

Figure 8–4
The effects of multipath.

Now let us see what happens after frequency division multiplexing. These multiplexed signals are at a much lower frequency and therefore have a much lower data rate. The top signal on the bottom half of Figure 8–4 shows one of the primary received (multiplexed) signals while the signal below it is its multipath signal. This signal experiences the same exact time delay as the one on the top of Figure 8–4.

Now when these two signals are combined as above, the resultant signal looks just like the original signal. In fact, with a little signal processing trickery, the original signal can be reproduced almost exactly. Frequency division multiplexing has conquered multipath simply by slowing down the data rate.

So what is OFDM? OFDM stands for *orthogonal frequency division multiplexing*. Say what? OFDM is a form of frequency division multiplexing, except here the carriers are orthogonal. Say what? As mentioned above, I said that frequency division multiplexing sacrifices information because it wastes some frequency on guard bands. Well, orthogonality allows the carriers to be placed very close to one another, in such a way that no guard bands are needed and therefore no information is sacrificed when using frequency division multiplexing.

OFDM is not without its challenges though. First, all that signal processing makes the hardware expensive. Second, there are several flavors of OFDM currently being debated for broadband fixed wireless and other applications. Which one will win out? Which one will become the standard? Stay tuned.

One of the newest applications for OFDM is in non-line of sight (NLOS) wireless systems. The theory is simple. Since an OFDM receiver can reproduce the intended signal by receiving it from multiple locations and at different times, the receiving antenna no longer needs to be in direct line of sight with the transmitting antenna. In fact there is one system being evaluated now that can work without receiving the primary (direct) signal at all. It can reproduce the intended signal just by receiving a bunch of reflected and re-directed signals from the transmitter.

WIRELESS NETWORKS..

Local Area Networks

A few years ago when someone said the word "network," everyone pretty much thought of computer networks. These *local area networks* or LANs were just a bunch of computers communicating over a special type of cable. Sometimes they communicated directly with each other or, more frequently, through a central computer called a server. Today, when you hear the word network, it can mean any number of different digital-based information devices communicating with each other including computers, personal digital assistants, network-ready peripherals, and from what I hear, pretty soon, your refrigerator too.

With all these new devices wanting to communicate with each other, it becomes a real challenge to get them to communicate over a cable, especially in light of the fact that many of these devices are mobile (think laptop). What is the answer? You already know: wireless networking. As you will soon learn, wireless networks come in many shapes and sizes and are intended to solve very different real-world problems. The subject of this section is the wireless local area network (WLAN).

Since there is much overlap in the functionality of all these different wireless networks, I differentiate WLANs by associating with them two unique characteristics. First, they are used primarily to connect computers and peripherals in a business setting and second, they have a very limited coverage area. So WLANs provide for some mobility. As long as you are in the coverage area, you can move around (at walking speed) and you will still be connected to the network.

Basic Architecture

The fundamental building block of a wireless LAN is the *basic service set* or BSS. The BSS contains a single *access point* (AP) and several other computers and peripherals (called nodes). (See Figure 8–5.) To establish the wireless link, each node and the AP uses a small RF radio, which includes an antenna, a transceiver, a modem, and some signal processing electronics.

All of the computers and peripherals communicate wirelessly with each other by using the AP as a bridge to relay the signals. The AP is analogous to the base-station used in cellular telephony. So the first role of the AP is to get all the nodes in the BSS to talk to each other. A typical access point is shown in Figure 8–6. Why do you suppose it has two antennas? Diversity!

NOTE: A wireless LAN can be set up without an AP in which all nodes communicate directly with each other. This peer-to-peer arrangement is referred to as an ad hoc network.

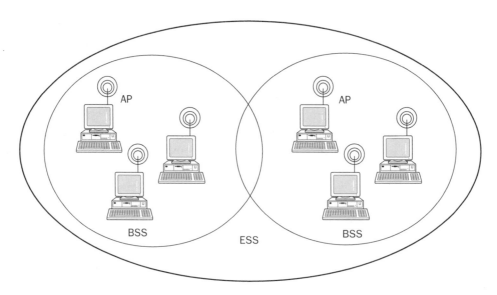

Figure 8–5
Basic wireless LAN system.

Figure 8–6
A typical wireless LAN access point. *Courtesy of Linksys, Inc.*

As long as you are in the BSS, which is essentially the RF footprint of the AP, you can connect wirelessly to the network. As an example, a BSS may be a single floor in a large office tower. But what if a company occupies more than one floor in an office tower, can users on multiple floors still connect wirelessly to the network? The answer is yes. First, each floor can be established as its own BSS with its own AP. Then the floors are combined into an *extended service set* or ESS by getting their individual APs to talk to each other. The second role of the AP is to function as a bridge between multiple LANs (either wireless or wired) to extend the overall coverage area.

802.11 vs. HiperLAN

In the world of wireless LANs, there are two international standards vying for world supremacy: 802.11 (originating in the United States) and HiperLAN (originating in Europe). These standards dictate every operational aspect of the wireless network from the frequency of operation to the type of air interface and modulation employed. Both of these standards are, to some extent, based on the Ethernet standard, which is the most popular wired LAN standard in the world. Following these standards is critical for interoperability.

The 802.11 standard is really a series of standards that have emerged over time as the technology has evolved. Subsequent standards updates reflect improvement in technology and/or the employment of additional spectrum. Each of these series of standards for 802.11 and HiperLAN are summarized in Table 8–3.

Table 8–3 Different Wireless Networking Options

Specification	Frequency	Band	Data Rate	Technology
802.11	2.4 GHz	ISM	2 Mbps	FHSS & DSSS
802.11a	5 GHz	UNII	54 Mbps	OFDM
802.11b	2.4 GHz	ISM	11 Mbps	DSSS & CCK
HiperLAN	5 GHz	UNII	20 Mbps	GMSK
HiperLAN II	5 GHz	UNII	50 Mbps	OFDM

Because in the U.S. wireless LANs are just not important enough to be allocated their own frequency bands, the standards for the most part have been written around the unlicensed bands mentioned previously in the section on broadband fixed wireless. As you already know, using unlicensed bands involves one very large technological obstacle: interference from everything else that is going on in the band. What is one way of dealing with all the interference? You already know: spread spectrum.

The 802.11 standard evolved out of the 2.4 GHz unlicensed ISM band. The real benefit to this band is that it can be used worldwide. To deal with the interference, it employs either direct sequence spread spectrum (DSSS) or another type of spread spectrum called *frequency hopping spread spectrum* (FHSS)—which you will learn about in the next section.

Note: 802.11 can also use diffuse infrared communications, but since nobody has ever built one commercially that uses it, we'll just ignore it.

Recall that for spread spectrum to work properly, the sending and receiving units must be synchronized to a master clock. The third role of the access point is to periodically send out a timing signal so that all the nodes are in time with the AP.

The DSSS version of 802.11 uses similar technology to that discussed in the section on CDMA, with one difference. Recall that with CDMA, every user has a different pseudo random code (PN), so that they can all transmit at the same time. With 802.11, all the nodes use the same PN code. Naturally they cannot all transmit at the same time and they don't. Instead, additional technology is used to sense when another node is transmitting. When one node is transmitting, all the other nodes must wait until it is done before they get a chance.

The first improvement to 802.11 is 802.11b, which is also known as 802.11hr and "Wi Fi." 802.11b takes the DSSS version of 802.11 and crams more than five times the digital information onto the same RF signal using something called *complementary code keying* or CCK. Let us just say that CCK is a sophisticated form of digital signal processing and leave it at that.

The next upgrade to 802.11 is 802.11a, which uses a higher (unlicensed) frequency band and OFDM. As mentioned above, OFDM is effective in dealing with multipath, which can be quite extreme in indoor situations.

The major benefit to the higher frequency band is that, unlike the 2.4 GHz band which has only 80 MHz of spectrum, the 5 GHz band has 300 MHz of spectrum. Other things being equal, more spectrum means higher data rates. To be sure there are even more improvements intended for 802.11 in the future with callouts like 802.11e, 802.11z, etc. Stay tuned.

HiperLAN in Europe works in a dedicated frequency band (for WLANs) and therefore does not have to use spread spectrum to deal with interference. And because it is Europe, much of the underlying technology for HiperLAN (like using GMSK modulation) comes from GSM, the European cellular standard. As you can see from Table 8–3, HiperLAN has much higher data rates than the earlier 802.11 systems, but also uses more expensive 5 GHz RF equipment.

HiperLAN II is a new standard that operates in the same frequency band as HiperLAN and utilizes OFDM. In fact, not only is the performance of HiperLAN II similar to that of 802.11a, they can use similar electrical components. Unlike 802.11a though, HiperLAN II can dynamically change the type of modulation it uses to increase or decrease the data rate, depending on varying conditions. Which wireless LAN standard (802.11a or HiperLAN II) is better? I think I'll let the free market determine that one.

Frequency Hopping Spread Spectrum

In a previous section you learned about direct sequence spread spectrum (DSSS) in which a pseudo random noise (PN) signal is modulated onto the RF carrier. When every user has a different PN code (like in CDMA), they can all transmit simultaneously. Even when all users have the same PN code (like in WLANs), DSSS is very effective in combating RF interference, which is abundant in the unlicensed bands. Well, there is another type of spread spectrum, called frequency hopping spread spectrum (FHSS), which is even better at combating interference, which is why it is used extensively in wireless LAN systems.

Like DSSS, FHSS uses a PN code. But instead of modulating the code onto the RF carrier as in DSSS, the code is used to determine a sequence of discrete frequencies. These discrete frequencies become the RF carrier. In essence, FHSS is an RF system in which the RF carrier is constantly hopping (ergo the name) from one frequency to another (within a defined range).

Figure 8–7 is a graphical depiction of FHSS. As you can see from the figure, as time goes by, the frequency hops from one value to another in a more or less random pattern. Once it hops to a given frequency, it only stays there for a very short time—just a fraction of a second—called the *dwell time*. When a system operates like this, the same phenomenon depicted in Figure 7–11 occurs: the signal's energy gets spread over a larger frequency range.

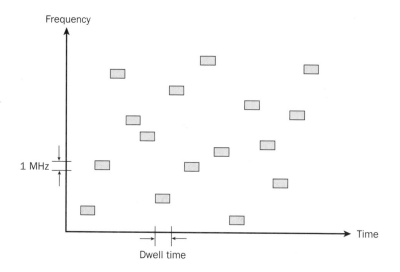

Figure 8–7
Frequency hopping spread spectrum.

As an example, suppose that each frequency depicted in Figure 8–7 is 1 MHz wide in the 2.4 GHz band and that there are 79 such 1-MHz wide frequencies to choose from. Every couple of microseconds, according to the PN code, another one of the 79 1-MHz frequencies is selected and that becomes the carrier frequency for the next few microseconds. If you viewed this signal's spectrum on a spectrum analyzer, it would appear 79 MHz wide.

Did You Know?

From the truth is stranger than fiction file, frequency hopping spread spectrum was first conceived by actress Hedy Lamarr and composer George Antheil during World War II. Talk about having too much free time.

What ingenious piece of RF hardware is responsible for rapidly generating the multitude of frequencies required in FHSS? If you said a synthesizer, give yourself a prize. In FHSS, the PN code is used to control the instantaneous frequency coming out of a synthesizer. And as long as both the transmitter and receiver use the same PN code and are synchronized (thanks to the AP), everything works just fine.

Which spread spectrum technology (DSSS or FHSS) is better? That depends. In FHSS, since the instantaneous frequency band may only be 1 MHz wide, the data rate will be less than that achievable through DSSS, which has no such bandwidth restriction. So if you want a higher data rate you need to use DSSS (that is what 802.11b uses). On the other hand, since FHSS uses a smaller instantaneous frequency, it is more resistant to multipath. Take your pick.

Personal Area Networks

The wireless LANs discussed in the previous section have one inherent limitation: the AP is usually in a fixed location. As a result, if you are within RF range of the AP you can tie into the network and if you aren't, there is not much you can do about it. But what if the AP were mobile? You would in essence have a "mobile" wireless LAN that could go anywhere the AP went. That is the theory behind a relatively new concept called the *personal area network* or PAN. In effect, you become the AP by carrying a mobile wireless device that serves as the AP for other wireless devices (fixed or mobile).

The are several keys to any PAN working properly. First and foremost is interoperability. It does you no good to be a walking AP if other wireless devices cannot communicate with you because they are using a different protocol or frequency. Everyone's got to be on the same wavelength, so to speak.

Next, the PAN must only cover a very short range otherwise it will interfere with other PANs. The good news is that short range means low RF power. And low RF power means a longer battery life, which is a good thing for mobile devices.

Finally, the real key to implementing a PAN is something called *self discovery* (also called *auto initiate*). It would be a real pain in the you-know-what if every time your mobile PAN device came within RF range of another device, you had to sit there and do some kind of software programming to get the two devices to talk to each other. With self discovery, every PAN device constantly "listens" for other PAN devices to come within RF range. When PAN devices sense each other, they immediately—and without you even knowing it—form a little network and start communicating. Those sly devils.

What are some applications for a PAN? Have you seen the hands-free mobile phone attachment, which is essentially a wire with an ear piece on one end, a microphone in the middle, and the other end plugged into the phone? With a PAN, you would not need to plug anything into the phone. You could wear a headset that communicates wirelessly with the cellular phone. As crazy as it sounds, you would no longer be tied to your mobile phone.

If you have ever taken photographs using a digital camera, you know at some point you need to get the picture into your computer (or someone else's computer). This typically involves connecting the camera to the computer using some kind of cable. With a PAN, you could upload your digital photographs into your computer sans cable.

There are hundreds of applications for PANs from wirelessly purchasing something from a vending machine to wirelessly connecting your laptop to the Internet at an airport. But before any of these can become reality, there needs to be a universally adopted standard to facilitate interoperability. And while there are a few PAN technologies vying for world supremacy, there seems to be one already that will emerge as the winner.

Bluetooth

Bluetooth, a specification for short range wireless communications (developed by Ericsson in Sweden), has emerged as the leading candidate for an internationally adopted standard for personal area networks. It is becoming so universally supported that it may even get its own IEEE standard (802.15). In fact, much of the Bluetooth standard is based on 802.11, the IEEE standard for wireless local area networks discussed in the previous section.

Did You Know?

The Bluetooth standard is named after Viking King Harald Blaatand (Bluetooth) II from 10th century Denmark who united and Christianized Denmark and Norway during his reign. It is rumored that he facilitated the remarkable feat while talking on a cellular phone. Of course it's only a rumor.

Bluetooth operates in the 2.4 GHz (ISM) frequency band. The real benefit here is that this band is allocated internationally so Bluetooth devices will work everywhere (in theory). Like 802.11, it also uses FHSS, which works well in noisy environments. Unlike 802.11 however, which uses a minimum of 2.5 frequency hops per second, Bluetooth changes frequency 1600 times per second. The high number of hops makes the system more immune to interference, but also limits the data rate. A summary of the Bluetooth specification is shown in Table 8–4.

As you can imagine, at that low a data rate (< 1Mbps) and that short of a range (30 feet), Bluetooth is not meant to replace wireless LANs. Now just as I say that, there is a second-generation Bluetooth specification in the works with a higher data rate (20 Mbps?) and longer range (300 feet?).

Table 8–4   Bluetooth Specification Summary

Item	Specification
Data rate	< 1Mbps
Range	30 feet
Frequency	2.4 GHz
Technology	FHSS
Hops/second	1600
RF power	1 mW

Bluetooth has two really nice features you should know about. First, it is designed to carry both voice and data, which makes it perfect for integrating into a cellular phone. Second, it facilitates the creation of something called a *piconet*.

A piconet is just a network of up to eight devices in which one device is designated as the master and the others are the slaves. All Bluetooth devices are capable of being either a master or a slave. Just like the access point in a wireless LAN, all communications in the piconet go through the master. The master is also responsible for selecting the hopping sequence for its slaves. Because different hopping sequences can be chosen, multiple piconets can operate in the same area (without interfering with one another). In fact, a Bluetooth device can be master of one piconet and slave in another. This feature really increases the scalability and extendibility of Bluetooth networks.

When might a piconet be formed? Picture a business meeting in a conference room where one person wants to make a slide presentation to seven others and each has a laptop computer. If all laptops are Bluetooth-enabled, the presenter could show the slides by bringing up the presentation on each person's laptop with no set-up and no wires. There's just no escaping PowerPoint.

Home Networks

Let's see, we have networked the office and the individual. What's left? How about the home? There are a lot of wireless LAN manufacturers who see an opportunity to expand their market by selling similar equipment to the newly emerging home networking market. But before they can sell their equipment to the consumer market, they have to make one big change: they have to make it cheap.

They also have to make another change. Office networking equipment is only responsible for moving data from one place to another. But for home networking equipment to be really useful, it has to not only move data from one place to another, it also has to be capable of carrying voice traffic.

HomeRF

In the home networking market, one approach—called HomeRF—has risen to become more or less the industry standard. HomeRF is nothing more than a bunch of equipment manufacturers that all agree to make their home wireless networking equipment to certain protocols and thus guarantee interoperability (always a good thing).

HomeRF is built around two very popular wireless technologies: 802.11 (which you learned about earlier in this section) and Digital Enhanced Cordless Telephone (DECT), which is the most popular cordless telephone specification in the world. And to ensure that HomeRF is widely adopted, it uses the 2.4 GHz unlicensed frequency band, which is generally available worldwide.

How does HomeRF work? Just like 802.11, only now, in addition to computers and peripherals, the network includes telephones, entertainment equipment, and other wirelessly enabled products. With HomeRF, the access point (AP) is called the control point (CP), just to be different. HomeRF not only handles data

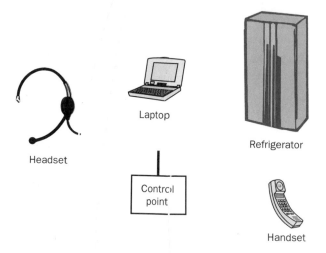

Figure 8–8
HomeRF networking functionality.

and telephony, but it is also optimized to handle entertainment-based communications like streaming audio and video. Figure 8–8 depicts the general functionality of a HomeRF network.

To put everything in perspective, I thought it would be interesting to compare the three big wireless networking technologies: 802.11b, Bluetooth, and HomeRF. Table 8–5 shows the comparison.

As you can see, HomeRF is really suited to the consumer with its lower price and support for entertainment. And with the lower data rate, it is not as good for heavily traveled corporate networks. You can also begin to see from Table 8–5 how crowded the 2.4 GHz band is becoming. In crowded RF environments, FHSS generally works better than DSSS, so the higher data rate of 802.11b does not come without some challenges.

Table 8–5 Networking Comparison

Item	802.11b	Bluetooth	HomeRF
Frequency	2.4 GHz	2.4 GHz	2.4 GHz
Technology	DSSS	FHSS	FHSS
Range	300 feet	30 feet	150 feet
Data rate	11 Mbps	< 1 Mbps	1.6 Mbps
Power consumption	Moderate	Low	Low
Price	Moderate	Low	Low
Voice support	None	Adequate	Good
Streaming media	None	Adequate	Good

The comparison in Table 8–5 is only valid for a single moment (today). As I write this, all of these technologies have their next generation coming out, which basically renders Table 8–5 out of date. The next generation 802.11 (802.11a) uses a different frequency and has a much higher data rate. The next generation Bluetooth has a higher data rate and longer range, and the next generation HomeRF has a higher data rate.

The bottom line is this, while 802.11 is designed for business networks, Bluetooth for PANs and HomeRF for the home, there is a lot of overlap and all of them can be used many different ways. And the reality is that 802.11 is just as popular in the home, or more so, than HomeRF.

IrDA

There is one more networking technology you should know about and it is called IrDA, which stands for *Infrared Data Association*. While not technically a home networking technology, it is certainly not for business LANs or PANs, so it ended up here. What is IrDA? A wireless data connection, using infrared light, which has a useful range of about three feet. And like HomeRF, IrDA is an industry association of companies that all agree to make their equipment to the same specification.

IrDA uses a direct infrared signal for point-to-point communications. It usually requires the user to walk up and point one device at another and unlike RF wireless communications, IrDA cannot go through walls. It has a maximum data rate (today) of about 4 Mbps.

With an effective range of only 3 feet and a true line-of-sight requirement, you must be wondering what in the world is IrDA good for? Plenty, and as things turn out, these two "limitations" (short distance and line-of-sight requirement), in reality provide three benefits. First, IrDA-enabled devices do not interfere with other wireless devices. Second, they are more secure because the signal cannot penetrate walls. And third, because of the limited range, many simultaneous users can operate IrDA devices in the same general area.

You may not know it, but IrDA communication is built into many of today's peripherals and electronic gadgets. Most PDAs are IrDA enabled. Many of the newer computer printers are IrDA enabled, as are digital cameras and some of the newer mobile phones. You can tell if a device is IrDA enabled if it has a small, dark red or black plastic radome on its outer surface. (The other way to tell is to read the user manual.)

What are some of the different ways to use IrDA? How about a wireless keyboard, mouse, or joystick? How about wirelessly transferring a photograph from a digital camera to a computer or printer? And how about faxing a memo from a PDA? I think you get the idea. Expect in the near future to see just about every mobile electronic device be IrDA enabled.

THE MOBILE INTERNET ....

What better combination of technologies than mobility and the Internet. You can go surfing while you go cruising. As you can imagine, accessing the Internet wirelessly is not without its challenges. First, mobile devices, like cellular phones and personal digital assistants (PDA), were not really designed to surf the Internet. They have small screens and no keyboard. Second, while the Internet is a packet-based communications medium, most wireless systems—at least initially—are/were circuit-based systems, which is very inefficient for data communications. And finally, even when these inefficient wireless systems are used, the data rates are painfully slow—often slower than dial-up modems.

Fortunately the incredible interest in accessing the Internet wirelessly is changing all of that. New systems are or will be coming on line soon that use packet switching technology and deliver data rates people at home can only dream about. Undoubtedly voice recognition will eventually help overcome even the lack of a keyboard. In short, there will soon be a time when you and the Internet will become as one for all time.

Technology

Since the power in a mobile unit is very limited, it cannot be expected to transmit signals very far, and thus must be in close proximity to a wireless receiver at all times. As a consequence, the "cellular" approach to wireless communications—in which a geographical region in divided up into cells—is the only one that makes sense. In this way, as you move from cell to cell, you are always in close proximity to a receiver.

But which cellular technology should be used? There are two basic choices: use some existing cellular infrastructure or build something new. So far, only a few companies have attempted to build one from the ground up—with limited financial success—and the reason is simple. It is really expensive. Nationwide, or even regional, coverage requires hundreds or thousands of basestations. It took the cellular providers many years to complete their national coverage and in some instances, they aren't done yet.

The only approach that really makes (financial) sense is to use the same antennas, towers, and amplifiers that are used to provide cellular phone service. I think it is safe to assume that mobile wireless Internet access is going to be provided by the same cast of characters that allow you to reach out and touch someone.

With that settled, there are still two challenges to wireless Internet access today. First, the existing infrastructure provides very low data rates (see Table 7–3). Second, most websites, with their extensive graphics and streaming media, are not really suited for viewing on mobile devices. What is the answer? Simple, upgrade the infrastructure to deliver higher data rates and somehow restrict the amount and type of information that can be accessed with a portable device.

From the previous chapter, you already know about the migration to 2.5G and 3G cellular technology. Well it is not happening to improve the quality of your voice calls. It is happening to increase the data rate for accessing the Internet. Now if they could only agree on a standard.

As for limiting the information quantity and type, that is already being done. It is accomplished by using a "restricted" programming language (e.g., C-HTML, HDML, etc.) when designing a website. It eliminates all of the fancy stuff and pretty much just communicates with pure text. Unfortunately, these restricted websites mean that a company must have two different versions of their website: one for regular traffic and one for mobile traffic. Such is the price of progress.

Frequencies

What frequencies can be used for the wireless Internet? Just about any which are or can be deployed in a cellular structure. Since all of the mobile telephony providers are trying to get in on the act, you should expect to see mobile Internet access at 800 MHz (SMR), 900 MHz (cellular), and 1900 MHz (PCS). The drawback in these cases is that the frequency bands—which are relatively small (25–30 MHz) to begin with—must be shared between Internet access and mobile telephony. That is not such a big deal today, but just wait until people start expecting to watch *Gone with the Wind* on their PDA. There may not be enough bandwidth (is there ever?).

To get around the bandwidth limitation of the cellular systems, some companies are looking to provide wireless Internet access using the unlicensed ISM frequency bands (900MHz, 2.4 GHz, and 5.8 GHz). Recall from Table 8–2, these ISM bands have up to 150 MHz to work with. Unfortunately, to use one of these bands requires building a system from scratch. But there is one advantage here. Since the unlicensed bands transmit very low power (less than one watt), the "base-station" can be made relatively small and relatively inexpensive. These so-called "micro basestations" are often small enough to hang from a utility pole. How widespread will these ISM services be? Stay tuned.

WAP

The best way for the mobile Internet to really take off is if everyone adopts the same standard. In this way, all of the hardware will be interoperable. Well after a lot of maneuvering, it seems one standard is set to become the de facto standard for the mobile Internet and it is called WAP, or *wireless access protocol*.

WAP is an open standard, which means anyone can use it. It is comprised of a programming language (for displaying websites on mobile devices) called *wireless markup language* (WML) and a set of protocols for communicating wirelessly. WAP can run over any technology and frequency. Not only will it work with all of the standard mobile telephone technologies, it will also work with Bluetooth and CDPD.

WAP functionality is similar to mobile telephony except for the addition of a piece of hardware called a WAP *gateway*. The WAP gateway mediates between the mobile device and the WAP server as shown in Figure 8–9.

If the system shown in Figure 8–9 is using existing cellular infrastructure, then at some point (not shown) the voice signals must be separated from the data signals, with the voice signals being routed to the PSTN and the data signals being routed to the Internet.

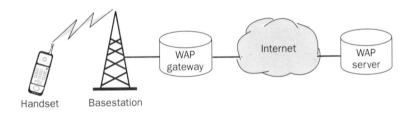

Figure 8–9
Basic infrastructure of a WAP system.

M-Commerce

There are a lot of things you can do with mobile access to the Internet, but all the companies spending billions of dollars are not upgrading their equipment so you can check a stock price or read your e-mail. The expectation is that you will use your wireless access to the Internet to shop (and the service providers will get a cut of every transaction). Purchasing something using a mobile device has been dubbed mobile commerce or *m-commerce* for short.

There are two different shopping scenarios using a mobile device. In the first scenario, you are cruising along in your car and suddenly you decide you need to purchase the latest John Grisham novel and for some strange reason, you need to purchase it in the next 30 seconds. So you dial up your favorite e-commerce web site and purchase the book (hopefully while stopped at a red light). As interesting as this scenario is, it does not demonstrate the true potential of m-commerce.

In the second scenario, you are cruising along in a rental car in a city you have never been and suddenly you decide you have to have a Big Mac (and in the next 30 seconds). So you use your mobile device to log onto the McDonald's website and request the location of their nearest restaurant. Within a few seconds, back comes an address and directions. Now that is pretty cool, but how is it done?

The website must know exactly where you are at the time you make the request, and it knows it by one of two ways. Either your mobile device is equipped with a GPS receiver or the mobile network itself is used to triangulate your location. (Technically, GPS is a form of triangulation.) Whether the wireless signals come from satellites or basestations, receiving signals from three (or more) different locations can be used to determine your position.

The ability to determine a mobile unit's location and then offer location-specific buying opportunities is expected to really drive the growth of m-commerce in the future. Of course knowing your exact location does come with some privacy issues, but that's another story.

THE BLEEDING EDGE ....

Why the bleeding edge? It is a tribute to the fact that those on the leading edge often experience a little pain. As fast as technology moves, it is hard to call anything leading edge. By the time this book is published, some of these new ideas may not be so new any more.

Did You Know?

In an effort to get around the limited availability of cellular basestation towers, there is now a company out there that is putting wireless transmitters on small blimps tethered 15,000 feet above the Earth. That's what I mean by bleeding edge.

Up-and-Coming Technologies

Ultra Wideband

RF engineers are constantly trying to come up with new and novel ways to cram as much information as possible into the limited amount of available bandwidth. One of the newer approaches is something called *Time Modulated-Ultra Wideband* (TM-UWB) or just plain old ultra wideband (UWB) for short. The theory is pretty simple to understand. It involves transmitting a single, unmodulated sine wave (like that shown way back in Figure 1–2), called a *monocycle*, every so often. Seems simple enough. Not so fast.

There are two problems with just transmitting a single, unmodulated sine wave every so often. First, without modulation, how can information be imparted onto it? Second, if the single sine wave occurs at a regular interval, it will in fact, be at a fixed frequency, the spectrum of which will look just like that in Figure 7–9a. And unless the FCC has given permission to transmit at this frequency, the chances are it will be interfering with the other wireless signals that are authorized to transmit at that frequency. What to do?

Let us solve the second problem first. What would happen if the sine wave wasn't transmitted at a regular interval, but rather it was transmitted at a random time interval? The same thing that happens to any spread spectrum signal: the peak signal level drops and the signal energy gets spread over a larger frequency band like that shown in Figure 7–11b. If you guessed that this is a form of *time-hopping spread spectrum* (THSS), then you should be writing this book instead of me. The signal drops down into the noise level and, up to a point, does not interfere with any other signal—even those authorized by the FCC. Problem two solved. Now to solve the first problem: no modulation.

In this system, the transmitter and receiver are both working from the same pseudo random noise (PN) code, which determines the random time interval of the monocycle. So when the transmitter transmits at a specific (random) time, the only receiver ready to receive the monopulse is the intended receiver. But what if instead of transmitting the monopulse at the exact random time, the transmitter sent the monopulse just slightly shifted in time? I'm talking a couple hundred picoseconds (trillionths of a second). In fact the monopulse could be slightly shifted in time two ways: shorter or longer. And to make the whole story complete, the shorter time shift could be assigned the digital bit "0" and the longer shift could be assigned the digital bit "1." Voilá, we have imparted information onto the sig-

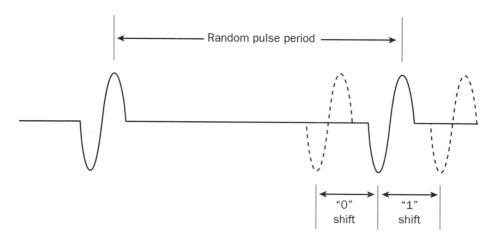

Figure 8–10
Graphical depiction of a TM-UWB signal.

nal. See Figure 8–10 for a graphical depiction. This imparting of information through the use of small time shifts in a signal is called *time modulation* or *pulse position modulation.*

There are a few other things you need to know about UWB technology. First, since the spreading of the signal typically covers a large spectrum (650 MHz to 5 GHz), encompassing many different authorized applications, it has not yet been approved by the FCC, but it is close. Second, it works well in dense environments and is effective in determining the position of things (think radar). And finally, the initial deployment of the technology will probably be for high-speed indoor wireless links.

MEMS

Microelectromechanical systems. Now you know why they call it MEMS. MEMS are nothing more than integrated circuits (IC) in which some part of the circuit actually moves—no small feat. (There are MEMS in which nothing moves, but they're boring.) MEMS differ dramatically from "normal" integrated circuits in which the only thing that moves are electrons. Also, MEMS are not made with transistors (yet), so they do not incorporate amplification.

MEMS have been around awhile but they are just now beginning to be used in RF systems. What kind of devices can be made as MEMS? Boring ones, like capacitors and inductors, and exciting ones like switches and oscillators. Why would an RF engineer choose to use a MEMS device rather than a more standard type? To understand why, I have taken the liberty of comparing a MEMS switch to two other, more traditional switch types used in RF systems. The comparison can be seen in Table 8–6.

Table 8–6   *MEMS Switch Comparison*

Parameter	PIN	Electromechanical	MEMS
Insertion loss	1 dB	0.1 dB	0.1 dB
Switching speed	microseconds	milliseconds	microseconds
Size	small	very large	very small
Power consumption	moderate	substantial	tiny
Price	low	high	very low

As you can see, the MEMS switch has the (low) insertion loss of an electromechanical switch with the switching speed of a PIN diode switch. It is also smaller, consumes less power, and costs less (in high volume) than either of the other switch types. Now you know why.

You should expect to see more and more MEMS-based devices in applications where small size, low price, and low power consumption are the driving factors (think cellular phones).

BLAST Technology

Just when you thought there were no other ways to cram more information into less bandwidth, along comes something called BLAST technology. Short for Bell Labs lAyered Space-Time, BLAST is a technological development in response to a challenge. The engineers of Bell Labs were challenged to see how much information they could cram into a given bandwidth. The result was 10 to 20 times more information into a given frequency band than had been done before.

The theory behind BLAST is simple to understand (and difficult to implement) because it depends on taking advantage of the multipath effect. In most wireless systems, multipath is bad and a variety of techniques are used to eliminate it. With BLAST technology, not only aren't the multipath signals eliminated, they are used to increase the information carrying capacity of the system. The multiplicity of scattered signals are really just parallel subchannels.

BLAST accomplishes the increase in data carrying capacity by breaking up a single, high-speed data signal into multiple lower speed signals and sending each of them to their own transmitter. All of the transmitters are spatially separated and transmit at the same exact frequency. If four transmitters are used, then theoretically four times as much data can be carried compared to a single transmitter. And since they are all using the same frequency, the data carrying capacity of that frequency (i.e., spectral efficiency) is four times higher (in bps/Hertz). See Figure 8–11 for a pictorial representation.

At the receiver just the opposite happens. Several receivers, spatially separated, are set to receive at the transmitter's frequency. Not only does each receiver receive the four direct signals (from the four transmitters), but they all receive all of the multipath signals too (what a mess). However, if the multipath effect is great enough, then all of the signals will scatter differently and sophisticated signal processing can then distinguish one substream from another. Each receiver picks out one of the substreams and they are all recombined into a single, high-speed data stream. I told you it was hard to implement.

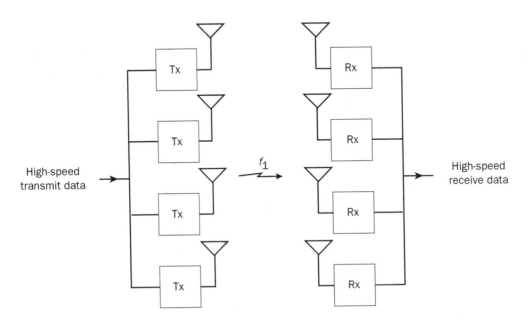

Figure 8–11
Pictorial representation of a BLAST system.

If the truth be told, BLAST is more of a breakthrough in advanced signal processing than in wireless technology, but I included it here anyway. BLAST is really only meant for fixed wireless applications. A mobile phone with four antennas would just require too much explanation.

RFID Systems

It is not so much that Radio Frequency IDentification (RFID) is an up-and-coming technology—it has been around since the early 1980's—it is that there has been an explosion in the applications for it recently. And it is entirely possible that the greatest applications based on RFID have yet to come to market.

RFID is a simple wireless system with just two basic components that is used to control, detect, and track objects. The basic block diagram of an RFID system is shown in Figure 8–12 (I told you it is simple).

The system consists of one *interrogator* (or reader) and many *transponders* (or tags). In most systems, the interrogator continuously sends out an RF signal and waits for a response. When a transponder enters the RF range of the interrogator, it senses the signal and returns one of its own. The interrogator then takes this information and does something with it (like entering data in a database or sounding an alarm).

In most RFID systems, the tag has a unique numerical code associated with it. In some systems, the code is preprogrammed at the factory by the manufacturer and in other systems, the code can be programmed by the user and can be changed as often as needed. When a tag senses the RF signal from the interrogator, it modulates its code onto a sine wave and continuously transmits it until the interrogator receives it. The interrogator demodulates the transponder's signal and then knows exactly which one it is by its unique code.

While the interrogator is usually a full-blown wireless system with a connection to a backend database, the transponder is much simpler. It consists of a printed antenna (on a small PCB), a power source, a single integrated circuit

Figure 8–12
Basic block diagram of an RFID system.

transceiver chip, and a small amount of memory (to hold the unique code among other things). Tags are purposely kept simple so they can be made very small and very inexpensive.

RFID systems come in many shapes and sizes but they all fall into one of two categories: active or passive. In an active system, the tag uses an onboard power source, usually a small battery. In a passive system, there is no onboard power system. The tag gets the energy it needs from the interrogator. How is that possible? The interrogator transmits a relatively high-power (e.g., 15 watts) RF signal and uses something called *magnetic induction* (don't ask) to couple energy onto the tag itself, where it stores the energy—very briefly—in an onboard capacitor. For this process to work, the tag must be held in close proximity to the interrogator.

RFID systems also fall into one of three frequency ranges: low (< 500 kHz), intermediate (10–15 MHz) and high (900 MHz, 2.4 GHz). As things turn out, most low-frequency systems are passive.

How do you decide whether to use an active or passive RFID system, or what frequency range to use? That depends on the application. Different systems and frequencies have their advantages and disadvantages, and the application itself determines which one is most appropriate. Table 8–7 compares active and passive RFID systems. For the sake of simplicity, I assumed that all passive RFID systems are low frequency, which is not entirely true.

The number of different uses for RFID is only limited by the imagination. You have no doubt (knowingly or unknowingly) run into this technology in your daily life. One of the most common ones is something called *electronic article surveillance* or EAS. EAS, which requires attaching a passive RFID tag to some article of merchandise, is used to prevent shoplifting from retail stores. In this realization, a tag in the normal state will set off an alarm upon passing through the not-so-unobtrusive "antenna gates" near the exit of a store. When you finally purchase a product, the salesperson will quickly apply a strong RF pulse (stronger than the interrogator) to the tag, which literally burns out the circuit (just like a fuse). A tag in this altered state is incapable of triggering the interrogator's alarm.

Table 8–7 Comparison of Active and Passive RFID Systems

Item	Active	Passive
Power source	Battery	Energy from the RF signal
Range	250 feet	1.5 feet
Output power of interrogator	Low	High
Frequency	900 MHz, 2.4 GHz	< 500kHz, 10–15 MHz
Numerical code	Re-programmable	Factory programmed
Memory	Some to a lot	Little to none
Advantages	Long reading range Can transfer large amounts of information	Lasts forever Inexpensive
Disadvantages	Battery must be replaced More expensive	Low data throughput Requires a high-powered reader
Applications	Toll road readers Inventory tracking	Auto immobilizers Cashless payments

Security Issues

With all the wireless signals floating around, there is naturally a concern about security (or lack thereof). But what are the risks of communicating wirelessly and what tools are available to combat them? Table 8–8 is a quick summary of the risks encountered when trying to communicate wirelessly.

The first thing you will probably notice is that the risks of communicating wirelessly are not a whole lot different from those in the wired world. But overcoming these risks in the wireless world is more challenging for several reasons.

First, physical security is more difficult. In a wired network, the end user device is usually a desktop computer, which is easy to secure physically and does not get lost very often. In the wireless world, the end user device might be a cellular phone or a PDA, which is difficult to secure physically and is very easily lost.

Table 8–8 *Summary of Wireless Security Risks*

Risk	What It Entails
Insertion attack	Unauthorized users and/or access points
Interception and monitoring	Data analysis, access point clone
Jamming	Denial of service
User-to-user attacks	Users can bypass access points
Brute force attacks	Repeated attempts to guess a password
Encryption attacks	Exploit a weakness in privacy protocols
Misconfiguration	Manipulated access points

Second, bandwidth and computer processing power (in a mobile device) is very limited. So robust encryption schemes can really slow down the data throughput.

Finally, wireless networks are made up of two segments: the wireless part and the wired part. If the same encryption scheme is not used on both segments, then at the point where the two segments meet, the data will need to be unencrypted and re-encrypted. It is at that point where the protected data gets exposed, albeit for a short time, and a potential security problem exists.

There are things that make some wireless systems inherently more secure than others. For instance, point-to-point systems are inherently more secure than point-to-multipoint systems. Why? Because point-to-point systems use narrow beam antennas focused on a single point. If you are not in that tightly focused beam, you cannot intercept the signal. Point-to-multipoint systems on the other hand use wide antenna beams focused on many points. These systems provide a lot of opportunity for someone to intercept the signal. Likewise, infrared systems are inherently more secure than RF systems because the signals cannot penetrate walls.

Protocols

Regardless of the type of system, data should be secured when transported wirelessly. The primary tool used to transport data securely (wirelessly or otherwise) is encryption. Encryption makes the data indecipherable to anyone who sees it except the intended receiver. How does encryption work? The process is very similar to that of direct sequence spread spectrum (DSSS). Recall that in DSSS, a pseudo random number (PN) is logically combined with the data. The result is a meaningless data string until the reverse process (de-spreading) is applied to it at the receiver. Encryption works in a similar manner, only instead of using a pseudo random number, a special number, called a *key,* is used to "multiply" the data. The key is a very long number and is (theoretically) only known by the sender and receiver. The reason spread spectrum is not secure by itself is because often the PN number is known by everyone.

Encryption only works if both the sender and receiver agree on the specifics of the encryption process. These specifics are called *protocols*, and in the wireless world there are only two of any consequence (today).

The first one is called WEP, or Wired Equivalent Privacy. WEP is the standard for encryption in 802.11 wireless LANs. WEP uses either a 40 bit or 128 bit key to encrypt the data and the same key is used for both encrypting and decrypting. One weakness with WEP is that many times a single key is shared between all the mobile stations and access points. Also, there has been a lot of testing recently, which has found security holes within WEP. Stay tuned.

The other protocol is WTLS, or Wireless Transport Layer Security. WTLS is the security layer of WAP. WTLS adds security to mobile devices, with little computing power, by making the encryption process efficient. At the present, it suffers from the two encryption problems discussed above. At the WAP gateway, the wireless data must be unencrypted from WTLS and re-encrypted into a wired encryption protocol like Secure Socket Layer (SSL). Work is being done on WTLS to overcome this problem. Stay tuned. The bottom line is that no network, wireless or otherwise, is 100% secure. It is an ongoing battle and requires day-to-day management of the network

Did You Know?

You knew it would not take long. Now there is a term to describe hacking into a wireless network. It is called whacking. Now that you know it, make sure your WAP doesn't get whacked.

Health Concerns

There has been a lot of concern recently about the hazards of exposure to RF radiation, particularly from cellular phones. As much as I would like to tell you that this section will clear everything up for you, it won't. There are two realities you need to face (today) when discussing the effects of RF exposure. First, much of the evidence is still inconclusive. Second, when the evidence finally does become conclusive, it will be statistical in nature. What does that mean? It means that conclusive results will read something like this fictitious statement: People who talk on mobile phones for more than a hour a day are three times more likely to come down with a certain type of cancer than people who do not. Common sense ought to tell you that.

Did You Know?

This should put your mind at ease. Separate studies in the UK and in Finland on human volunteers actually showed improved reaction time from those who used cellular phones compared to those who did not. Take it for what it's worth.

This section briefly discusses the different ways RF energy can be hazardous to you. Hazard effects from RF exposure are a function of at least three different parameters as shown in Table 8–9.

Table 8–9   Parameters Affecting RF Exposure

Parameter	Comment
Frequency	Different frequencies affect the body differently
Power density	The higher the power density, the worse it is
Time duration of exposure	The longer the exposure, the worse it is

Generally speaking, there are two ways electromagnetic energy can adversely affect the human body and they are a function of frequency. The first way is called *ionization*. Above a certain frequency—about where ultraviolet and X-rays occur—a phenomenon called ionization takes place. Here, if the energy is sufficient, electrons can be stripped from atoms. These molecular changes lead to tissue damage, including effects on DNA, which can potentially lead to cancer and birth defects. This explains why ultraviolet rays from the sun can cause skin cancer. At the frequencies at which wireless systems operate, ionization is not a problem.

The other way that electromagnetic energy can adversely affect the human body is through heating. This *thermal* effect causes heating of the body's tissue when the water within it absorbs the RF energy. This is the same phenomenon responsible for heating in microwave ovens. Not surprisingly, the thermal effect is also a function of frequency. The human body most efficiently absorbs RF energy between 30–300 MHz, with the peak somewhere between 80–100 MHz.

Power density is also a critical parameter in determining the amount of body heating from RF energy. The higher the power density, the faster things heat up. As an example, microwave ovens, which produce power densities on the order of 100 mW/cm^2, heat water-based things up very quickly. Measurable tissue heating occurs between 1–10 mW/cm^2. As a comparison, measurements made below a cellular basestation tower show power densities on the order of 1 μW/cm^2 (microwatt). The main thing to know about RF power density is that it decreases exponentially as you move away from the transmitting antenna. Therefore, moving twice as far away cuts the power density by more than half.

The real key to adverse thermal effects of RF radiation is can the body dissipate the heat? Since blood flow is the mechanism the body uses to cool off, the real vulnerable parts of the body are those with the least blood flow, like the eyes and the testes.

The FCC publishes a guide to limits on power density exposure, which is summarized in Table 8–10. There are several things to note when viewing Table 8–10. First, it applies to the general population in uncontrolled exposures. Second, it applies to whole-body exposure. A separate table is used for partial-body exposure (like that from a cellular phone). Third, it is an average measured over a 30-minute period. Since most people do not measure their personal RF exposure, as long as these maximum limits are never exceeded, everything should be okay. And finally, if you look closely, you will notice that some of the limits are a function of frequency as represented by the letter "f."

Table 8–10 *Power Density Limits*

Frequency (MHz)	Maximum allowable power density (mW/cm^2)
0.3–1.34	100
1.34–30	$(180/f^2)$
30–300	0.2
300–1500	$f/1500$
1500–100,000	1.0

As mentioned above, a separate table is used for partial-body exposure. I did not reproduce it here as it is somewhat difficult to interpret because it depends on something called the *specific absorption rate* (SAR), measured in W/kg (watts per kilogram). There are only two things you need to know about SAR. First, in the U.S., the maximum allowable uncontrolled exposure (to the head) is 1.6 W/kg and second, the FCC only approves for use cellular phones that do not exceed this limit.

Finally, for power densities below that which can cause measurable body heating, evidence of harmful biological effects is ambiguous and unproven. Such effects have been termed "non-thermal" effects. The bottom line with cellular phones is that you are more likely to be injured in a car accident while you (or somebody else) is talking while driving, than you are from direct exposure to RF energy.

Glossary

Absorption

Describes the process by which RF energy penetrates a material or substance and gets converted to heat. RF energy, of the appropriate frequency, will experience severe absorption when it encounters rain.

Adapter

A short, two-sided connector used to enjoin connectors from different families. It is primarily used to connect a cable (with a connector from one family) to a cable or component (with a connector from a different family).

Air interface

A general term describing any one of several techniques used to increase the signal carrying capacity of a wireless system. Examples include CDMA, TDMA, and FDMA.

Altimeter

A device that uses radar technology to determine an airplane's altitude by reflecting an RF signal off the ground.

Amplifier

An active RF component used to increase the power of an RF signal. Amplifiers come in three varieties: high power, low noise and "other." Other includes variable gain amplifiers and limiting amplifiers. Amplifiers are mostly solid state today, but they can also be traveling wave tubes.

Amplitude modulation

A form of modulation that works by superimposing an information signal onto an RF carrier by varying the amplitude of successive sine waves of the carrier.

Analog

An electrical signal that varies over time and can take on any value between its minimum and maximum values.

Antenna

An RF component used to transform an RF signal, traveling on a conductor, into an airborne wave and vice versa. For antennas to work properly, their size must be similar to that of the wavelength of the signal they are intended to radiate. Antennas can be active or passive components.

Antenna diversity

A technique that uses more than one receiving antenna to help overcome the problem of multipath.

Antenna pattern

A graphical tool used to show a birds-eye view of the RF energy radiating out from an antenna.

Attenuation

Describes the amount by which an RF signal is made smaller as it moves from one point to another. It is used interchangeably with the term insertion loss and it is measured in decibels.

Attenuator

An RF component used to make RF signals smaller by a predetermined amount, which is measured in decibels. There are two general categories of attenuators: fixed and variable. Fixed attenuators are also referred to as pads. There are two categories of variable attenuators: voltage variable attenuators and digital attenuators.

Balanced amplifier

An amplifier configuration that combines two amplifiers in parallel to provide redundancy and improved match.

Bandwidth

A measure of the usable frequency range of a component or application. It equals the difference between the upper frequency and the lower frequency and can be expressed in Hertz or as a percentage.

Baseband

The lowest frequency signal in a transmitter or receiver. It is the modulated RF signal after it is fully downconverted in a receiver or before it is upconverted in a transmitter.

Basestation

The wireless access point of a cellular system. It consists of all the necessary infrastructure to enable wireless communications including a tower, antennas, cables, RF transceivers, and power supplies. It is also referred to as a cell site.

Beamwidth

An angular measure, in degrees (of a circle), used to describe the width of the RF energy radiated from an antenna. It is also a measure of the width of an antenna pattern.

Bidirectional

Used to describe any RF component that works equally well in both directions. It can also be referred to as dual-directional. Antennas are almost always bidirectional while amplifiers are never so.

Bit error rate

A measure of the number of digital bits that are incorrectly received per million. It is a measure of a wireless link's reliability.

Broadband

Used to describe a characteristic of an RF component or wireless application with a "wide" bandwidth. It is also referred to as wideband. A rule of thumb is that any bandwidth greater than 50% is considered broadband.

Broadcasting

An RF system in which a single transmitter is used to communicate with a multitude of geographically dispersed receivers.

Cable assembly

A combination of bulk coaxial cable with coaxial connectors attached to each end.

Capacitor

A small, passive component used to shape electrical signals, which is found in every electrical circuit.

Carrier

An RF signal—ideally a perfect sine wave—which has an information signal superimposed upon it, through modulation, to carry it as a wave over the air.

Cavity

Describes a family of RF components made by utilizing uniquely constructed hollow metal containers. Cavity components are primarily used for high-power applications.

Cell site

See Basestation.

Cellular

A general term used to describe any one of several mobile wireless telephony applications that divide up a given geographical area into smaller sub-regions called cells.

Channel

A frequency subdivision of a bandwidth. Most RF applications divide their allocated bandwidth into different channels.

Chipping rate

The frequency of the chips used in direct sequence spread spectrum.

Chips

A string of 1s and 0s used in direct sequence spread spectrum to spread (and de-spread) the information signal.

Circuit

An organized interconnection of passive and active electrical components to accomplish some electrical objective. A circuit can be further described as analog, digital, or RF, depending on the application.

Circulator

A three-port, passive RF device made of magnets and ferrite material that is used to control the direction of signal flow in an RF circuit.

Coaxial cable

Media used to transport an RF signal. It is comprised of an inner conductor (wire) surrounded by dielectric material (insulator) and covered by an outer conductor (shield). It is frequently referred to by its "RG" number.

Code division multiple access

A type of air interface that describes a technique of adding signal-carrying capacity to a given bandwidth by allowing multiple signals to occupy the same frequency at the same time and assigning each one the unique "address" of the intended receiver. It is also used to describe a form of direct sequence spread spectrum.

Collision avoidance

A radar system, mounted on the front of an automobile, which is used to determine the appropriate driving distance from the car in front.

Combiner

A passive RF device used to add together, in equal proportion, two or more RF signals.

Component

Any object an electrical signal encounters in a circuit. Used interchangeably with the term device, all components are either active or passive.

Connector

A cylindrical, metallic object firmly attached to a cable or component that is used to facilitate joining one to the other. It is also referred to as a coaxial connector.

Continuous wave

Any RF signal that is never turned off. It is primarily used to describe a type of radar in which the transmitter is always on.

Continuous wave radar

A type of radar in which the transmitted signal is always on. See also Doppler radar.

Conversion loss

The insertion loss a signal experiences in a mixer as it goes from the RF port to the IF port or vice versa. It is measured in decibels.

Coupler

A passive RF component in which the input signal is split unevenly and the smaller one is siphoned off to be used somewhere else in the system. This type of coupler can be directional or bidirectional. There is another type of coupler called a Lange or quadrature (or quad) coupler in which the signal is split evenly between two ports, but one of the outputs is phase-shifted from the other. Quad couplers are also referred to as quad hybrids.

Current

Electrons on the move, either on a conductor or inside a component.

Decade

A bandwidth in which the upper frequency is ten times bigger than the lower frequency.

Decibel

A mathematical conversion, utilizing logarithms of a ratio, which is used as a unit of measure for RF signals. It is primarily used to describe the (power) gain and (insertion) loss of RF components.

Demodulation

The process of separating the RF carrier from the information signal in a modulated signal.

Demodulator

An RF device used to perform demodulation. It is a complex component that is comprised of active and passive devices, especially mixers.

Detector

A passive RF component used to convert an RF power signal into a voltage signal. It is used to supply a voltage, which is proportional to the RF power signal, to another component or piece of test equipment that is not designed to handle an RF power signal.

Device

See Component.

Dielectric

Any material that does not conduct electricity (an insulator). When used in the context of RF, dielectric material is a special type of insulator that is designed to minimize the insertion loss of an RF signal being carried on a conductor attached to it.

Digital

An electrical signal that varies over time and can take on only one of two values: high and low.

Digital signal processing

Describes the process of using sophisticated mathematical computations and signal processing to pack a lot of information into a digital signal.

Diode

A semiconductor device used in many RF components. There are several different types of RF diodes that are each manufactured differently to optimize different performance parameters.

Diplexer

See Duplexer.

Dipole

A straight-line (omnidirectional) antenna that is one half of a wavelength long.

Direct broadcast satellite

A high-power, geosynchronous orbit satellite that transmits broadcast signals to be received by small antenna dishes attached to the home.

Direct sequence spread spectrum

A form of spread spectrum in which the signal is spread by encoding it with a pseudo random number.

Directional coupler

A coupler that only works in one direction.

Discrete component

An electrical component that performs a single function and is housed in its own package.

Distributed circuit

A type of RF circuit philosophy in which some passive components are made from uniquely shaped circuit traces.

Divider

A passive RF device that equally divides an RF signal into two or more RF signals.

Doppler radar

A type of radar that utilizes the return signal's frequency shift to determine an object's velocity.

Downconverter

Another name for a mixer in a receiver, it is used to lower the frequency of the RF signal.

Downlink

The path an RF signal travels from a satellite to the ground.

Downstream

The path an RF signal travels from a base-station to the end user.

Dual directional coupler

A coupler that works equally well in both directions.

Dual mode

Describes mobile phones that can communicate in both first-generation cellular (analog) and second-generation cellular (digital) modes.

Duplex

Describes an RF system that has the ability to transmit and receive simultaneously. Used most frequently with regard to telephony.

Duplexer

A passive RF device that contains two band-pass filters with different passbands. It is also called a diplexer.

Dynamic range

A measure of how large a signal an RF component can handle without distorting it. It is the key performance parameter of any device operating in a digital wireless system. One measure of a component's dynamic range is its third order intercept point, measured in dBm. Sometimes the dynamic range is specified as a combination of a component's third order intercept and its noise figure. The term is often used interchangeably with the term linearity.

Earth station

The name given to the ground facilities that communicate with a satellite.

Effective isotropic radiated power

A mathematically derived measure of the effective power leaving an antenna, which is calculated by comparing the actual power leaving the antenna to that of an isotropic antenna. It is also used to describe the amount of RF energy from a satellite that reaches the Earth within the satellite antenna's footprint.

Electronically scanned array

An antenna, made up of many small transceivers, that can sweep an antenna pattern without moving anything mechanically.

Feedback

An electrical circuit technique whereby a signal at one point in the system is sampled and "fed back" to a prior point in the system and used to make adjustments or corrections.

Ferrite

A composite material with excellent magnetic properties used to make isolators, circulators, and transformers.

Filter

A passive RF component that passes or rejects a signal solely on the basis of its frequency. There are four main categories of filters: low pass, high pass, band pass, and band reject.

Fire control radar

A type of radar system, used in fighter aircraft, to control the targeting of a missile.

Footprint

The antenna pattern that the antenna on a satellite projects onto the Earth.

Free space loss

Describes the attenuation a signal experiences as it travels away from an antenna. It is the result of the signal spreading out as it moves.

Frequency

The measure of how many complete sine wave cycles occur in one second in an RF signal, measured in Hertz.

Frequency division duplexing

Dividing up a frequency range into two different frequency ranges for the specific purpose of accommodating a two-way conversation. Each frequency range is used solely to carry information in one direction.

Frequency division multiple access

A type of air interface that describes a technique of adding signal-carrying capacity to a given bandwidth by dividing it up into smaller frequency bands.

Frequency division multiplexing

Dividing a frequency range into multiple, smaller frequency ranges, usually for the purpose of sending multiple signals.

Frequency hopping spread spectrum

A spread spectrum technique that involves constantly changing the RF carrier's frequency in such a way that only the intended receiver can decipher it.

Frequency modulation

A form of modulation that works by superimposing an information signal onto an RF carrier by varying the frequency of successive sine waves of the carrier.

Frequency response

A graph of amplitude gain or loss, versus frequency, for an RF component. It is used to describe how the particular component behaves as the signal's frequency changes.

Frequency reuse

Describes the unique feature of mobile wireless telephone services in which more than one party can use the same exact frequency, at the same time, in a given geographical location.

Gain

The increase in size of the output signal of an amplifier with respect to the input signal. It is measured in decibels.

Gallium Arsenide

A compound semiconductor material, made of Gallium and Arsenic, used to make RF diodes and transistors. It is the preferred semiconductor material choice for very high frequency RF products.

Geostationary orbit
See Geosynchronous orbit.

Geosynchronous orbit
An orbit, 22,000 miles above Earth, in which satellites rotate around the Earth at the same speed as the Earth's rotation, giving them the appearance of not moving.

Global positioning system
A system of 24 satellites that continuously transmit special signals used by special receivers to determine location.

Handoff
Describes the process whereby a mobile telephone call is transferred from one cell site to another with no interruption of service.

Hertz
The unit of measure for frequency, it measures a signal's "cycles per second."

Hybrid
When used in the context of circuit technologies, it is used to describe an RF circuit made by combining chips and discrete components onto a ceramic substrate, which is also referred to as a microwave integrated circuit (MIC). When used in the context of coupling, it describes a Lange coupler.

Impedance
A measure of an RF component's input and output "size," expressed in ohms. In RF systems, the standard size used by all components is 50 ohms.

Impedance matching
The process of converting the output impedance of some RF device—which is not 50 ohms—to 50 ohms, so that it can be operatively connected to some other component.

Impedance ratio
A number used to quantify a transformer's ability to convert one impedance value to another. A transformer with a two-to-one (2:1) impedance ratio can convert a 100 ohm impedance to 50 ohms.

Inductor
A small passive component used to shape electrical signals, which is made by winding a wire into a spiral. It is found in most electrical circuits.

Insertion loss
A measure of how much smaller the output signal of a passive device is with respect to the input signal. It is measured in decibels.

Insulator
Any material that does not conduct electricity.

Integrated circuit
Combining more than one active and/or passive device onto a single piece of semiconductor material.

Intercept point
See Third order intercept.

Interference
Any unintended or unwanted RF energy that interferes with the proper reception of the intended signal at the receiver.

Interleaving
Describes the process of alternately combining the voice information and the signal information when conducting a cellular call.

Intermediate frequency
The name of the signal between the two mixers in a two mixer receiver. It is also used to identify one of the ports of a mixer.

Interrogator

That part of a wireless RFID system that is used to detect and communicate with the transponder.

Isolation

A measure of the insertion loss in the "open" path of an RF switch, or between any two ports in a passive RF component. Like insertion loss, it is measured in decibels.

Isolator

A two-port passive RF device made of magnets and ferrite material that is used to protect other RF components from excessive signal reflection. Isolators are circulators in which the third port is connected to a heat-dissipating load.

Lange coupler

See Coupler.

Limiting amplifier

An amplifier that is used to protect the RF device that comes after it by limiting its output power to a predetermined level, regardless of the input power.

Linearity

See Dynamic range.

Local loop

The telephone circuit from the home (or office) to the local telephone company and back.

Local multipoint distribution service

A fixed wireless application operating around 28 GHz that is ideally suited for wireless local loop service.

Local oscillator

The source of a perfect sine signal, it is connected to one of the ports of a mixer.

Loss

A measure of the decrease in size of an output signal from a passive component, with respect to the input signal. It is measured in decibels.

Lumped element circuit

A type of RF circuit philosophy that utilizes packaged passive components.

Macrocell

The family of cell sites with the greatest signal carrying capacity. They require relatively high power RF transmission.

Match

A measure of how perfectly two RF components "fit" together, which results in less of the RF signal between them being reflected. Match is measured by VSWR, which is expressed as a ratio of X:1, and by return loss, which is measured in decibels.

Microcell

The family of cell sites that results from subdividing macrocells. They require a relatively moderate amount of transmitted RF power.

Microelectromechanical systems

Describes a family of integrated circuits in which a part of the circuit actually moves.

Microwave

A term loosely used to describe a range of frequencies between 1 and 40 GHz.

Microwave integrated circuit

See Hybrid.

Millimeter wave

A term loosely used to describe a range of frequencies greater than 40 GHz.

Mixer

A three-port RF component used to change the frequency of one of the input signals. It is sometimes referred to as an upconverter (in a transmitter) or a downconverter (in a receiver). Mixers can be active or passive devices, although most are passive.

Mobile commerce

Also called m-commerce. Describes a set of wireless applications in which a mobile device is used to transact business.

Mobile switching center

The central communications hub of a cellular telephone system that is responsible for routing all the calls from the various basestations to other basestations, or to the public switched telephone network and for billing. It is also referred to as the mobile telephone switching office.

Mobile telephone switching office

See Mobile switching center.

Modem

A modulator and demodulator combined in a single unit.

Modulation

Superimposing an information signal onto an RF carrier by varying some aspect of the carrier. There are two fundamental types of modulation: amplitude modulation and phase modulation. Frequency modulation is a subset of phase modulation.

Modulator

A device that superimposes an information signal onto an RF carrier. It has two inputs (the carrier and the information signal) and one output (the modulated signal).

Monocycle

A single, isolated sine wave.

Monolithic microwave integrated circuit

An integrated circuit designed for RF purposes. It can be made of several different semiconductor materials, but the two most common are Silicon and Gallium Arsenide.

Monopole

A straight line (omnidirectional) antenna that is one quarter of a wavelength long.

Multipath

The phenomenon in which a single wireless signal takes two different paths to the intended receiver.

Narrowband

Used to describe a characteristic of an RF component or wireless application with a "narrow" bandwidth. A rule of thumb is that any bandwidth less than 50% is considered narrowband.

Noise

Any unwanted changes to an RF signal. Noise usually manifests itself as unwanted changes in the sine wave's amplitude, referred to as AM noise, although FM noise is also possible. Mixers are notorious for injecting noise onto an RF signal.

Noise figure

A measure of how much noise an RF component injects onto an RF signal. Noise figure, which is measured in decibels, is most often mentioned with regard to low noise amplifiers.

Notch filter

Also called a band reject filter, it allows all frequencies to pass except those in a narrowly defined frequency range.

Octave

Describes a bandwidth in which the upper frequency is twice as big as the lower frequency.

Omnidirectional

Describes an antenna that radiates RF energy out equally in all directions.

Oscillator

An active RF component with a sole purpose to produce a perfect sine wave at a predetermined frequency. It is also referred to as a source.

Pad

A fixed attenuator (its insertion loss is constant).

Passband

The frequency range of a bandpass filter that has low insertion loss and therefore allows the signal to pass. A passband is defined by identifying its upper and lower frequency.

Personal area network

A form of local area network in which a human being, carrying a mobile wireless device, acts as the access point of the network.

Personal communication services

Second generation (digital) cellular services in the United States.

Phase locked loop

An oscillator that incorporates feedback in an effort to produce a more perfect sine wave. A phase locked loop can be part of a very sophisticated oscillator called a synthesizer.

Phase modulation

A form of modulation that works by superimposing an information signal onto an RF carrier by varying the phase of successive sine waves of the carrier. This modulation has a similar effect to frequency modulation.

Picocell

The smallest family of cell sites. They provide for the least signal carrying capacity, cover the smallest area, and require the lowest amount of transmitted RF power.

Piconet

A wireless network using the Bluetooth protocol, which contains up to eight nodes.

Polarization

Refers to the fact that RF sine waves have spatial orientation to them as they travel in the air. The three types of polarization are horizontal, vertical, and circular.

Power density

A measure of the RF energy in the air that passes through a given area and has the unit of watts per square meter.

Power divider

See Divider.

Printed circuit board

Describes a circuit technology in which metal traces are mounted on a plastic composite material that is used to interconnect electrical components. The motherboard inside a personal computer uses a printed circuit board.

Propagation delay

The time it takes for a signal to travel from the Earth to a satellite and back again. For satellites in geosynchronous orbit, the delay is about a quarter of a second.

Pseudo random noise

A digital bit stream that appears random (when viewed on a spectrum analyzer), but in reality repeats itself over some long period of time.

Quadrature (Quad) coupler
See Coupler.

Quadrature (Quad) hybrid
See Coupler.

Radar
A wireless system that uses reflected RF energy to detect an object's range, location, and velocity.

Radar cross section
The effective area to reflect RF energy of an object being sensed by radar.

Radiate
A term used to describe the process by which an RF signal changes into an airborne wave.

Radio frequency
Shame on you. Used to identify a class of high frequency electrical signals intended to be radiated as waves. It is also used to describe a range of frequencies less than 1 GHz.

Radome
A hard protective shell that covers an antenna and protects it from the elements while letting the RF pass through it.

Receiver
One of the two main building blocks of a wireless system that is responsible for collecting the RF energy from the antenna and reducing the signal's frequency down to where it can be accepted by the demodulator.

Reflection
A term used to describe an RF signal's behavior when it encounters an impedance mismatch or a solid object. With an impedance mismatch, some (or all) of the RF energy is reflected back in the direction from which it came. With a solid object, the RF energy bounces off the object at the same angle at which it encountered it.

Repeater
A general term used to describe an RF system that is designed to geographically extend the RF coverage of a macrocell.

Resistor
A small, passive component used to reduce the size of electrical signals that is found in every electrical circuit.

Return loss
A measure of match between two RF components, expressed in decibels. The better the match—the less energy reflected—the higher the return loss.

Saturation
The behavior of all amplifiers when the input power exceeds a certain point, the amplifier no longer amplifies, and the output is more or less constant. When an amplifier is in the saturated region, it is said to be non-linear and it causes distortion to the RF signal.

Scanning
Electrically or mechanically moving a radar's antenna pattern to achieve radar coverage over a large area.

Self-resonant frequency
The frequency at which an object will oscillate if sufficiently excited by electrical energy. Almost all solid objects have a self-resonant frequency.

Signal
Electrical energy that is made to vary, over time, in a controlled manner.

Silicon
A semiconductor material used to make RF diodes and transistors. Because it is low

cost, it is the preferred material choice for low-frequency RF products.

Simplex
Describes an RF system that can only transmit in one direction at a time.

Skin effect
A term used to describe an RF signal's behavior when it is on a conductor. Because of their high frequency, RF signals do not penetrate into a solid conductor, but rather exist exclusively on the outer surface.

Source
See Oscillator.

Specialized mobile radio
A cellular-like service in the United States that combines standard cellular operation with dispatch capability.

Spectral efficiency
A measure of the data-carrying capacity of a wireless system, which has the units of bits per second per Hertz.

Spectrum
A term used to describe a range of frequencies for a specific application.

Spectrum analyzer
A tool used by RF engineers to visualize the RF energy over some range of frequencies. It is a plot with the horizontal axis in units of frequency and the vertical axis in units of power.

Spread spectrum
A digital modulation scheme that increases the signal carrying capacity of a given bandwidth by allowing multiple signals to occupy the same frequency and distinguishing each one by its unique "address."

Station keeping
The practice, by satellites, of using small bursts of propellant to change position to ensure that they do not stray very far from their intended location in geosynchronous orbit.

Stopband
The frequency range of a band reject filter that has high insertion loss and therefore stops signals from passing. A stopband is defined by identifying its upper and lower frequency.

Subassembly
See Subsystem.

Subsystem
An RF item, in a single container, that performs more than one function and utilizes more than one component. For example, a combination of a mixer, a filter, and an amplifier in a single box is considered a subsystem.

Surface acoustic wave
An electrical signal converted to a sound wave. In surface acoustic wave devices, the sound wave travels along the surface of the device, rather than inside of it.

Switch
An active RF component that switches a single input between one or more outputs. RF switches are characterized by their number of poles (switches) and throws (outputs).

Synthesizer
A very sophisticated oscillator incorporating other electronic circuitry, plus feedback, to make a more perfect sine wave.

T/R switch

A single-pole, double-throw switch situated between a transmitter, a receiver, and an antenna.

Thermal impedance

A measure of how hot a component gets for a given amount of power dissipated. It is expressed in °C/Watt.

Third order intercept

The measure of an RF component's linearity or dynamic range, expressed in dBm. It is also referred to as the intercept point. The higher the measure, the more linear the component and the less distortion of the RF signal.

Time division duplexing

Dividing up a single communication channel into multiple time slots for the specific purpose of accommodating a two-way conversation. Alternating time slots are used for alternating directions.

Time division multiple access

A type of air interface that describes a technique of adding signal-carrying capacity by breaking up each frequency allocation into multiple time slots and assigning each signal a specific slot.

Trace

A small, thin piece of metal on a dielectric material used to carry signals.

Transceiver

A combination transmitter and receiver in a single package.

Transfer curve

A graph of output power versus input power of an amplifier.

Transformer

A passive RF component used in impedance matching, among other things. It is defined by its impedance ratio.

Transistor

A semiconductor device utilized primarily in amplifiers to create gain, they can also be used by other RF components to perform switching. There are many different varieties of transistors that are made from different semiconductor materials.

Transmitter

One of the two main building blocks in a wireless system that is responsible for taking the signal from the modulator, increasing its frequency and power, then radiating it out the antenna.

Transponder

An RF subsystem on board a satellite that is responsible for receiving the uplink signal, converting it to the downlink frequency, and then re-transmitting it. It is also the name given to that part of a wireless RFID system that gets detected by the interrogator.

Traveling wave tube

An older technology RF amplifier that amplifies RF signals in a vacuum inside a cavity.

Triangulation

A method for determining position by receiving three different wireless signals from three different locations.

Triplexer

A passive RF device that contains three bandpass filters with different passbands.

Tuner

An RF device, used in a receiver, to frequency select individual channels.

Upconverter

Another name for a mixer used in a transmitter, which is used to raise the frequency of the RF signal.

Uplink

The path an RF signal travels from the ground to a satellite.

Upstream

The path an RF signal travels from the end user to the basestation.

Varactor

A diode used to vary the frequency in a voltage controlled oscillator.

Variable gain amplifier

An amplifier with an external control that is used to vary its gain.

Very small aperture terminal

An RF system in which many small Earth stations use a satellite to communicate with a single receiver.

Voltage

Electrical potential. There are two types: AC (alternating), like the kind in a wall outlet, and DC (direct), like the kind in a battery.

Voltage controlled oscillator

An oscillator with an external control that is used to vary its output frequency.

Voltage standing wave ratio

A measure of match between two RF components, expressed as a ratio of X:1. The lower the X, the better the match.

Watts

Unit of measure for any kind of power, e.g., RF, heat, etc.

Waveguide

Pipes, with rectangular cross sections, used to carry RF signals from one point to another. Inside, the RF signals move as waves and the waveguide serves to guide and control their movement.

Wavelength

A measure of the length of an RF signal. The higher a signal's frequency, the shorter its wavelength.

Wideband

See Broadband.

Wireless

A marketing term, generally used to describe the newer RF applications.

Wireless local area networks

A local area network of computers that communicate via wireless signals.

Wireless local loop

An RF system that allows communication with the local telephone company, wirelessly.

Appendix A—Acronyms

This appendix includes the most commonly used acronyms in the RF and wireless industry. Some of the more arcane acronyms have been omitted because they do not experience widespread use. Because of the nature of the wireless industry, this list will almost certainly be incomplete. (The darn engineers can abbreviate things faster than publishers can publish.)

A/D   *Analog to digital,* signal conversion.

AC   *Alternating current,* power from a wall outlet.

ADC   *Analog to digital conversion,* signal conversion.

AGC   *Automatic gain control,* control of a variable gain amplifier.

AM   *Amplitude modulation,* a type of modulation.

AMPS   *Advanced mobile phone service,* first generation cellular in the United States.

ASIC   *Application specific integrated circuit,* a custom integrated circuit.

BER   *Bit error rate,* the number of errors per second in a transmitted signal.

BJT   *Bipolar junction transistor,* a type of transistor.

BLAST   *Bell Labs layered space time,* a new air interface.

BPF   *Band pass filter,* a type of filter.

BPSK   *Bi-phase shift keying,* a type of phase modulation.

BSS   *Basic service set,* all the computers in a section of a wireless LAN.

BTA   *Basic trading area,* a small geographical area allocated for PCS.

BTS   *Base transceiver station,* cellular basestation.

CCK   *Complimentary code keying,* a form of modulation used in wireless LANs.

CDMA   *Code division multiple access,* spread spectrum for mobile phones.

CDPD   *Cellular digital packet data,* wireless data communication using cellular phones.

CL   *Conversion loss,* the insertion loss of a mixer.

CONUS   *Continental United States,* geography covered by some satellites.

CW   *Continuous wave,* an RF system in which the transmitter is always on.

D/A   *Digital to analog,* signal conversion.

DAC   *Digital to analog conversion,* signal conversion.

D-AMPS   *Digital AMPS,* a digital version of AMPS.

dB   *Decibels,* a relative measure of signal strength.

DBS   *Direct broadcast satellite,* TV signals from satellites direct to the home.

DC   *Direct current,* power from a battery.

DCS   *Digital communication services,* second generation cellular in Europe.

DECT   *Digital enhanced cordless telephone,* an international standard.

DGPS   *Differential GPS,* more accurate GPS.

DPDT   *Double pole-double throw,* a type of RF switch.

DQPSK *Differential quadrature phase shift keying,* a type of phase modulation.

DRO *Dielectric resonator oscillator,* a type of oscillator.

DSL *Digital subscriber line,* a high speed telephone connection.

DSP *Digital signal processing (*or *processor),* a type of electrical signal processing.

DSSS *Direct sequence spread spectrum,* a type of spread spectrum.

DTH *Direct to home,* a type of satellite service.

DTO *Dielectrically tuned oscillator,* a variable DRO.

DVB *Digital video broadcast,* broadcast which modulates a digital signal.

EAS *Electronic article surveillance,* an RFID application.

EDGE *Enhanced data rate for global (GSM) evolution,* an advanced GSM system.

EGPRS *Enhanced GRPS,* enhanced GPRS.

EHF *Extremely high frequency,* frequency between 30 and 300 GHz.

EIRP *Effective isotropic radiated power,* the power radiated from a satellite's antenna.

EMC *Electromagnetic compatibility,* acceptable levels of EMI.

EMI *Electromagnetic interference,* a type of RF noise.

ESS *Extended service set,* all of the computers in a wireless LAN.

FCC *Federal Communications Commission,* U.S. government airwaves regulators.

FDD *Frequency division duplexing,* duplexing signals by frequency.

FDMA *Frequency division multiple access,* breaks up conversations by frequency.

FET *Field effect transistor,* a type of transistor.

FHSS   *Frequency hopping spread spectrum,* a type of spread spectrum.

FM   *Frequency modulation,* a type of modulation.

FSK   *Frequency shift keying,* a type of digital modulation.

FSS   *Fixed satellite systems (or service),* a type of satellite service.

GaAs   *Gallium Arsenide,* a type of semiconductor material.

GEO   *Geosynchronous orbit,* 22,000 miles above Earth.

GMSK   *Gaussian minimum shift keying,* a type of phase modulation.

GPS   *Global positioning system,* a satellite constellation used to deter-mine location.

GRPS   *Generalized packet radio system,* an advanced GSM system.

GSM   *Group special mobile,* a popular cellular standard in Europe.

HBT   *Heterojunction bipolar transistor,* a new type of fast transistor.

HDTV   *High definition television,* next generation digital TV.

HEMT   *High electron mobility transistor,* a very high frequency transistor.

HF   *High frequency,* frequency between 3 and 30 MHz.

HPA   *High power amplifier,* a type of amplifier used at the output of a transmitter.

HPF   *High pass filter,* a type of filter.

Hz   *Hertz,* the measure of a signal's frequency in cycles per second.

IC   *Integrated circuit,* multiple electrical components on a single semiconductor.

IEEE   *Institute of Electrical and Electronics Engineers,* a standards body.

IF   *Intermediate frequency,* one of the signals used by a mixer.

IL   *Insertion loss,* the loss a signal experiences in a passive component.

IMD   *Intermodulation distortion,* a type of RF signal noise.

IMT   *International mobile telephone*, third generation cellular.

InP   *Indium phosphide*, a compound semiconductor material used in RF.

IrDA   *Infrared data association*, a standards body for infrared communications.

ISM   *Industrial, Scientific, Medical*, a family of frequency allocations for such use.

ISP   *Internet service (or satellite) provider*, supplies Internet service.

ITU   *International Telecommunications Union*, the FCC for the world.

JTACS   *Japan TACS*, Japanese version of TACS.

Kbps   *Kilobits per second*, thousands of bits per second.

LAN   *Local area network*, computers hooked together.

LCC   *Leadless chip carrier*, a type of RF component package.

LDMOS   *Laterally diffused metal oxide semiconductor*, a type of transistor.

LED   *Light emitting diode*, a diode which gives off light.

LEO   *Low Earth orbit*, a few hundred miles above Earth.

LHC   *Left hand circular*, a type of polarization.

LMCS   *Local multipoint communications system*, a high frequency set of applications.

LMDS   *Local multipoint distribution service*, a high frequency fixed wireless service.

LMR   *Land mobile radio*, a wireless application.

LNA   *Low noise amplifier*, a type of amplifier, used at the input of a receiver.

LNB   *Low noise block converter*, an LNA and a mixer in the same package.

LO   *Local oscillator*, one of the inputs to a mixer.

LOS   *Line of sight,* when the transmitting antenna can see the receiving antenna.

LPF   *Low pass filter,* a type of filter.

LTCC   *Low temperature co-fired ceramic,* a multilayer MIC circuit.

Mbps   *Megabits per second,* millions of bits per second.

MCM   *Multi-chip module,* an RF subsystem hybrid.

MCPA   *Multi-carrier power amplifier,* a type of very linear power amplifier.

MDS   *Multipoint distribution service,* a set of wireless services.

MEMS   *Microelectromechanical systems,* ICs with moving parts.

MEO   *Medium Earth orbit,* between LEO and GEO.

MESFET   *Metal semiconductor field effect transistor,* a high frequency transistor.

MIC   *Microwave integrated circuit,* a particular circuit technology.

MMDS   *Multichannel multipoint distribution service,* a wireless service.

MMIC   *Monolithic microwave integrated circuit,* an RF integrated circuit.

MOSFET   *Metal oxide semiconductor field effect transistor,* a low frequency transistor.

MSA   *Metropolitan statistical area,* an urban geographical area allocated to cellular.

MSC   *Mobile switching center,* the brains of the cellular system.

MSK   *Minimum shift keying,* a type of phase modulation.

MSS   *Mobile satellite systems (or service),* a type of satellite service.

MTA   *Metropolitan trading area,* a large geographical area allocated for PCS.

MTSO   *Mobile telephone switching office,* the brains of the cellular system.

NADC   *North American digital cellular,* a digital cellular standard.

NF	*Noise figure,* the measure of quietness of an LNA.
NLOS	*Non-line of sight,* when the transmitting antenna can't see the receiving antenna.
NMT	*Nordic mobile telephone,* a cellular standard used in Scandinavian countries.
NODS	*Near object detection system,* a radar system for the rear bumper of a car.
OCXO	*Oven controlled crystal oscillator,* a type of oscillator.
OEM	*Original equipment manufacturer,* a manufacturer.
OFDM	*Orthogonal frequency division multiplexing,* a new type of frequency multiplexing.
PA	*Power amplifier,* same as HPA.
PACS	*Personal access communication systems,* U.S. version of PHS.
PAE	*Power added efficiency,* a measure of a power amplifier's efficiency.
PAN	*Personal area network,* a wireless network that moves with the person.
PCB	*Printed circuit board,* a particular circuit technology.
PCN	*Personal communications network,* a new wireless application.
PCS	*Personal communication services,* second generation cellular in the United States.
PDA	*Personal digital assistant,* a fancy new gadget.
PDC	*Personal digital cellular,* a Japanese cellular standard.
PHEMT	*Pseudomorphic high electron mobility transistor,* a very high frequency transistor.
PHS	*Personal handyphone system:* Japanese cellular phone standard.
PLL	*Phase locked loop,* a feedback technique used in an oscillator.

PLO   *Phase locked oscillator,* an oscillator which utilizes a PLL.

PM   *Phase modulation,* a type of modulation.

PN   *Pseudo random noise,* a noise-like signal used in spread spectrum.

POTS   *Plain old telephone system,* the system used to make landline calls in the U.S.

PSTN   *Public switched telephone network,* the local phone company.

QAM   *Quadrature amplitude modulation,* a type of amplitude modulation.

QPSK   *Quadrature phase shift keying,* a type of phase modulation.

RBOC   *Regional Bell operating company,* the baby Bells.

RF   *Radio frequency,* shame on you.

RFI   *Radio frequency interference,* unwanted RF signals.

RFIC   *Radio frequency integrated circuit,* self explanatory.

RFID   *Radio frequency identification,* a wireless application for tracking things.

RHC   *Right hand circular,* a type of polarization.

RSA   *Rural statistical area,* a rural geographical area allocated for cellular.

SAR   *Specific absorption rate,* a measure of thermal heating of the body.

SAW   *Surface acoustic wave,* an electrical signal as a sound wave.

SDMA   *Spatial division multiple access,* dividing up a wireless system spatially.

Si   *Silicon,* a type of semiconductor material.

SiGe   *Silicon germanium,* a compound semiconductor material used in RF.

SMR   *Specialized mobile radio,* a cellular-like mobile phone service.

SMS   *Short message service,* a wireless application.

SMT	*Surface mount technology,* a method of mounting components on a PCB.
SPDT	*Single pole-double throw,* a type of switch.
SPST	*Single pole-single throw,* a type of switch.
SSPA	*Solid state power amplifier,* a power amplifier made from transistors.
TACS	*Total access communications systems,* similar to AMPS.
TCXO	*Temperature controlled crystal oscillator,* a type of oscillator.
TDD	*Time division duplexing,* duplexing signals by time.
TDMA	*Time division multiple access,* breaking up signals into multiple time slots.
THSS	*Time hopping spread spectrum,* a form of spread spectrum.
TVRO	*Television receive only,* a television service.
TWT	*Traveling wave tube,* a type of RF amplifier.
TWTA	*Traveling wave tube amplifier,* same as a TWT.
UHF	*Ultra high frequency,* frequency between 300 MHz and 3 GHz.
UMTS	*Universal mobile telecommunications system,* a 3G cellular system.
UNII	*Unlicensed national information infrastructure,* an unlicensed frequency band.
UWB	*Ultra wideband,* wider than wideband.
VCO	*Voltage controlled oscillator,* a type of oscillator.
VCXO	*Voltage controlled crystal oscillator,* a type of oscillator.
VGA	*Variable gain amplifier,* a type of amplifier.
VHF	*Very high frequency,* any frequency between 30 and 300 MHz.

VSAT   *Very small aperture terminal,* a multipoint-to-point satellite system.

VSWR   *Voltage standing wave ratio,* the measure of a component's match.

VTO   *Voltage tuned oscillator,* same as VCO.

VVA   *Voltage variable attenuator,* an attenuator whose attenuation can vary.

WAP   *Wireless application protocol,* a wireless protocol for mobile devices.

WCDMA   *Wideband CDMA,* CDMA used for PCS telephony.

WEP   *Wired equivalent privacy,* security measures for a WLAN.

WLAN   *Wireless local area network,* computers connected without wires.

WLL   *Wireless local loop,* wireless local telephone service.

WML   *Wireless markup language,* the markup language for WAP.

WTLS   *Wireless layer transport security,* the security protocol for WAP.

YIG   *Yttrium-Iron-Garnet,* an alloy used in oscillators.

YTO   *YIG tuned oscillator,* a tunable YIG oscillator.

Appendix B—Specifications

This appendix is intended for people working in the RF industry who need to understand the arcane language of component performance. Contained herein are the most common electrical performance characteristics of RF components. Each parameter is broken down by its specification name, its most common symbol or acronym, the unit of measure, and where it is most often used.

Specification	Symbol or Acronym	Unit of Measure	Typically Measures
Amplitude unbalance		dB	The difference in insertion loss on two paths of a power divider.
Attenuation		dB	The amount of signal loss in an attenuator or other passive component.
Bandwidth	BW	MHz, GHz	The useful frequency range of a component.
Bit error rate	BER	10^{-6}	The number of digital bit errors per one million bits received.
Compression point (output)	P_1dB	dBm	The linear power output capability of a component.
Compression point (input)		dBm	The linear power input capability of a component.
Conversion gain		dB	The signal gain in an active mixer.
Conversion loss	CL	dB	The insertion loss in a passive mixer.

Specification	Symbol or Acronym	Unit of Measure	Typically Measures
Coupling		dB	The amount of the signal which is "siphoned off" in a directional coupler.
Directivity		dB	The ability of a directional coupler to direct RF energy onto the desired port.
Gain	G	dB	The amount a signal increases as it passes through an amplifier.
Gain flatness	ΔG	dB	How much the gain of an amplifier varies over its bandwidth.
Harmonics (suppression)		dBc	The amount of unwanted signals, in a particular bandwidth, which are a frequency multiple of the desired signal.
Image rejection		dB	The amount of attenuation of the unwanted signal coming out of a mixer.
Impedance	Ω	ohms	The resistance a signal experiences when entering a component.
Impedance ratio	N:1		The impedance changing ability of a transformer.
Insertion loss	IL	dB	The loss a signal experiences as it travels through a passive component.
Intermodulation distortion	IMD	dBc	The amount of unwanted signals as a result of mixing two signals.
Isolation	ISOL	dB	The insertion loss in the open path of a switch, or between two ports on a passive device.

Specification	Symbol or Acronym	Unit of Measure	Typically Measures
Match	VSWR		How well a signal is transferred from one component to another.
Noise figure	NF	dB	The input sensitivity of a low noise amplifier.
Noise temperature		°K	The input sensitivity of very low noise figure LNAs.
Phase noise		dBc/Hz	Signal distortion resulting from unintended phase modulation.
Phase shift	$\Delta\phi$	degrees	The angular shift in an RF signal as it travels through a component.
Phase unbalance		degrees	The difference in phase shift on two paths of a power divider.
Power added efficiency	PAE	%	The efficiency with which a power amplifier turns DC power into RF power.
Power density		W/m^2	The RF energy in the air which passes through a given area.
Pulling factor		MHz	The change in the output frequency of an oscillator when the input impedance of the device it is driving changes.
Pushing factor		MHz/V	The change in the output frequency of an oscillator when the power supply voltage changes.
Return loss	RL	dB	The amount of the signal which is reflected at the interface of two components.
Reverse isolation	S_{12}	dB	The isolation from the output to the input of a component.
Saturated power	Psat	dBm	The maximum amount of power an amplifier can put out.

Specification	Symbol or Acronym	Unit of Measure	Typically Measures
Second order intercept	Ip2	dBm	The linearity of a component.
Selectivity	Q		The efficiency of a filter to tune out unwanted frequencies.
Settling time		msec	The time it takes for a VCO's output to stabilize after a frequency change.
Spectral efficiency		bps/Hertz	The data carry capacity of a wireless system.
Spurious noise (spurs)		dBc	Random noise in an RF signal.
Stability		ppm	The change in output frequency of an oscillator over time.
Switching time	t_{sw}	msec, nsec	The time for a switch to change positions.
Thermal impedance	θjc	°C/W	The rise in temperature of a component which is dissipating power.
Third order intercept (output)	Ip3, OIP	dBm	The linearity of a component's output signal.
Third order intercept (input)	IIP	dBm	The linearity of a component's input signal.
Tuning sensitivity		MHz/V	The change in the output frequency of a VCO with a change in the control voltage.

Bibliography

Chang, Kai, *Handbook of Microwave and Optical Components, Volume 1*, John Wiley & Sons, 1989.

Cheung, Stephen W., and Levien, Frederic H., *Microwaves Made Simple*, Artech House, 1985.

Danzer, Paul, *The ARRL Handbook for Radio Amateurs*, American Radio Relay League, 1999.

Dornan, Andy, *The Essential Guide to Wireless Communications Applications*, Prentice Hall, 2001.

Elbert, Bruce R., *Introduction to Satellite Communications,* Artech House, 1987.

Hurn, Jeff, *GPS: A Guide to the Next Utility*, Trimble Navigation, 1989.

Lebow, Irwin, *Information Highways & Byways*, IEEE Press, New York, 1995.

Nellist, John G., *Understanding Telecommunications and Lightwave Systems*, IEEE Press, New York, 1992.

Smith, Clint, *Practical Cellular & PCS Design*, McGraw-Hill, New York, 1998.

Stimson, George W., *Introduction to Airborne Radar*, Hughes Aircraft Co., 1983.

Synergy, *Designer's Handbook*, Synergy Microwave, 1999.

About the Author

Carl Weisman attended the Pennsylvania State University where he earned a BSEE in 1980. From there he went to work for the Hughes Aircraft Company as a design engineer working on airborne radar for fighter aircraft. During his nine-year stay there, he was awarded a Hughes Fellowship, which enabled him to earn an MSEE from the University of Southern California while working full time.

Carl spent the next eight years working in sales and marketing of RF and wireless hardware for several companies including Avantek-Hewlett Packard and M/A-COM-AMP. During this period he spent a great deal of time conducting product training for non-technical sales people in the industry, which served as the inspiration for this book.

Carl also earned his MBA from Loyola Marymount University, where he graduated with honors. He is currently a professional trainer and offers a seminar on RF and Wireless Technology. Carl lives in Redondo Beach, CA, and can be reached at cjweisman@yahoo.com

Index

Numerals

2.5G, 220, 222

802.11, 243, 244, 245

    Wi-Fi, 244–247

A

Absorption, 26

AC (alternating current), 6

Access point, 241, 243

Adapters, 133–134

Adaptive cruise control, *See* Collision avoidance

Air interface, 203

    CDMA (code division multiple access), 205–206

    CDPD (cellular digital packet data), 206–207

    FDMA (frequency division multiple access), 203–204

    TDMA (time division multiple access), 204

Altimeter, 159–160

AM (amplitude modulation), *See* Modulation

Amplifier(s), 17, 49–57

    balanced, 55–56

    block diagram, 49

    function, 49

    fundamental properties, 49–54

    gain, 49

    high power (HPA), 50–51

    how they work, 54

    limiting, 55

    linear region, 53

    linearity, 52–54

    low noise (LNA), 50–51

    noise figure, 50

    nonlinear region, 53

    output power, 50–51

    saturated output power, 53

    saturation, 53

    transfer curve, 52–53

    types, 50

    variable gain (VGA), 56–57

AMPS (advanced mobile phone service), 218

Analog signal, 8–9

Antenna diversity, 190

Antenna(s), 38–49, 75

    active, 39

    array, 47

    block diagram, 38

    dipole, 46–47

    directional, 39

    dish, 48

    function, 38

    gain, 44–45

    horn, 47

    how they work, 42

    intelligent

        See Antenna(s), smart

    isotropic, 45

    monopole, 46–47

    omnidirectional, 39

    passive, 39

    patch, 47

    patterns, 43–44

    radiated signal directions, 41

    radiated signal strength, 41

    shape, 39

    size, 39

    smart, 48–49

ASIC (application specific integrated circuit), 111

Attenuation, 17

Attenuator(s), 84–88

    block diagram, 84

    digital, 86–87

    fixed, 85

    function, 84

    pad, 85

    variable, 86

    voltage variable (VVA), 86

B

Balanced amplifier, *See* Amplifier(s)

Bandwidth, 22–23

    percentage, 22–23

Baseband (signal), 67, 148

Basestation, 7, 197

Basic service set (BSS), 241

Beamwidth, 154–155

Bidirectional, 79

Bidirectional coupler, *See* Coupler(s)

Binary amplitude shift keying (BASK), *See* Modulation

Binary phase shift keying (BPSK), *See* Modulation

Bipolar transistor (BJT), *See* Transistor(s)

Bit error rate (BER), 236

BLAST technology, 259–261

Bluetooth, 248–249, 251

Broadband fixed wireless, 228

    supercell, 229

Broadcast auxiliary microwave, 187

Broadcasting, 143–152

    characteristics, 143–144

    constraints, 144–145

    frequency allocation, 145–146

ghost, 147

signal propagation, 147

tuner, 148–149

BSA (basic trading area), 195

C

Cable assembly, 131

Cable(s), 128–131

construction, 128–130

designation, 130–131

types, 130–131

Capacitors, 111, 112

Carrier (signal), 13

Cavity (components), 117–118

CDMA (code division multiple access), 209–218

channels, 217

cdmaOne, 223

CDPD (cellular digital packet data), *See* Air interface

Cell site, 197

Cells, *See* Cellular topology

Cellular infrastructure, 197–198

sectors, 197

use of omnidirectional antennas, 197

Cellular mobility, 198–199

Cellular phone block diagram, 206

Cellular telephony, *See* Mobile telephony

Cellular topology, 195–196

cells, 195

Channels, 144, 173, 236

Chipping rate, 211

Chips, 211

Circuit, 6, 111

Circuit switched technology, 218

Circuit traces, *See* Traces

Circulator(s), 93–94

block diagram, 93

how they work, 93

system use, 94

Coaxial adapters, 133

Coaxial cables, 129

Coaxial connectors, 131

Collision avoidance, 162

Combiner(s), 88–89

Common carrier microwave, 187

Complementary code keying (CCK), 244

Component(s), 16

active, 16

passive, 16

Connector(s), 131–133

families, 132–133

in cable assemblies, 131

Continuous wave (CW), 13

Control point, 250

CONUS, 169, 182

Conversion loss, *See* Mixer(s)

Coplanar waveguide, 136

Coupler(s), 90–92

bidirectional, 91

block diagram of a directional coupler, 90

block diagram of a Lange coupler, 92

directional, 91

function, 90

Lange, 91–92

quadrature (quad), 91–92

quadrature (quad) hybrid, 91–92

sample port, 90

Current, 6

D

dBm, 50

to power conversion, 51

DBS (direct broadcast satellite), 171

DC (direct current), 6

Decade, 23

Decibels (dB), 19

conversion, 19

mathematics, 19–20

Demodulation, 119, 127–128

Demodulator, 119, 127–128

Detector(s), 98

block diagram, 98

function, 98

Device(s), *See* Component(s)

Dielectric, 129

Digital attenuator, *See* Attenuator(s)

Digital compression, 174

Digital enhanced cordless telephone (DECT), 250

Digital signal, 8, 12

Digital signal processor (DSP), 207

Diode(s), 106, 107

Gunn, 106, 107

Impatt, 106, 107

PIN, 106, 107

Schottky, 106, 107

Tunnel, 106, 107

uses, 107

varactor, 106, 107

Diplexer, *See* Filter(s)

Directional coupler, *See* Coupler(s)

Discrete circuit (technology), 114

Discrete components, 111

Dish antenna, *See* Antenna(s)

Distributed circuit(s), 111, 113

Divider(s), 88–89

block diagram, 88

function, 88

system use, 89

Doppler radar, *See* Radar

Doppler shift, 158–159

Doubler, *See* Frequency doubler

Downconverter, 65

Downlink, *See* Satellite(s)

Downstream, 182, 202

DSSS (direct sequence spread spectrum), *See* Spread spectrum

DTH (direct to home) satellite, 171

Dual mode, 219

Duplex, 166, 202

Duplexer, *See* Filter(s)

Dwell time, 245

Dynamic range, 54

E

E911, 175–176

Earth station, 165

EDGE (enhanced data for GSM environment), 222

Effective isotropic radiated power (EIRP), 45, 168

Electromechanical switch, *See* Switch(es)

Electronic article surveillance, 263

Electronically scanned array, 158

Energy, 6

Equalizer, 208

Extended service set (ESS), 243

F

FCC (Federal Communications Commission), 16, 58–59, 143–144, 166

FDD (frequency division duplexing), 236–237, 238

FDMA (frequency division multiple access), *See* Air interface

Feedback, 57

    as implemented with couplers, 90

    used in synthesizers, 72–73

    using variable gain amplifiers, 57

Ferrite (material), 93

FHSS (frequency hopping spread spectrum), *See* Spread spectrum

Field effect transistor, *See* Transistor(s)

Filter(s), 57–63

    band reject, 59

    bandpass, 59

    block diagram, 57

    duplexer (diplexer), 61

    frequency response, 59–61

    function, 58

    high pass, 59

    low pass, 59

    notch, 59

    pass band, 61

    SAW (surface acoustic wave), 61–62

    stop band, 61

    superconducting, 62–63

Fire control radar, *See* Radar

First generation (1G) cellular, 218

Fixed satellite service (FSS), 172

Flexible cable, 130

FM (frequency modulation), *See* Modulation

Footprint, *See* Satellite(s)

Fourth generation (4G) cellular, 224

Free space loss, 25

Free space optics, *See* Wireless fiber

Frequency, 7, 9

    bands, 11

    of various applications, 10

    range definitions, 11

Frequency doubler, 68

Frequency hopping spread spectrum (FHSS), *See* Spread spectrum

Frequency reuse, 201–202

Frequency shift keying, *See* Modulation

G

Gain, 16–18

Gallium Arsenide, 105

Gateway, *See* WAP

Geostationary orbit, *See* Geosynchronous orbit

Geosynchronous orbit, 164

Ghost, *See* Broadcasting

GPRS (general packet radio service), 222

GPS (global positioning system), 174–178
    function, 174–175
    theory of operation, 176
    uses for, 177–178
GSM (group special mobile), 222

H

Handoff, 199
HEMT, *See* Transistor(s)
Hertz, 9
Heterojunction bipolar transistor (HBT), *See* Transistor(s)
High power amplifier (HPA), *See* Amplifier(s)
HiperLAN, 243, 245
HomeRF, 250–251
Hybrid (MIC) circuit technology, 114, 135

I

IF (intermediate frequency), 66
Impedance, 28
    matching, 31
Impedance ratio, *See* Transformer(s)
IMT-2000, 221, 222
Indirect GPS, 178
Indium Phosphide (InP), 105
Inductor, 111, 112
Insertion loss, 18
Insulator, 129
Integrated circuit(s) (IC), *See* MMIC
Intercept point, 54
Interference, 48

Interleaving, 208
Interrogator, 261
Ionization, 266
IrDA, 252
IS-136, 223
IS-54, 223
IS-95, 223
ISM , 232–233, 244, 248
Isolation, 80
Isolator(s), 95–96
    function, 95
    system use, 95
ITU (International Telecommunications Union), 166, 221

L

LAN (local area network), 240
Lange coupler, *See* Coupler(s)
LDMOS, *See* Transistor(s)
LEO (low Earth orbit) satellites, 179–181
    theory of operation, 180–181
Limiting amplifier, *See* Amplifier(s)
Linearity, *See* Amplifier(s)
Line-of-sight (LOS), 144, 147, 162, 230
LMDS (local multipoint distribution service), 230–231
LO (local oscillator), 68
Load, 95
Local loop, 227
Loss, 16–17
Low noise amplifier (LNA), *See* Amplifier(s)
LTCC (low temperature co-fired ceramic), 116
Lumped circuit(s), 111–112

M

Macrocell(s), 196, 199

Match, 28–29

    consequences of an imperfect, 30

M-commerce, 255–256

MEMS, 258–259

MEO (medium Earth orbit), 179

MESFET, *See* Transistor(s)

MIC (microwave integrated circuit), 114

Microcell(s), 196, 199

Microstrip, 136

Microwave relay, 187

Microwave(s), 7

Millimeter wave(s), 7

Mixer(s), 63–68

    block diagram, 63

    configuration, 67

    conversion loss, 66–67

    double balanced, 68

    function, 64

    how they work, 65–66

    mathematics, 64

    port(s), 65

    single ended, 68

    triple-balanced, 68

MMDS (multichannel multipoint distribution service), 229–230

MMIC (monolithic microwave integrated circuit), 110

    circuit technology, 114

    performance, 110

Mobile satellite service (MSS), 172

Mobile switching center (MSC), 197

Mobile telephone switching office (MTSO), 197

Mobile telephony, 193–224

    cellular, 193

    dual mode, 219

    frequency allocation, 193

    roaming, 218

Modulation, 12, 119–127

    AM (amplitude modulation), 120–121

    binary amplitude shift keying (BASK), 121–122

    binary phase shift keying (BPSK), 125

    FM (frequency modulation), 122–123

    frequency shift keying (FSK), 123

    PM (phase modulation), 123–126

    QAM (quadrature amplitude modulation), 126–127

    quadrature phase shift keying (QPSK), 125

Modulator, 119, 127–128

Monocycle, 257

MOSFET, *See* Transistor(s)

MSA (metropolitan statistical area), 195

MTA (metropolitan trading area), 195

Multipath, 189–190, 238

N

Narrowband, 24

Nodes, 234, 241

NODS (near object detection system), 159, 162

Noise, 65

    from a mixer, 65

on AM signals, 120

sensitivity of FM signals, 123

Noise figure (NF), 50, 66

Noise spectrum, 209–210

Non-line-of-sight (NLOS), 240

O

Octave, 23

OFDM (orthogonal frequency division multi-plexing), 240, 244

Ohms, 28

Omnidirectional antenna, *See* Antenna(s)

One dB compression point, 53

Oscillator(s), 68–73

block diagram, 68

how frequency is determined, 71

how they work, 69

types, 70

P

P₁dB point, 53, 62

P₁dB power, 53

Packet switched technology, 220

Pad, *See* Attenuator(s)

Pass band, *See* Filter(s)

PCB (printed circuit board), 6, 113, 135

PCS (personal communications services), 193, 220

Personal area network (PAN), 247

Phase, 99, 123–124

Phase detector(s), 100–101

function, 100–101

Phase shift, 99–100, 123–126

Phase shifter(s), 99

block diagram, 99

function, 99

Phase-locked loop (PLL), 73

PHEMT, *See* Transistor(s)

Picocell(s), 193, 200

Piconet, 249

PIN, *See* Diode(s)

PM (phase modulation), *See* Modulation

Point-to-point microwave, 187–190

operation, 188–190

uses, 187–188

Polarization, 45–46

Port(s), 65–66, 93

Power, 6

Power density, 25

Power divider(s), 88

Power management, 203

Private operational fixed microwave, 187

Propagation delay, 166

Pseudo-random noise (PN), 211

PSTN (public switched telephone network), 197, 198

Pulse position modulation, 258

Pulsed Doppler radar, *See* Radar

Pulsed radar, *See* Radar

Pulsed RF, 13

Q

QAM (quadrature amplitude modulation), *See* Modulation

Quadrature (Quad) coupler, See Coupler(s)

Quadrature (Quad) hybrid, See Coupler(s)

Quadrature phase shift keying (QPSK), *See* Modulation

R

Radar, 153–162

    continuous wave (CW), 158

    cross section, 155

    definition, 153

    Doppler, 158, 161

    factors affecting frequency selection, 154

    fire control, 161

    frequency allocation, 153

    how it determines direction, 157

    how it determines distance, 156

    how it determines velocity, 158–159

    pulsed Doppler, 159, 161

    pulsed systems, 156–159

    scanning, 157

Radio frequency (RF), 5

Radome, 188

Receiver(s), 8, 36–38, 75

    block diagram, 37, 74

    detailed operations, 75

    generic description, 8

Reflection, 27, 30

Repeater, 200

Resistor, 95, 111

Return loss, 30

RF (radio frequency), *See* Radio frequency

RFID, 261–263

Roaming, *See* Mobile telephony

RSA (rural statistical area), 195

S

Sample port, *See* Coupler(s)

Satellite(s), 162–186

    bent pipe architecture, 170

    dish, 166–167

    downlink, 165–166

    footprint, 168–169

    frequency allocation, 166, 172–174

    function, 162

    Internet downstream, 182–185

    Internet service using, 181–186

    Internet upstream, 186

    spacecraft, 170–171

    spot beams, 183

    station keeping, 171

    topologies, 171–172

    transponder, 169–170

    uplink, 165–166

Saturation, *See* Amplifier(s)

SAW (surface acoustic wave), *See* Filter(s)

Schottky, *See* Diode(s)

SDMA (spatial division multiple access), 48

Second generation (2G) cellular, 219

Security protocols, 265

Security risks, 264–265

Selective availability, 175

Semi-flex cable, 130

Semi-rigid cable, 130

Shift keying, 121

Signal, 8

Signal spectrum, 209–210

Silicon, 105

Silicon Germanium (SiGe), 105

Sine wave, 9

Skin effect, 24–25

SMT (surface mount technology), 116

Solid state technology, 104

Source(s), *See* Oscillator(s)

Spatial diversity, 190

Specialized mobile radio (SMR), 194

Specific absorption rate (SAR), 268

Spectral efficiency, 237

Spectrum, 150

Spectrum analyzer, 210

Spread spectrum, 204, 209–216

    de-spreading, 214

    direct sequence (DSSS), 211, 244, 246

    frequency hopping (FHSS), 244, 245

    spreading, 211–213

    time hopping (THSS), 257

Station keeping, *See* Satellite(s)

Stop band, *See* Filter(s)

Stripline, 136

Subassembly, 117

Subsystem, 117

Superhetrodyne receiver, 67

Switch(es), 79–83

    block diagram, 79

    electromechanical, 80

    function, 79

    performance, 79–80

    poles, 82–83

    solid state, 81

    T/R, 83

    throws, 82–83

Synthesizer, 72–73

    use in cellular phones, 208

T

T/R switch, *See* Switch(es)

T1 line, 198

TDD (time division duplexing), 236–237

TDMA (time division multiple access), *See* Air interface

Telematics, 178

Thermal effects of RF radiation, 267

Thermal impedance, 18

Third generation (3G) cellular, 221

Third order intercept (Ip3), 54, 62

Time hopping spread spectrum (THSS), *See* Spread spectrum

Time modulation, 258

Traces, 113, 135–137

Transceiver, 8

Transfer curve, *See* Amplifier(s)

Transformer(s), 96–98

    block diagram, 96

    function, 96–97

    impedance ratio, 97

Transistor(s), 107–110

    as used in amplifiers, 54, 108

    bipolar (BJT), 104

    block diagrams, 108

    field effect (FET), 107

    HEMT, 109

    heterojunction bipolar (HBT), 108

    LDMOS, 109

MESFET, 109

MOSFET, 108

PHEMT, 109

Transmitter(s), 8, 36–38, 75

    block diagram, 37, 74

    detailed operation, 75

    generic description, 8

Transponder, *See* Satellite(s)

Triangulation, 176

Tubes, 104, 105

Tuner, *See* Broadcasting

TWT (traveling wave tube), 117–118

TWTA (traveling wave tube amplifier), *See* TWT (traveling wave tube)

U

Ultra wideband (UWB), 257–258

UMTS (universal mobile telecommunication system), 222

UNII (unlicensed national information infrastructure), 233

Unlicensed spread spectrum, 233

Upconverter, 65

Uplink, *See* Satellite(s)

Upstream, 182, 202

V

Vacuum tubes, *See* Tubes

Varactor, *See* Diodes

Variable gain amplifier (VGA), *See* Amplifier(s)

Voltage, 6

Voltage controlled oscillator (VCO), 71–72

    block diagram, 72

    how they work, 72

    role in frequency modulation (FM), 72

Voltage variable attenuator (VVA), *See* Attenuator(s)

VSAT (very small aperture terminal), 172

VSWR (voltage standing wave ratio), 29

W

WAP, 255

    gateway, 255

Watts, 6

    as related to dBm, 51

Waveguide, 134–135

Wavelength, 42

WEP (wired equivalent privacy), 265

Wideband, 24

Wideband CDMA (WCDMA), 222–223

Wideband PCS, 220

Wi-Fi, *See* 802.11

Wireless, 5

Wireless communication, 13

Wireless fiber, 234–236

Wireless local area network (WLAN), 241

Wireless local loop (WLL), 228–229

WML (wireless markup language), 255

WTLS (wireless transport layer security), 265

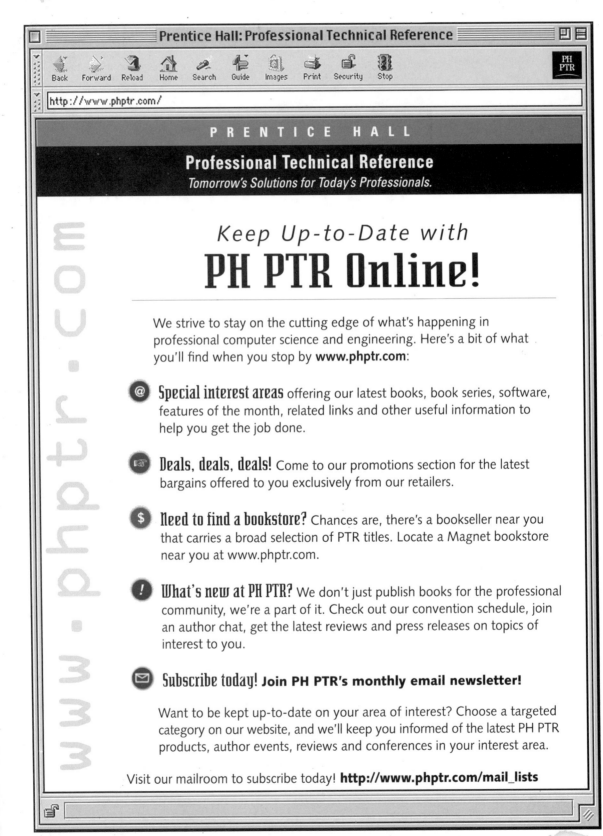